AJS and MATCHLESS— THE POSTWAR MODELS

OSPREY
COLLECTOR'S
LIBRARY

AJS AND MATCHLESS— THE POSTWAR MODELS

Lightweight and heavyweight singles and twins from 1945

Roy Bacon

Published in 1983 by Osprey Publishing Limited
12–14 Long Acre, London WC2E 9LP
Member company of the George Philip Group
Reprinted winter 1985

British Library Cataloguing in Publication Data
Bacon, Roy
AJS and Matchless.
1. AJS motorcycles 2. Matchless motorcycles
I. Title
629.2′275 TL448.A/
ISBN 0-85045-536-7

Editor Tim Parker
Design Roger Daniels
Filmset and printed in England by
BAS Printers Limited, Over Wallop, Hampshire

Contents

Right **Williams exiting from Parliament Square in the 1973 Senior in which he finished second to Agostini**

Below **Peter Williams and the Arter Matchless with its cast wheels and disc brakes**

Foreword by Peter Williams

This book is a catalogue of the motorcycle range and the modifications and changes to it that make up the evolution of the AJS and Matchless after World War 2. It is an objective report written largely without comment. It is remarkable, then, that the magic wands of nostalgia kept prodding me as I read it.

How is it that the names AJS and Matchless should be so emotive? Anyone who has 'played' with one—let alone ridden one—knows why. The obvious reason for me is that I was brought up with them and much of my racing life was spent with the two great marques.

I was particularly delighted to find the mention of the 7R AJS Special which John Surtees built. It was an indication of how good the 7R was that he chose the engine to power what my entrant, Tom Arter, and I called the Surtees Special. I had admired his machine so much, even before I started racing that I could not believe my luck when I was given the chance to ride it in 1966. It was this machine and derivitives of it which gave us four Isle of Man TT second places.

The materialists will say that I was wasting my time not going with trends of Japanese two-strokes—and they may well be right, of course. But when the foundations of engineering are as firm as they were with AJS and Matchless an engineer finds it difficult to leave them behind; as a rider I found them a joy.

The fascination of AJS and Matchless, once the mainstay of the biggest motorcycle group in the world, is now something akin to the fascination that steam engines, traction engines, railways and fairground machinery has for many of us. It has to do with trying to continue or hang on to our engineering heritage of which we can be so justly proud.

The book's factual presentation therefore mentions the engineers but the names of management are conspicuously absent. I hope it is my prerogative to pose the quetion whether the non-existence of the industry now is because of management inadequacy or because history passed it by?

The reader will get a flavour of this problem, I hope, as he realises that the annual model modifications become fewer and less understandable and even frivolous. Some may even be identified as being made in a sort of panic. These were the tragic death throes of the once great company.

Thanks to Roy Bacon we have a record of those wonderful motorcycles in those good years.

Peter Williams
2nd place, 1973 Senior TT, Arter Matchless
Southampton
June 1983

Acknowledgements

My memories of AMC are diverse for they range from a 350 trials model I tried up and down a few hills to a 7R I did a little work on and was allowed to push to bring to life.

I can recall the lovely lines of the first Matchless twin with its then novel dualseat and megaphone silencers. At the race circuits in the 1950s there were 7Rs with massive megaphones and G45s with chronic carburation. No one seemed to be able to get them to run clean. Later on I enjoyed a speed trial with a 650 sidecar and passengered the same machine, but different chair, in the Exeter.

My thanks for help in writing this book go especially to Deryk Wylde of the AMC owners club who not only answered my many telephone queries but also checked the manuscript. As well as reading it himself he arranged for the club experts to inspect their appropriate chapters and make suitable comments and my thanks go to all of them.

I had help from Don Morley once again and Vic Willoughby while Jock West kindly cleared up an obscure point and my *Classic Bike* colleague Ken Hallworth lent me material on the war-time Matchless.

The National Motor Museum at Beaulieu was a most useful reference point and I have to thank the library staff for their ever helpful assistance. They were also able to help with some of the pictures as did the Imperial War Museum who always have some good action shots in their files.

Most of the pictures and line drawings came

from the files of the magazines and once more I am indebted to Bob Berry and Peter Law of *Motor Cycle News*, Mick Woollett and Graham Sanderson of *Motor Cycle Weekly* and Jim Lindsay of *Mechanics*. S. R. Keig of Douglas again found me pictures as in the past and others from the professionals were taken by Cecil Bailey, Málcolm Carling, K. Holmes, K. G. Jones, Manx Press, Thomas McCleary, Nick Nicholls, L. J. Nicholson, Rene Par, Ken Price and Bill Salmond.

As usual all the pictures were returned to their files after publication and I have tried to make contact to clear copyright. If my letter failed to reach you or I have used an unmarked print without realising this please accept my apologies.

To close I must thank Peter Williams for kindly writing the foreword and, once more, Tim Parker for making the book happen.

Roy Bacon
Niton, Isle of Wight
June 1983

1 Establishment and amalgamation

AJS and Matchless started as two separate companies that ran on diverse, then converging, then parallel and finally a single track. They followed their own, very individual, paths while working alone, and then joined as AMC, Associated Motor Cycles. For a while they ran together with the same model range but retained a small flavour of individuality. At the end they became as one with only badges and colour to distinguish them and thus badge engineering disillusioned not one but two sets of enthusiasts.

The melancholy final act was far off in the future when, at the turn of the century, Joe Stevens and four of his sons first became involved in engines. Joe was an engineer and his firm produced high grade work near Wolverhampton in the '90s of the late Victorian period. He became interested in the idea of using internal combustion engines to power stationary equipment and, in time, acquired a small American Mitchell engine.

With this the family moved into the transport field in 1897 and built their first motorcycle with the engine clipped to the downtube of the frame. Most of the machine was bicycle but the direct belt drive to the rear wheel did have a jockey which gave far more belt contact on the engine pulley than was usual.

The father and sons did not pursue the idea of building complete machines immediately but, for most of the Edwardian era, just manufactured engines which were used by a number of firms. In time they also began to make frames, and in 1909 returned to the idea of a complete machine.

Billy Jones with the Junior AJS on which he finished 4th in 1914. This machine has a three speed gearbox and was used on the road into the 1950s before being restored

They wanted a new name, as the Stevens engines were already associated with too many other makes, and decided to use the initials of the elder brother – Albert John. Thus the famous AJS name came into being. Elder brother, in fact known as Jack, was keen on the sporting aspects of motorcycling and often rode in speed events and trials so when the ACU announced a Junior class for the 1911 TT he decided to compete.

Single cylinder entries were limited to 300 cc, twins were 340 cc, and two AJS machines were entered and both finished. They were of simple construction with side valve engines and countershaft gearboxes with chain and belt drive. The frame was a simple diamond and Druid forks were fitted.

Pressure of business building road machines for customers kept the brothers away from the TT in 1912 but they were back again the next year with a tenth and a retirement. For 1914 they decided that the way to success was to forget about modifying standard machines and to build a proper racing model.

The Junior capacity limit had been raised to 350 cc in 1912 and AJS had taken advantage of this to adopt dimensions of 74 × 81 mm. They kept to these in 1914 and built a team of machines with very special engines with the complete cylinder and fins machined from a solid billet of steel and the piston also made in the same way. The result of extensive testing was an

The skimpy build of a competition motorcycle in 1921 is exemplified by this $2\frac{3}{4}$ AJS. Rider is said to be Geoff Boston

engine speed of 5000 rpm, which was phenomenal for the period, and reliability. The engine drove a two-speed countershaft gearbox and the choice of ratios was doubled up by fitting two primary chains with a selector at the engine sprockets. The magneto sat in front of the engine driven from the exhaust camshaft, while the frame continued a simple diamond with Druid forks. A stirrup front brake was fitted.

The outcome of all the effort was complete domination, with Eric Williams winning from Cyril Williams and the other three AJS models entered finishing 4th, 6th and 29th. Not all had the dual transmission, for Billy Jones had a three-speed gearbox on his model.

Sales of the road machines took off to such a degree that new and much larger premises were needed and so the firm moved to Wolverhampton north-west of Birmingham. There production was quickly built up until war broke out and the plant was turned over to munitions work. During the conflict what odd spare moments were available were spent on development and in thinking about engine design.

The result was that after the war AJS returned to the TT with a new advanced engine design but with the 1914 dimensions. The side valves had gone and in their place was a very advanced hemispherical combustion chamber with overhead valves. The transmission was still the prewar two-speed box combined with two-speed

Howard Davis in 1921, the year he won the Senior on his 350 cc AJS and took second place in the Junior

primary drive and this was to prove one of their problems in the race. The additional power of the ohv engine was too much for the mainshaft and the cylinder pressure was too much for the head to barrel joint.

Seven machines entered the Junior but only two survived, the others succumbing to inter-team battles. Fortunately one of the finishers came home first by a ten minute margin, and this despite an engine failure four miles from home, so that Cyril Williams had to coast and push his way to the finish.

For 1921 there were no mistakes. The fragile, temperamental transmission was replaced by a three-speed gearbox with chain drive, the head joint improved and the valve angle decreased. The frame and many of the details were improved but curiously the stirrup front brake was retained. The marque totally dominated the Junior that year with Eric Williams leading them home in the first four places.

The Senior TT brought an even bigger sensation, for Howard Davies kept close to the leaders for much of the race and then took over to give AJS a double victory and a unique Senior win with a 350 cc machine.

The next year, 1922, saw the first appearance of the big port model with further improvements including drum brakes, and once more AJS took home the Junior trophy. This was to be their last TT win in the 1920s as, although they finished in the first three on many occasions, outright victory was to elude them for a while.

Meanwhile their competition success had brought its reward in demand for the road models and to meet this AJS built a range of side and overhead valve singles backed by the then traditional big vee-twin for sidecar work. Finished in black and gold these were some of the finest of vintage machines with a good performance, light weight, and excellent detail work.

In 1927 they produced their first camshaft engine and it took a form it kept throughout its life. The camshaft lay across the cylinder head and was driven by a chain with a Weller tensioner; virtually a clock spring pulled out straight whose natural curvature took up the slack in the drive and coped with expansion as the engine warmed up.

The first engines were built in both 350 and 500 cc sizes, but success in the TT still eluded the marque until 1930 when a 250 cc version was prepared and ridden to victory by Jimmy Guthrie. The year before the camshaft engine, in various sizes, was used to take a large number of world records at Brooklands and Montlhéry and the firm was contemplating an attack on the world's fastest record.

As the vintage decade ended so things changed for the Stevens' brothers. They had expanded well outside the pure motorcycle field with their own sidecars, a light car, a motor coach chassis, and even into wireless sets in the days when such things were built into massive plywood boxes and relied on large, hot valves for reception.

The company was over-extended for the depression of the 1930s and entered that period with a very revized range of models. Away went the lean, light and lithe flat tank machines of the vintage era and in their place came the rounded lines of the early thirties with sloping engines, then all the rage, low seats and saddle tanks. The weight went up and the performance down, while the precise handling became more mundane.

Despite the hard times AJS were enterprising on the design side and for 1931 announced a transverse vee-twin of 500 cc with side valves. The gearbox was driven by shaft but final drive remained the usual chain.

It was soon after this model appeared that the company went into liquidation but without loss to its creditors, all of whom were fully paid out in the end. The BSA company were one that tried to take over the AJS name, but it went to the Matchless concern and the Collier brothers. They moved the AJS production to their works

Above **The 996 cc blown AJS built around 1930 for a world's fastest attempt in its 1933 form with massive supercharger**

Below **Early Matchless from the Edwardian era, around 1907**

Harry Collier and his 496 Matchless-JAP on which he finished 3rd in the 1912 Senior TT

at Plumstead in south London, while the Stevens' brothers remained in the Midlands and built a range of models under their own name during the thirties.

So AJS were amalgamated with one of the oldest names in the industry, Matchless, and one that had won three TTs before AJS had even reached the Isle of Man. The founder, Henry Collier, registered the Matchless trademark in 1891 for use on a bicycle he intended to market with a partner. In the event the partner withdrew so Collier continued alone building up his business.

In 1899 he and his sons, Harry and Charlie, built their own engine and mounted it over the front wheel of one of their own bicycles. They soon came to realise that this was not a good position and experimented with others. Charlie Collier was already competing in cycle races, often held on banked tracks, so when motorcycle races began to be held at the same venues it was natural that he should ride in these as well.

In 1902 the Colliers built their first production machine and this soon led to a range of models during the Edwardian era. Both brothers rode in the International Cup and from the problems of that event came the TT in 1907 with both on the starting line for that year and each succeeding one up to 1914. They were very successful in those early days with Charlie winning the very first TT and finishing second in 1908. It was Harry's turn to win in 1909 and in 1910 they took the first two places with Charlie in front. While less successful in the TT after that, the brothers continued to ride at Brooklands with many successes in that far off pre-war time.

When the First World War broke out, motorcycle production continued for a while on a reduced scale with much of the factory taken over to munitions work. In 1916 the sale of motorcycles to the public was banned and the whole firm given over to the war effort. In 1917 a flat twin was shown in an interim catalogue but only one was made and, when the conflict ended, Matchless built their by now traditional vee-twin engined sidecar models.

These were soon joined by a range of singles and for a year or two they also built a small car powered by a flat twin engine. An overhead camshaft engine was designed for the 1923 TT but could not be finished in time. It was used, however, when the marque next ran in the Isle of Man in 1926 but without success.

By the late twenties Matchless had a range that stretched from 250 to 1000 cc with side or overhead valves and one or two cylinders. They were successful in the reliability trials of the day and on occasion still surprised the field at track racing, one such occasion being the 1928 Hutchinson 100 won by Philip Brewster at over 93 mph. Late in 1928 the Collier brothers went public, the father having died in 1925, and the company became Matchless Motorcycles Limited. By that time the success of the sidecar outfits caused them to open a separate works on a site near the Woolwich Ferry for the production of the sidecar bodies.

For 1930 they had a new, enterprising vee-twin just as AJS were to have the next year. The Matchless one was called the 'Silver Arrow' and had its two very narrow angle longitudinal cylinders in one block with their side valves. The oil tank bolted to the front of the crankcase to eliminate pipes, and the machine had a sprung frame and an instrument panel. It was a sophisticated model of limited performance, built in response to the cries from press and public for a clean, quiet, smooth machine. As usual when a maker responded, there were few sales for the Arrow was too clean, too quiet and too smooth and as usual the enthusiasts waited to see how it performed.

A year later the firm produced a model that was just as enterprising but decidedly more exciting. This was the Silver Hawk which was powered by a 600 cc narrow angle vee-four en-

The Matchless Silver Arrow introduced for the 1930 range. 400 cc, narrow vee twin with oil tank bolted to crankcase front

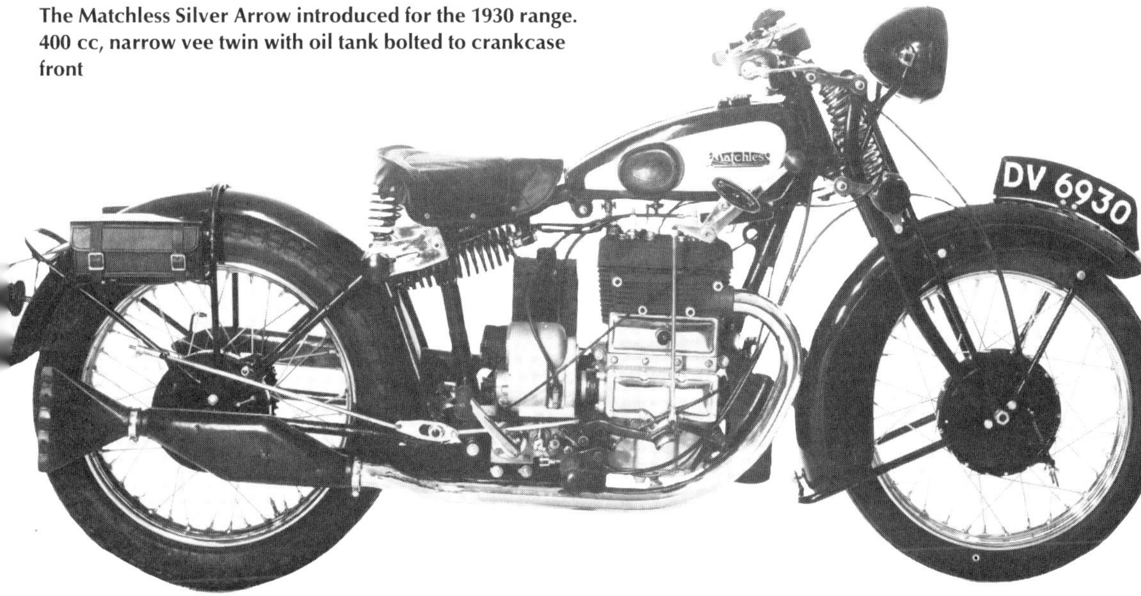

Above **The road model AJS vee four with overhead camshafts introduced at the 1935 Olympia Show**

Top **Matchless Silver Hawk of 1931 with vee four engine and overhead camshaft**

Right **Harold Daniell at Governor's Bridge in the 1936 Senior in which his blown, air cooled AJS 4 retired**

gine with overhead camshafts. It retained the sprung frame of the Silver Arrow but even with better performance was too exotic for the depressed years of the early thirties.

In 1931 the firm adopted the big letter 'M' on its tanks and took over AJS, whose production they moved to their own works. There followed a year or two without the camshaft AJS, while the works stabilized, and the transverse twin was only built for a short period. Then the two ranges began to run more alongside one another.

By the end of the decade the singles had much in common but with one obvious variation, for

CE
WS CHRONICLE
5

Above **Walter Rusk and the watercooled four on which he finished 11th in the 1939 Senior and later lapped in Ulster at a level 100**

Below **1944 prototype springer using Teledraulic leg principle for rear suspension**

the AJS carried its magneto in front of the cylinder and the dynamo in the rear engine plates just above the gearbox, while the Matchless kept the dynamo in the same location but mounted the magneto on a platform above it. In both marques the dynamo was chain driven from the crankshaft, the chain being enclosed in the primary chaincase, and the magneto chain driven from the nearest camshaft, inlet for Matchless and exhaust for AJS, in either case under a monogrammed cover.

Alongside the singles ran the 990 cc vee-twins for sidecar use, and the Matchless engine came to be the choice for both marques and others also, for Brough Superior, Coventry Eagle, OK Supreme, OEC and Morgan (three wheeler) all used the Plumstead motors.

On the AJS side of the fence the camshaft single reappeared in 1933 but its steady development was completely overshadowed in 1935 when, at the Olympia show, AJS introduced a vee-4 road model. It had overhead camshafts, was air cooled and with provision, it was said, for a supercharger to be mounted in place of the dynamo in front of the crankcase. Two of the fours were raced in the TT in 1936 when they retired, and one in 1938 by which time it was fitted with rear suspension but again retired.

For 1939 the four was water-cooled and the spring frame revised. However, the handling was still dreadful and Rusk and Foster had to fight the machines home in the Island. Late in the year in the Ulster the four finally showed how quick it was. Despite the handling Walter Rusk took the lead on the Clady straight and on lap 3 broke the lap record at exactly 100 mph. Sadly he was forced out on the next lap when the lower, right fork link snapped, but there was no doubt that the AJS, on a circuit that was not too demanding on handling, had the legs of the blown Gilera four, then considered the leading machine on the European racing scene.

The 4 did make two further appearances after the war in 1946 before blowers were banned. It was given an airing at North Weald airfield ridden by Jock West to carry out plug tests, and then run in the Grand Prix des Frontieres at Chimay in Belgium where West finished ahead of a BMW and an FN. He later rode it at Albi in France, but a big end seized and, although a rough attempt was made to repair it at the time, it remained untouched until Sammy Miller rebuilt the complete machine in 1980, truly one of the really great restoration projects.

From the mid-thirties the road ranges began to take on model numbers some of which were to continue for many years postwar. Most of the Matchless range were given the prefix letter 'G' used for all the later machines, so the 250 became the G2, the 350 the G3 and the 500 the G80, with suffix 'C' for competition. The Special Clubman models with tuned engines were the G4 (350) and G90 (500), to emphasize their added performance. On the AJS side the three basic sizes were coded 12, 16 and 18 and available in standard, sports and competition forms. These ohv models were backed up by 500 singles and 990 vee-twins with side valves.

In 1937 the Matchless company took over the Sunbeam firm but relinquished it to BSA in 1940. At the time, with three very respected firms in the group, a decision was taken to register a new name for it; 'Associated Motor Cycles' or AMC as it was henceforth known. About the same time the board took exception to the occasional unfavourable comment on their models in road tests in the magazines of the day. They thus decided not to supply machines any more and this policy was continued until the late 1950s. Curiously, the press failed to defend its right to report by simply borrowing machines from dealers or private owners, while strangely the ban does not seem to have applied to competition models.

In 1938 the large letter 'M' on the Matchless tanks gained its wings and as war drew nigh AMC were in a sound financial position. During the conflict they were able to continue building motorcycles and produced a single model, the

G3L and BSA M20 at the municipal airfield in Naples in October 1943 (IWM)

A G3L among very top brass at Gibraltar in May 1943. The Prime Minister, Winston Churchill, inspects the defences (IWM)

350 cc Matchless. A few AJS were built in the very early days but production centred on the G3 with a detuned engine and appropriate service finish to the tune of some 80,000 machines.

Early in the war an experimental lightweight 250 was built and tried by the War Office along with prototypes from other makers, but after Dunkirk there was no time for such exercises, only for manufacture. The only really major and important change made to the Matchless came in 1941 when it gained telescopic front forks and became the G3L. The forks were hydraulically damped and became known as 'Teledraulics'. They were the first to be adopted by a British machine and the result of development work following the acquisition of a set of BMW forks.

The G3L became a favourite of the forces for convoy duty for it was fast and comfortable, although the earlier G3 was said to be faster still. Maintenance was less popular for in some areas the Matchless was not easy to work on. The dynamo was nearly hidden from view under the magneto and embedded in the engine plates. Its drive chain shared the primary chaincase and the case seal was a notorious rubber band and clamp rim that was hard to get oiltight with pristine new parts. Once dented or strained it had no hope of retaining the oil, and generations of riders were to curse it and its seal and clip.

Those points aside, it was a good machine and well able to stand up to the rigours of service use. In addition, it meant that when peace finally came in 1945 AMC had four years of telescopic fork experience under their belt and a factory able to switch to peacetime production virtually by changing the paint in the spray guns.

2 Heavyweight singles

As the war in Europe drew to a close AMC began to dust off their plans for civilian production. All firms were beset by many problems at that period for on the one hand was the Government crying for exports and on the other were restrictions, rationing, shortages and a prolification of wartime regulations administered by Government officials often, it seemed, determined to put obstacles in everyone's way.

There was no time to think much about fresh designs, what was needed were machines in large numbers and at that time AMC advertized that theirs were the product of the world's largest factory devoted solely to the making of motorcycles.

So they did the obvious and settled for a two model range in each make, the models being nearly identical singles of 350 and 500 cc. They came while Matchless G3Ls were still being shipped to the army in the Far East as well as the Occupation Forces in Germany.

In June 1945 the two AJS models were announced followed by their Matchless cousins a week later in July. Following tradition the magnetos were carried fore and aft of the barrel respectively and type numbers were 16M and G3L for the smaller AJS and Matchless, and 18 and G80 for the larger. To save constant repetition it is not proposed to write the marque names after every model but to put them in alphabetical order as above. Anyway, *all* Matchless codes begin with the letter 'G'.

All four 1945 models were based on the tried and tested AMC design with all iron, single cylinder engine, four-speed gearbox with foot-change, Teledraulic forks and rigid frames.

The engines were based on a common 93 mm stroke with 69 mm bore to give 348 cc, and 82·5 mm to give 497 cc. Their construction was very typical of the English industry and thus the substantial flywheels had separate mainshafts held on the timing side on a taper by a nut, and on the drive by a parallel press fit, a key and another nut. The crankpin was a parallel fit in the flywheels and had the big end bearing sleeve pressed onto it. Nuts on each end of the pin held the assembly together and three rows of rollers in a Duralumin cage acted as the bearing in a hardened sleeve pressed into the big end eye of the connecting rod.

At its other end the rod was bushed for the gudgeon pin held, fully floating, in the piston by circlips. The piston itself was conventional with one oil and two compression rings and gave a compression ratio low enough to suit the indifferent pool petrol then in use. It ran in an iron barrel held on four studs and this was capped by the iron head held by four bolts. The head was a straightforward design with pressed-in valve guides, while the valves were restrained by double coil springs retained by collars and cotters.

On top of the head went the rocker box casting which acted as a cover to the valve wells in the head as well as carrying the rockers. Each rocker was in three pieces with the end arms splined to the spindle which oscillated in bronze bushes in the casting. On the right side went a cover plate held on three studs and this gave access to the tops of the push rods where the valve clearance adjustors were situated.

The push rods reached down to flat based tappets and were enclosed by tubes that sealed on to the crankcase top and up into the cylinder head. The tappets ran in bushes pressed into the aluminium crankcase which was split on the ver-

Girder forked G3 for the army needed this attention to keep it properly oiled

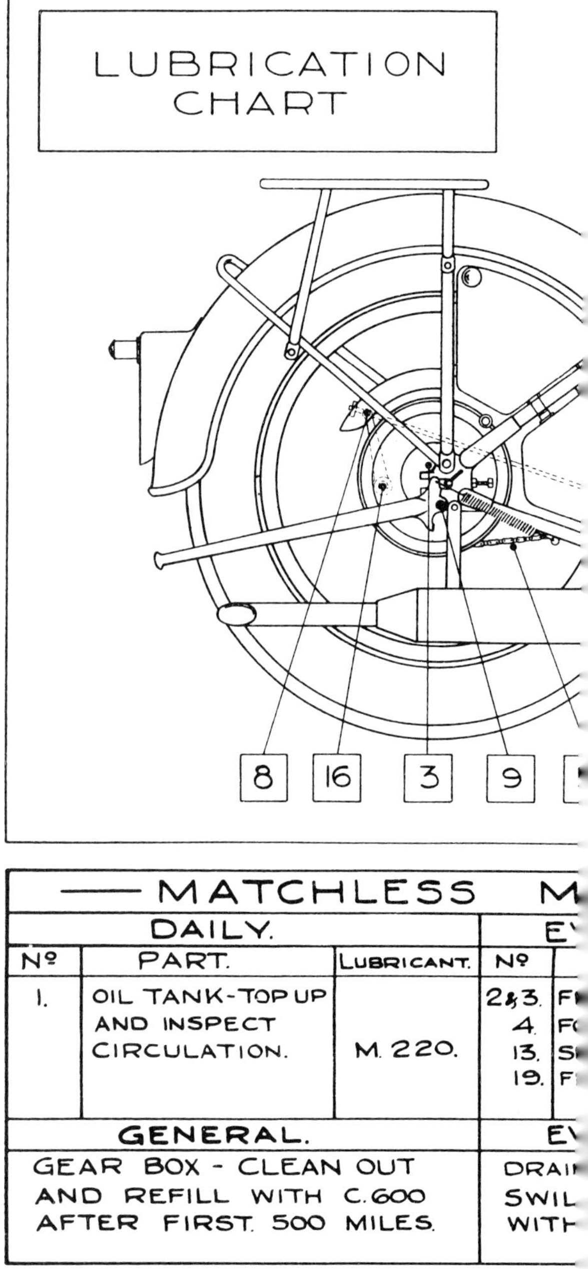

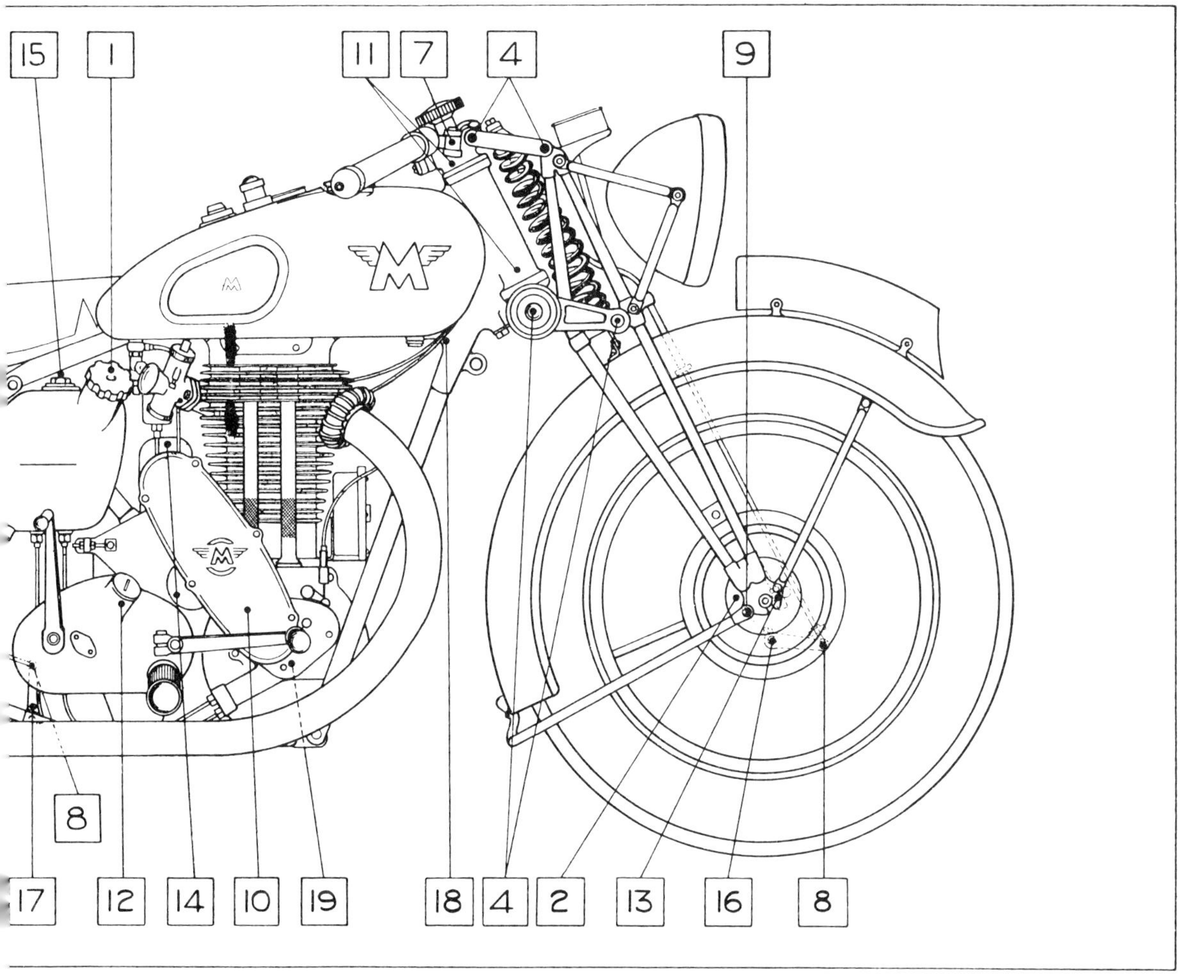

CYCLE. TYPE- 40/G3. MILITARY MODEL. ——							
OO MILES.		EVERY 1000 MILES.			EVERY 1500 MILES.		
	LUBRICANT.	Nº	PART	LUBRICANT	Nº	PART	LUBRICANT.
AR HUBS	GREASE	18	BOWDEN CABLES	C. 600	15.	REMOVE THE OIL FILTER & CLEAN IT	
DLES.	GREASE	12	GEAR BOX	C. 600			
RBOX	GREASE	10	MAGNETO CHAIN	GREASE	5.	REAR CHAIN	TALLOW
NCASE.	M. 220.	11	STEERING HEAD.	GREASE	9.	FRONT & REAR STANDS.	GREASE.
		16	BRAKE CAMS.	GREASE			
OO MILES.		8	BRAKE ROD JOINTS	M. 220	EVERY 10000 MILES.		
NK - Nº6.		7.	CONTROL LEVERS.	M. 220.	DISMANTLE- CLEAN- ADJUST & REPACK BEARINGS WITH GREASE DYNAMO AND MAGNETO. Nº 14.		
ND REFILL		17.	BRAKE PEDAL.	GREASE			

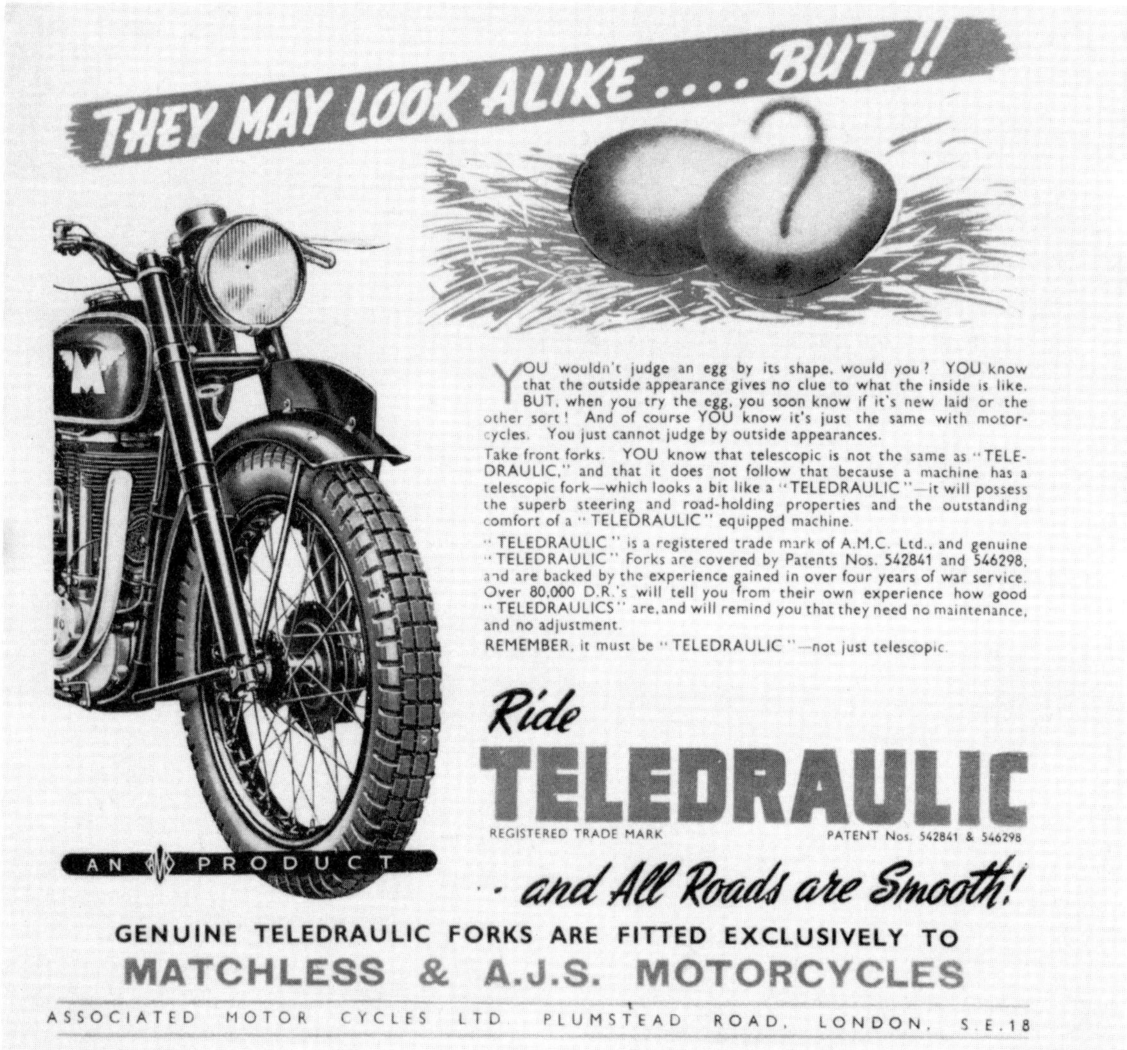

Motor Cycling **front cover advert in late 1945 emphasising AMC Teledraulics. Edward Turner of Triumph was annoyed by it**

tical centre line. The drive side carried two ball races to support the crankshaft but in the timing side went a single bronze bush and a roller bearing. The underside of the bush was cut away to enable a worm cut on the mainshaft to mesh with a pinion on a shaft positioned fore and aft and beneath the mainshaft. This acted as the oil pump and had two diameters each with a machined flat, the larger size acting as the scavenge pump and the smaller as the pressure. The pump shaft was forced to move axially as well as rotate and this was done by a screwed pin running in a cam groove in the rear, larger, diameter. At each end of the pump housing went small blanking plates and the front one carried a union for a feed pipe connected to the rocker

Above **The 1946 AJS model 18, a typical English 500 cc single of the times which had to do sterling service week in, week out**

Top **The competition G3C of 1946, really the road model less lights**

Right **Works competition Matchless for 1947 Scottish Six Days. Viney won for AJS but Ratcliffe was second, possibly on this machine**

oil-jets. Surplus oil drained to the valve guides and then fell down the push rod tubes to lubricate the tappets and cam gear on its way to the sump. The inlet valve guide feed had an adjustor to restrict the quantity of oil supplied.

Oil went under pressure to the big end bearing and, under the control of a ball valve, to feed holes in the cylinder wall to lubricate the piston skirt. All the oil drained to the crankcase sump from where it was picked up by the scavenge pump and returned to the oil tank. A flap valve breather was fitted into a boss behind the drive side main bearing housing in the left crankcase.

The pump housing was incorporated in the crankcase below the timing chest in which sat the two cam wheels side by side. Each was driven from the crankshaft and rotated with its cam on a live spindle in bronze bushes in the crankcase and the outer cover. Above the timing chest and between the push rods went the valve lifter to raise the exhaust when needed.

It was at the timing cover that the engines took on their marque personality and this affected the camshaft spindles, one of which had to pass through the cover to carry the magneto sprocket. For AJS it was the exhaust and for Matchless the inlet, but it made little real difference even on the assembly line. Once set with magneto fore or aft the drive chain was enclosed by an outer cover carrying the appropriate marque legend.

In both cases the dynamo went in the engine plates above the gearbox and behind the crankcase where it was driven by chain from a sprocket inboard of the main primary one.

Carburation was looked after by Amal and the exhaust gases went down a low level pipe to a silencer on the right.

The left mainshaft carried a sprocket driven via a face cam shock absorber connected by a single strand chain to a Burman four-speed footchange gearbox. This was of conventional English design with concentric mainshaft, carrying clutch, and sleeve gear with gearbox sprocket,

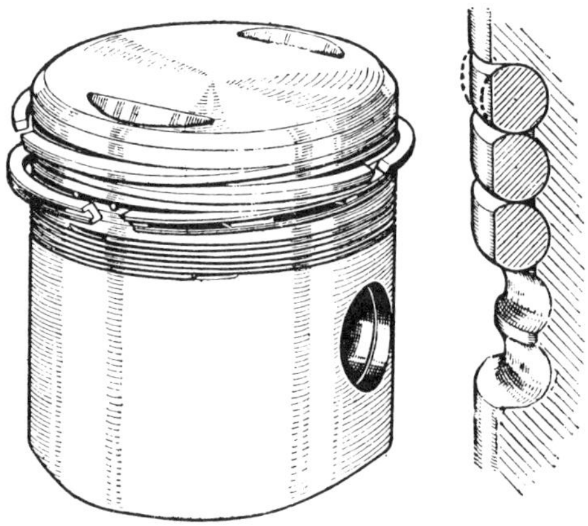

Above **The wire wound piston and a cross-section showing how the turns fit into grooves and are then ground**

Top **1947 Matchless advert taken from a** *Motor Cycling* **front cover and indicating the extent of their export market**

Right **November 1948** *Motor Cycling* **advert for AJS and their show stand**

A·J·S
QUALITY
MOTOR CYCLES
STAND No 69
EARLS COURT
A·J·S MOTOR CYCLES • PLUMSTEAD ROAD • LONDON, S.E.18

The 1949 G3L with hairpin valve springs, valve lifter in cylinder head and new frame with sidecar lugs

both on the left. The layshaft was sited below the mainshaft, the positive stop mechanism enclosed on the right, and a kickstart lever fitted on the same side.

The primary and dynamo chains were enclosed by the normal AMC case comprising two steel pressings, a rubber seal and a metal clamping band. A hole in the outer gave access for checking chain tension and a means of pouring the lubricant in. The rear chain was guarded on the top run only by another steel pressing which also carried the tyre pump.

The frame was constructed in two parts bolted together, each comprising tubes brazed into forged lugs. The front part had single top, seat and down tubes, the last terminating in a lug with twin arms. These bolted to the crankcase and also to the rear frame which had twin tubes running back to the rear wheel lug and up and forward from that lug to the top of the seat tube. Cross-tubes held the two main sides apart and also supported the rear mudguard.

At the front of the frame went the Teledraulic forks which carried a front wheel with single leading shoe brake matched by that at the rear.

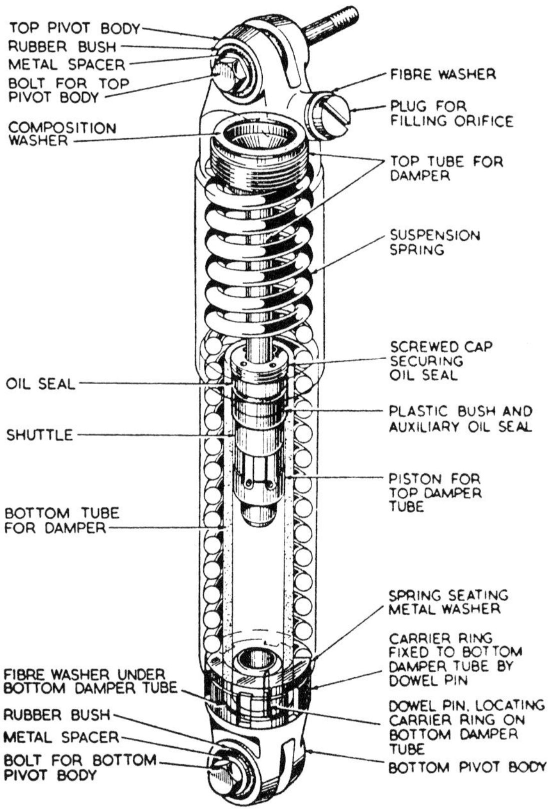

The first slim-line rear suspension unit offered by AMC and known as the candlestick. Not renowned for long life damping

The front mudguard was unsprung and its rear stay could be hinged down to act as a front stand. A rear stand was fitted plus a prop stand attached to the left lower frame member.

Rider comfort was attended to by a well sprung saddle, and a mudguard pad plus pillion rests were available as extras. The oil tank for the dry sump system went on the right above the gearbox and behind it went a toolbox attached to the frame and a mudguard stay. On the left went the battery and this served a headlight mounted on pairs of short strips and a rear lamp on a boxed-in rear number plate. The dynamo control unit went under the saddle and the horn was behind the engine on the AJS but in front of it on the Matchless, in each case occupying

The 1949 model 18S with swinging fork rear end controlled by candlesticks. Saddle and pillion seat still used

The 1949 Matchless equivalent, the G80S with the same cycle parts

1950 Matchless springer with offset silencer and chrome plated petrol tank. Mudguards became ribbed and front brake gained a torque arm

the area left vacant by the magneto position.

The speedometer was an option although a legal requirement, as was then normal practice, and fixed to the top fork crown and, while the fuel tanks were common, the kneegrips were individual to the marques and the tank finishes were traditional to the names. Thus the AJS was in black with gold lining and lettering to the tank, while the Matchless was lined with a broad silver strip with a red central pinstripe and its flying 'M' in the same colour. Aside from a few chrome plated details, the major parts were all in black and the tank motifs for both marques were transfers.

So AMC were very quickly back into the production of civilian models even if home purchasers had to have a 'licence to acquire', issued by the Ministry of War Transport, before they could buy one. Late in 1945 two patents were taken by the company, the first related to the use of cams on the rear wheel spindle to aid wheel alignment when the chain was adjusted. The second was for a swinging fork bearing that carried a reserve of oil in the bearing tube able to maintain a supply to the working surfaces and came as the result of a prototype springer G3L built in 1944 which had rear legs based on the Teledraulic front fork design.

In January 1946 came news that the first consignment of British postwar machines reached Argentina in the form of 20 Matchless models but of more interest to enthusiasts was the March news that AMC were to produce competition versions of their range. Only a small batch was promised with 50 of each marque split as 30 of 350 cc and 20 in the larger size.

As with the road models, all four were substantially the same with a special frame head angle, altered trail, tucked in exhaust system with upswept silencer, increased ground clearance, folding kickstarter, competition tyres and alloy mudguards; all modifications carried out to make the machines more suited to trials use. The gearing was lowered and lights became an option, while both clutch and throttle cables were duplicated.

Late in the year the changes for 1947 were announced and with production the key issue there were few alterations and these mainly details. Also, to whet the appetite, there was news of an impending ohc road racing machine for the 350 cc class, but this was not to reach the

December 1950 advert in *The Motor Cycle* showing the world wide range of satisfied customers—or the service department mail

MATCHLESS
LONDON
British Made – World Famous
MODEL G80S 498 c.c. O.H.V.
MATCHLESS
Clubman
TCHLESS MOTOR CYCLES · PLUMSTEAD ROAD · LONDON. S.E.18 · ENGLAND

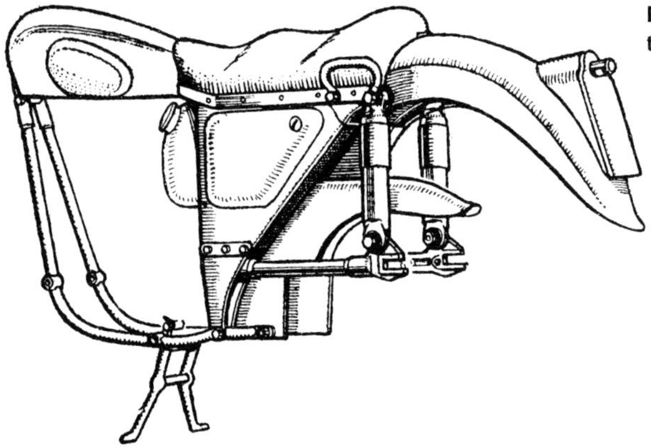
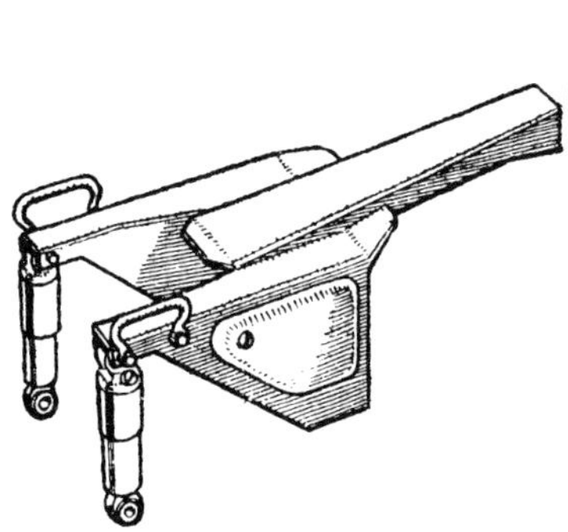

Line drawings of the AMC frame made using pressings and tubes, the prototype crashed on test

programme for some time and is dealt with in a later chapter.

The standard range had the lubrication system improved by the adoption of a two-start worm drive to the pump and in the same region a single plain flanged bush was used as the timing side main. This deleted the smaller roller race and retained the underside cut-out for the worm to drive through. Internally the connecting rod was shortened by half an inch and the gudgeon pin hole lowered by the same amount to allow the outside to remain unaltered.

On the outside the exhaust pipe of the 350 was changed to the form of the 500 so that it ran under the footrest in a cleaner and straighter line. At the front end the forks were given three-rate springs and added buffer springs, while both number plates were improved and the rear chain-guard flared to curtail where the oil could be thrown. A lifting handle was made part of one of the rear mudguard stays and a small but welcome change was an increase in the length of the chaincase clamp screw to give owners a better chance of joining the seal clamp ends together.

The finish was brightened with the flying 'M' becoming a chrome plated badge and the adoption of chrome plated handlebars and rims, the latter with black centres lined gold or silver to suit the marque. The AMC finish was in fact very good with three coats of Pinchin Johnson's best black enamel stoved on to a rust proof Bonderized base. It looked, and was, durable and well able to stand up to the rigours of the road.

Minor changes were again the order of the day for 1948 except for the brakes which became 7 in. diameter for both wheels. As before, the ends of the shoes were designed to be spaced from the cam as the lining wore, although the method used was totally new. The front forks were also new with revised hydraulic damping and a two bolt location for the brake backplate, which was chrome plated. The fork top yoke was modified to a smoother shape and the handlebar clamp changed to a four bolt design.

Details that altered included a section increase for the rear tyre on the 500, adjustable mountings for the saddle springs, further improvements to the oil pump, a chrome plated battery strap and domed headlamp glass. The competition models were fitted with the new brakes plus a polished finish for the alloy mudguards, while lights continued to be an option.

Early in 1948 came news of a change in piston design to the wire-wound type. This was developed by Automotive Engineering in conjunction with AMC and had an 18 swg high tensile steel wire wound into a groove machined into the piston skirt just below the scraper ring. Groove and wire went round for five turns like a screw thread

Cut-open show model engine and gearbox assembly from 1951

M

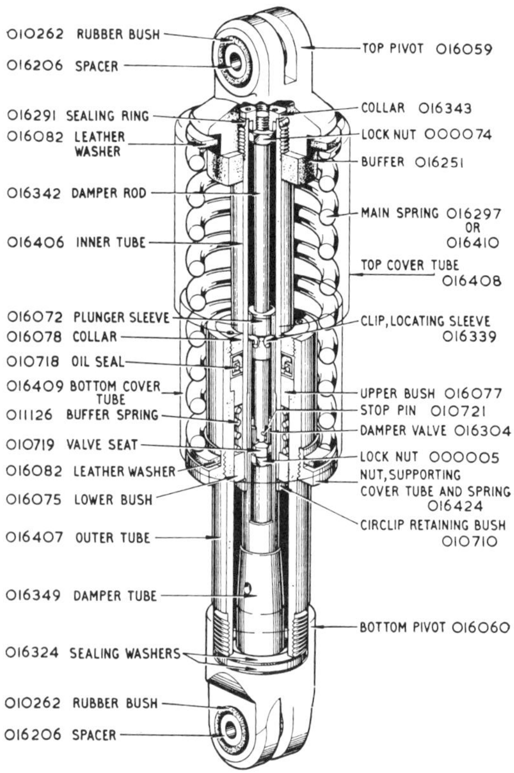

and the wire ends went through small holes at each end to be spot-welded on the inner wall of the piston. The assembly was then ground to take the wire down flush with the skirt. The result was even piston expansion without distortion and thus closer running clearances and less piston slap. This design was adopted for the 500 cc engines during the year and taken up by the 350 in the following one.

During 1948 the crankcase and crankshaft assembly of the 500 cc engine was adopted by the 350 so both used common parts. Of interest to riders seeking better comfort was a rear wheel springing conversion kit offered by Geoffrey Siddaway. This bolted to the existing rigid frame and gave three inches of movement with hydraulic damping in both directions adjustable by metering screws.

This, and other similar kits, filled a gap for a while especially as, when springer AMC models

Left **Line drawing of the jampot which superseded the candlestick for 1951**

Right **Showtime advert linking the AJS racing background to their road models**

Below **1952 competition Matchless G80C, 500 cc of plonking single**

STAND
Nº 32
Earls Court
6
The Race-bred Motor Cycle

were announced for 1949, they were labelled export only along with the new twins introduced at the same time. The home range thus remained the same but not without modifications. The main one to the engine was the adoption of hairpin valve springs which entailed a new iron cylinder head with wider valve wells and a matching rocker box. At the same time the barrel fins were made deeper to match the new head and the valve lifter moved to the rocker box, which cleaned up the appearance a little, shortened its operating cable, and simplified the tappet and its guide. The 350 engine was fitted with the wire wound type piston and the dynamo speed increased a trifle to give more output at low speed.

The revised engines were given new frames much as before but with sidecar lugs built in. The frame changes improved accessibility and allowed the fitting of an air cleaner, although this remained an option and was not supplied as standard. The oil tank was made larger but continued to contain its detachable filter as before, while across the frame the dynamo regulator was bolted to the rear of the battery carrier, not to lugs on the rear frame below the saddle. At the front went new handlebars and headlamp shell and at the rear a new lamp of rectangular form with chrome plated cover. The saddle nose was drilled to provide a choice of seating heights.

The new frames used for the home market were built in two parts and it was by changing the rear one that the new swinging fork frame was produced. Thus any rigid model could be converted if the owner wished and could find all the necessary parts. The sprung models were four in number, all export at first and built in both engine sizes and marques. The addition of the letter 'S' to the type reference distinguished them as the 16MS and G3LS of 350 cc, and 18S and G80S in the 500 cc size.

The Matchless single with front mounted magneto as built from 1952 to 1954, a G3L

The frame design utilized the patent taken out some time before so that the bearing tube carried an oil reservoir to lubricate the working surfaces. By removing a small screw in the right end cap this supply could be replenished with the screw also acting as a level. At the end of the rear fork went the two suspension and damper units which were made by AMC and as used by them on their road racing models.

The units used for that year were slim and the internal pressures high so they were very sensitive to the amount of oil in them and prone to leaking it away and losing all damping. Due to their shape they became known as 'candlesticks' and had one feature unique to AMC, clevis ends top and bottom to straddle the fixing to frame and fork. Other firms used a single overhung pin or made the frame part the clevis, but AMC stuck to their special way for many years.

Early in 1949 a G3L won an economy test held on the other side of the world in New Zealand when John Dale recorded a remarkable 238 mpg. Later in the same year he went a little better to reach 246·4 mpg, and Matchless took a front cover advert in *Motor Cycling* to publicize the achievement alongside a petrol coupon—rationing still being in force in the UK.

For 1950 the range was not extended and few changes occurred on the road models other than to details. These included ribbed mudguards, a new prop stand, a centre stand for the springers, the toolbox moved to between the chainstays on the rigid models, a new silencer with offset ends and a longer carburettor body which allowed a spacer in the inlet tract to be deleted.

Further changes were the adoption of a long torque arm for the front brake and a five-spring clutch in place of the older four-spring one on all except the road 350s.

As well as the brake arm and clutch the competition machines received some major changes. The engines became all alloy with cast-in valve seats and iron cylinder liner, the head being retained by four sleeve nuts screwed to

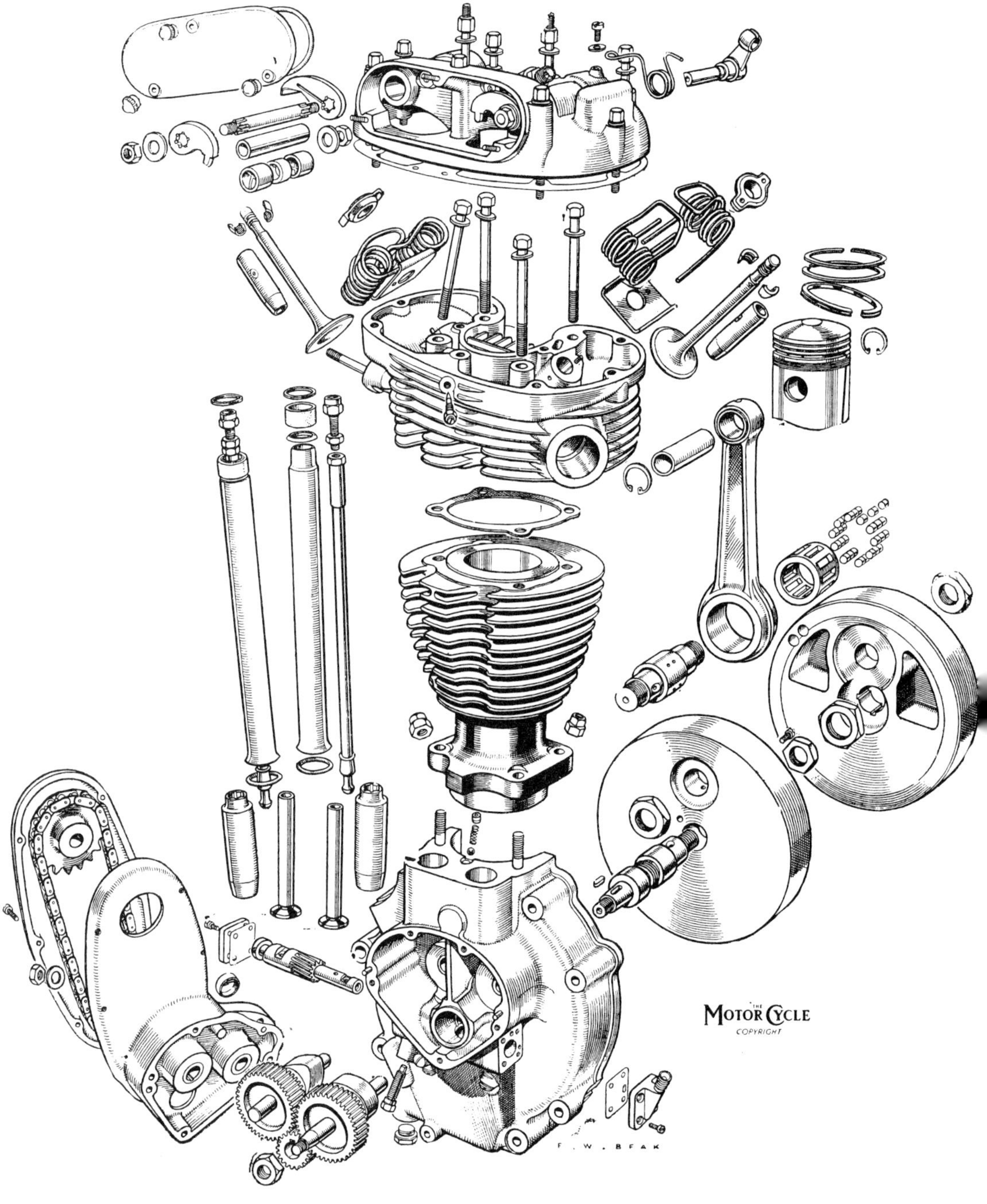
THE MOTOR CYCLE
COPYRIGHT
F. W. BEAK

Exploded single cylinder AMC engine around 1954. Classic English construction with built up crankshaft and overhead valves

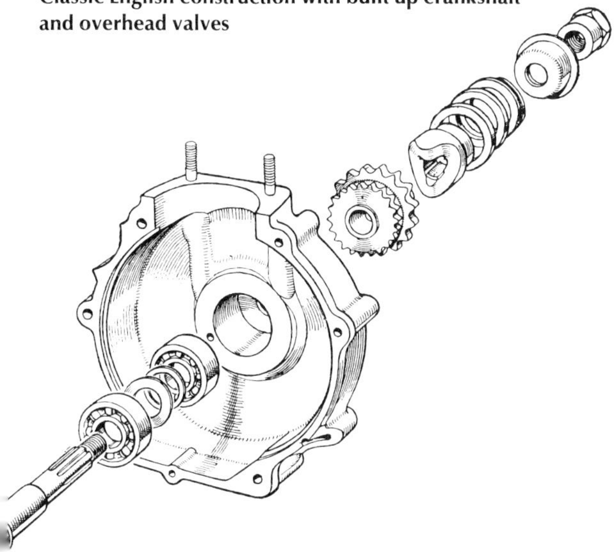

long studs in the crankcase. This followed the line taken by the works trials bikes over the previous year or two. A much more functional appearance was gained by the fitment of a smaller 2 gallon petrol tank, handling was improved with a shorter frame, and the toolbox became a small tubular canister under the saddle with a quick-action wing nut lid fastener like a filler cap. The competition engines also benefitted from the fitting of the Lucas 'wader' magneto, fully waterproofed and with its breather connected to a high rise pipe.

AMC are often thought of as a staid firm producing sound but unexciting designs. An inkling of what they could think of occurred early in 1950 when a patent applied for in 1946 was accepted. This was for a frame constructed from both sheet pressings and tubes, the first assembled to make a spine frame with means of enclosing many of the machine's accessories within the pressings. To this structure was attached twin down tubes to loop under the engine. Rear suspension with swinging fork was envisaged and a dualseat was specified. The fuel tank was freely mounted so devoid of frame stresses and the spine frame was to be built using Duralumin light alloy sheet rather than steel.

The design was by Phil Walker and a prototype was built, but sadly it crashed on test killing its rider and after that work on the project ceased.

In August 1950 New Zealander, John Dale, visited England and demonstrated his art of obtaining phenomenal mpg with a G3L at MIRA. His method was to fit 3·00 in. section ribbed tyres to both wheels, a smaller bore carburettor, to remove the electrics, and pour thin oil into the engine and gearbox. The machine went off in third or top gear and Dale rode flat on the tank, feet on pillion rests and hands holding the fork tubes, when heading into the wind, and bolt upright where it could assist him. His speed was a very steady 18 to 20 mph and he took well over eight hours to use half a gallon of petrol, with which he covered 155 miles to achieve 310 mpg —a remarkable figure even allowing for the methods used.

1951 saw the introduction of a good few changes, some detail and some more major, plus a further two models for the sportsman, competition springers with the letters CS added as a suffix to their marque and type number. The road singles were fitted with a die-cast light alloy cylinder head with cast-iron valve inserts and, as the exhaust port angle was altered a little to be more horizontal, the pipe sweep was also changed. With the alloy head went alloy push-rods to maintain the clearances as the engine warmed up, but otherwise the internals remained as before except for a minor improvement to the big end. On the outside the magneto drive cover of the Matchless models was cleaned up and polished to improve appearance.

On the cycle side the most obvious change was to the rear suspension units which became much fatter and known as 'jampots'. The redesign was done to reduce the loads on the seals and give a little more tolerance to the quantity of oil used in the dampers. They were still prone

The 1957 G80S, 500 cc, dualseat, twin pilot lights and usual excellent AMC finish

1958 AJS 16MCS plus lighting equipment, really a street legal scrambler and thus a fifties enduro bike

to leaking and great variation in damping as the oil warmed up, but AMC continued to persevere with them for some years. The new rear units were matched at the front by forks with the insides changed once more so they were much as the original design. A detail improvement was the recessing of the drain plugs to stop them being wiped off by high kerbs when parking.

The lower fork crown became a forged steel part and a new chaincase seal was adopted in an endeavour to make the task of assembly a little easier but the stories of the mystique needed to stop the oil coming out continued to circulate round the clubs. An improved dynamo with ball race bearings at both ends of the armature was fitted, while the horn mounting was

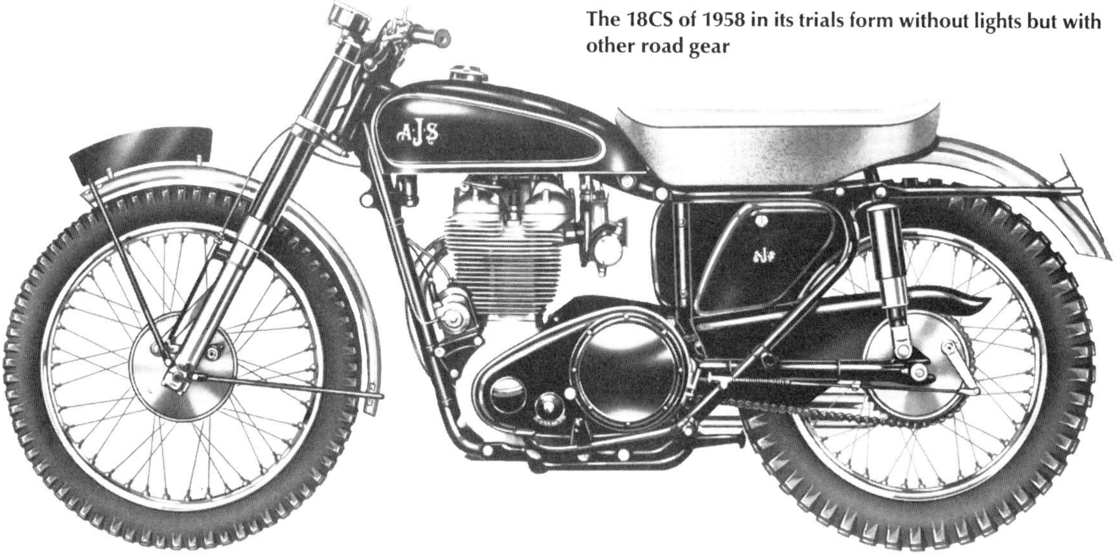

The 18CS of 1958 in its trials form without lights but with other road gear

1958 road model AJS 500, the 18S with alloy chaincase, alternator and coil ignition

made more flexible to inhibit fractures. The control cables and wiring were tidied up a good deal and the horn button screwed into the right handlebar with its wire passed internally to the harness. The AJS models adopted an oval metal tank badge in place of the transfers.

The competition springers came in both sizes and both marques with the all-alloy engine in the swinging fork frame. The silencer was uptilted but the toolbox, just as on the roadsters, tucked into the sub frame loop behind the oil tank. The gearbox fitted was the heavyweight BA Burman, and the footrests were very sturdy indeed.

Also available for the competition rider were light alloy petrol tanks and silencers but made for Paramount products by Ted Frend as a piece

Offside of the 1958 model 16MS. Without the front magneto the appearance is much changed from earlier machines

of private enterprise despite his involvement with the company as a rider. They were in practice sold by Taylor Matterson who was best known as a Norton specialist.

In August 1951 a new Burman gearbox was announced and this was adopted by the whole of the AMC range for 1952. The new box was called the B52 and was based on that used for the road racing ohc model. It replaced both the BA and CP units and featured a short, sturdy gear train, much simplified positive stop mechanism, better oil sealing and an improved clutch. The layout was conventional for the period with sleeve gear concentric with mainshaft and running in ball races with the layshaft underneath and rotating in bushes, unlike the racing unit which employed loose rollers in most places.

Gear selection was by moving one gear on each shaft and the selectors were controlled by a drum cam moved directly by the change mechanism housed under the right hand cover. Under this also went the kickstarter quadrant and a new form of clutch lift mechanism, although the old type was still available for firms who perferred it. The new design used three ball bearings held between two steel pressings with ramp recesses to take them. One pressing was held in the end housing and the other turned by the clutch cable so the balls ran up the ramps and moved the push rod.

The clutch itself had four or five friction plates, depending on its use, and an adjustor screwed into the pressure plate. Access to this was gained via a small cover added to the primary chaincase for the 1952 machines. A cable adjustor screwed into the box outer end cover and access for hooking the cable to the lift mechanism was by the removal of a screwed cap.

As well as the new gearbox there were a number of other noticeable changes for the 1952 models. Perhaps the most obvious only applied to the Matchless marque for the magneto moved from behind the cylinder, where it had been since the G3 had been introduced in 1935. Thus the two marques became even more similar with just the magneto cover making the difference. One advantage from this and the new gearbox was that the dynamo could now be removed from the right so was less of a chore to service. Inside the engine went an altered timing side main with bigger flange and chrome plated top piston rings. On the 500 the compression plate was removed and the barrel lengthened to compensate so that seekers of a higher ratio had to

Above **1959 AJS, either a 16 or an 18, in this example encased with side shields and carrying a fairing with screen**

Below **The model 18 in 1959 with chrome tank sides**

fit another piston. The competition units retained the plate which served as an easy means of changing the ratio to suit trials or scrambles. At the top the seating for the hairpin springs was altered to make spring changing easier and alignment automatic.

On the outside the front brake backplate became alloy and polished, while the lower fork legs were left unpainted and were also polished. The fork top crown had a material change from aluminium to malleable iron and was reformed to make the speedometer mounting neater. The headlight unit was new and the shell incorporated the infamous and useless underslung pilot light forced on the public at that time. The wiring to it and the other electrics was made easier to connect up by the use of colour coding and at the same time a positive earth was adopted and the dynamo control unit rubber mounted. Because of the magneto change, the horn on the Matchless was moved behind the cylinder into the AJS position.

Due to restrictions then in force because of a nickle shortage, the finish was altered to the earlier mainly black with gold or silver tank lining. Wheel rims were no longer chrome plated but finished by a process called 'Argenizing', which gave them a matt aluminium appearance and their centres were no longer painted or lined.

Competition Matchless at the 1960 show with Jock West (centre) showing points to Douglas Bader

1961 G80CS with oil tank on the left and tubular air filter attached to massive GP carburettor

Other side of equivalent AJS, the 18CS, built to the same specification and also from 1961

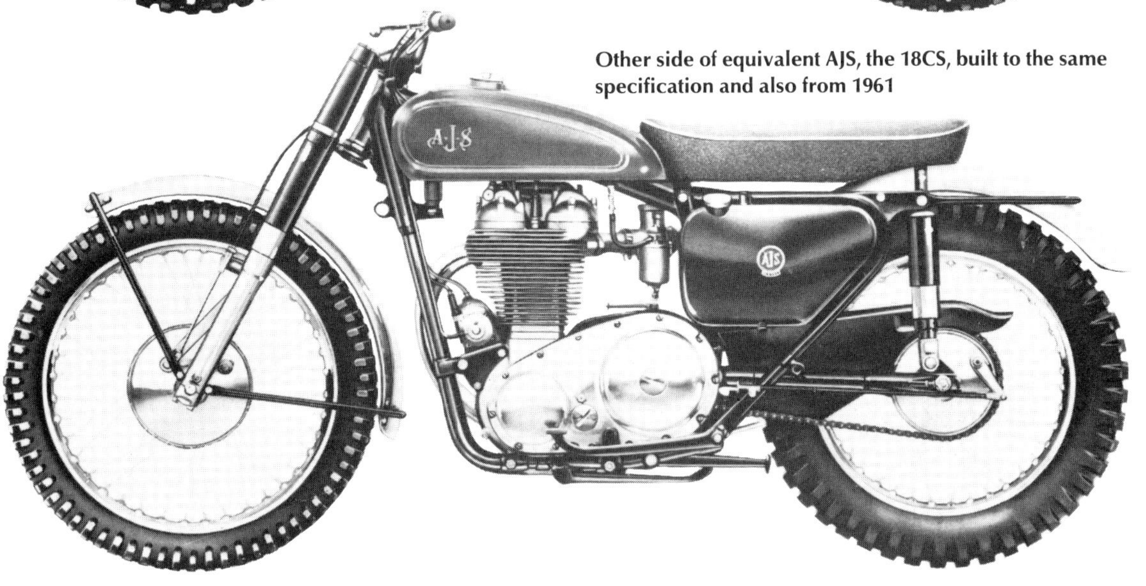

The tank badges were both new and both light alloy die-castings. The AJS one comprised the three letters attached to a single crossbar which bolted to the tank, the letters alone having a gold anodised finish. For Matchless the badge became small and round with a letter 'M' on a red background and with the flying wings to each side.

Another alloy petrol tank came on to the market late in 1951, this being the Lyta of 2 gallons capacity and available painted black or left in the natural aluminium. Early in 1952 AMC announced a new form of pillion seat that went partway to a dualseat. It was the usual pad with coil springs at the back but attached directly to the saddle at the front. A curious arrangement to be offered for a spring frame machine, especially as AMC had a dualseat fitted as standard on one of their existing twins and in practice the device never reached production.

The need for this odd seat went when the 1953 range was announced as all the springer road models were fitted with a dualseat as standard. Otherwise it was mainly details that year, although the front brake was revised with the cam lever pointing forward and the cable anchorage moved to suit. Some details of the front forks changed and the lower crown was altered to take a steering locking bar and pad-

1961 competition AJS 16C with small tank, saddle and front brake

Road 16 or 18 from 1961, a staid single

lock. The fork shrouds became free to turn to suit export packaging, while rubber washers held them firmly until the headlamp was fixed.

At the rear end a Lucas Diacon lamp was fitted which was larger than that used before and allowed a stop lamp to be offered as an option. Also the rear part of the rear mudguard was made separate and no longer hinged to the main piece. Nearer the front the centre stand was made sturdier, the chaincase seal made endless and the magneto shield smaller with the lead taken forward and through it. For export only some chrome plating came back on the rims and tank but for the home market the austerity finish continued.

Matchless version, the G3 or G80 in 1961, only tank, transfers and badges were different

Right side of the 1961 road Matchless single with chrome plated tank panels

The sixteen different models that AMC managed to squeeze out of one basic engine design and two frames ran on into 1954 with quite a number of changes. Inside the engines went new cams, mildly stronger for the road machines and more so for the sprung competition models, which also had a raised compression ratio and produced more power. In the bottom half went lighter flywheels except in the rigid competition engines intended for trials where low speed plonk was essential.

The new flywheels had a larger diameter timing side mainshaft which was a parallel press fit in the wheel and in turn this meant a change to the main bearing on that side. In the rocker box a controlled bleed fed oil to the rocker contact points and the valve springs via grooves in the rocker arms, while on the outside went larger carburettors.

The ignition system for the road 500s was changed to a Lucas SR1 rotating magnet magneto with automatic advance, and to accommodate the mechanism, which was embodied with the drive sprocket, a bulge appeared in the drive chain cover. On the other side of the machine the dome in the primary chaincase for the clutch was made a separate piece so that maintenance of that unit could be more easily carried out.

The most obvious chassis change was the adoption of a full width light alloy front hub with central cooling fins and shrunk-in liner. A less obvious but very useful improvement was the fitting of straight spokes in the new hub. A further easily seen change was to a pair of pilot lights positioned either side of the main headlight.

Other alterations were flared mudguards, a new prop-stand spring, flexible fuel lines, cable lubricators and the moving of the dynamo regulator under the seat. The tanks were modified with the capacity of that used on the 500 cc road models increasing and the filter in the oil tank becoming easier to change. Finally, the tank badges became plastic mouldings on the road models.

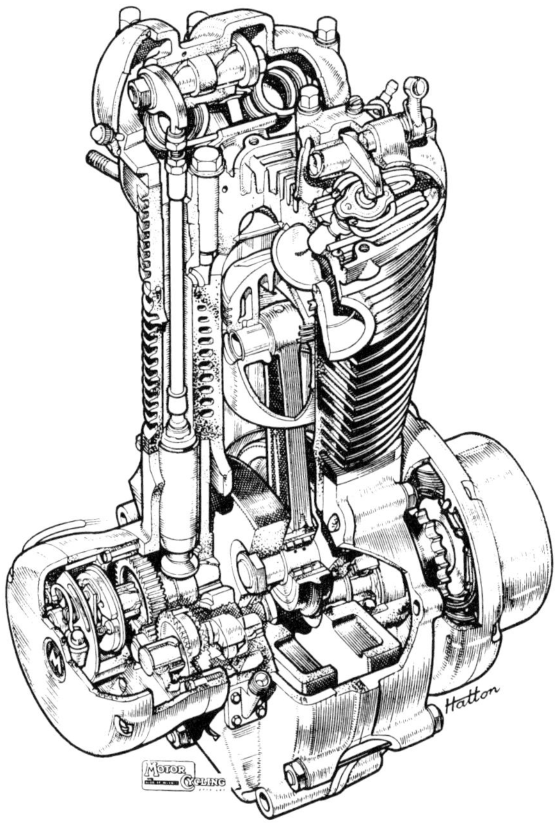

Line drawing of the 1962 350 cc single with integral pushrod tunnels in barrel

For the competition machines the front half of the rigid frame became a lighter all-welded part and these models had a change to the gearbox ratios. The springers were given revised rear damper units with a stiffer action and a dualseat. All competition models had the gearbox mainshaft to chaincase seal improved and a new filler cap for the oil tank that was more tucked in and less likely to dig into the rider's leg. To top off the changes, the petrol tank became light alloy but remained the same capacity.

1955 brought a further long list of relatively minor changes, for AMC policy was one of very steady development—some said so steady as to be barely discernable. The competition

A 1962 G3S outside a dealer of that time waiting for its buyer

machines had polarized to a degree with the rigid ones used for trials and the springers for scrambles, but either could be supplied to suit whichever branch of the sport the customer wished to participate in. Otherwise the range plodded on with adequate if unexciting performance from the 500 and rather less than this from the 350, which had to drag the weight of the larger machine along. A common practice in the industry at that time.

Changes for the year were to the hubs, which were trued after spoking, with the front reducing in width with greater dishing of backplate and end cover, plus the fins taking a barrel profile. The rear hub also became full width in light alloy with a quick detachable facility for the springers but not the rigid frames. On the former, screw chain adjustors were adopted in place of the cams used before. The jampots were further modified as were the front forks, which had new top covers and crowns, also bigger fork tubes.

The new top crown was shaped to match a new and deeper headlamp shell that carried the speedometer plus lighting switch and ammeter. The front mudguard lost its front stay and gained a central bridge, while the frame seat tube had a casting fitted into it with a hole through its centre for the air hose plus bosses for studs supporting both the oil tank and the battery carrier. The air cleaner itself remained an option and the pillion footrest supports became pressings incorporating one of the sidecar connection points.

A deeper chainguard was fitted and a neater rear brake pedal and spring, while the saddle springs, when fitted, became barrel shaped. The oil tank connections were revised, a rear reflector added and new silencers fitted. All models had the new Amal Monobloc and internally the timing side bush was given a bigger flange and the inner drive side main ballrace made larger.

The road 350 received the larger petrol tank and the SR1 magneto with automatic advance that had been fitted to the 500 the previous year so also had the chain cover with bulge. The rigid competition models reverted to a 2·75 in. front tyre section and the springers got another dualseat and, for scrambles use, a TT carburettor.

The singles range was really by now rather dated and the rigid models in particular showed their pre-war ancestry. So for 1956 the rigid models were dropped and a new trials model with swinging fork frame appeared along with new scramblers with short stroke engines.

The road machines received a new frame with vertical seat tube running down to the fork pivot but, as it was also used for a new large twin, it did nothing to enliven the 350s performance. It did enable the appearance of the models to be styled more with a long thin oil tank tucked into the right subframe and a matching container on the left. This housed the battery, tools and regulator with a front panel across the frame, while the horn went under the dualseat which was increased in length.

Further smoothing of the edges took the form of a snap-on cover over the primary chain adjustor above the gearbox, grouping of the control cables and their location to the fork crown, a combined horn button and dipswitch on the left bar and a chrome plated embellishing disc riveted to the backplate of the rear brake. The adjustor for this moved to the front end of the operating rod, while at the front the backplate was rotated to bring the cam lever to the top where it lay behind the left fork leg but still pointed forward. Also at the front, the stand was deleted so the mudguard support became a simple stay.

Internally, compression ratios rose as did power outputs and a magnetic oil filter in the crankcase replaced the fabric one in the old oil tank. Finally, the AJS tank badge was made a little larger.

The new trials model was only available in 350 cc form as the 16MC or G3LC. It thus

The Matchless G3 in 1962 when it was called the Mercury by AMC alone and sported massive tank badges

repeated the designation of the older rigid competition model to everyone's confusion as the new machine had a swinging fork frame. The new frame was all-welded and a short wheelbase was achieved by mounting the rear fork pivot to the front of the vertical seat tube. The compression ratio of the engine remained a modest 6·5:1.

The 16 MCS scrambler and its larger version the 18CS/G80CS were fitted with all-alloy short stroke engines. These had the push rod tunnels cast integral with the cylinder and forged steel flywheels with a racing style connecting rod and single row of big end rollers. The stroke of both was 85·5 mm which with a 72 mm bore gave 348 cc, and with 86 mm an oversquare 497 cc. Compression ratios were 9·9 and 8·7:1 and valve timing as the earlier sports engine, while Monobloc carburettors were fitted. The machines were supplied with a centre stand and a silencer which was changed for a plain extension when racing.

The frame was very similar to the road range but had an extra brace between the tops of the rear damper supports. The suspension was stiffer than on the road models.

In the middle of the year came news of a major change for all the models, a new gearbox which became known as the AMC type. In fact it was based heavily on the Norton box whose ancestry went back to 1935 in its own right and further still in its original Sturmey-Archer form. The reasons behind this change were partly the AMC takeover of Norton in 1953 and a massive tooling investment programme begun around the same time. With their own gear cutters to hand and a policy of standardization already underway with the London based marques, it was inevitable that one gearbox would be used for all the larger machines.

The box retained all the good features of the Norton unit with a revised positive stop mechanism and the Norton clutch. What was lost was the big mushroom end of the clutch push rod which did much for the clean Norton change by ensuring the clutch plate lifted square regardless of the spring loads. This was replaced by a floating lever device that required an adjustor in the clutch centre and a good feature was lost.

In other respects the gearbox was excellent, well sealed and compact. It went on to all models for 1957 and, as the clutch contained a shock absorber, the face cam one on the engine shaft

The 1962 AJS Southerner better known to owners as the 18CS and built for scrambling

was deleted and the clearance dome for it in the chaincase reduced in size.

Among other changes for the year was the fitting of Girling rear units in place of the AMC ones but still with the clevis end at the bottom, although the top fixing was the normal eye so the frame had to be changed to suit. Small ribs were added to the sides of the oil tank and the toolbox lid. Push-on oil pipes were adopted, a new inlet cam fitted, and chrome tank panels offered as an option. The 350 alone continued with the 1956 frame but modified to use Girlings and for the one year was fitted with seat and oil tank to suit.

While the embargo on road test machines seemed just as rigid as always, the firm was more flexible over competition models and allowed *The Motor Cycle* to play with one of 50 special Matchless' early in 1957. The venue was Brands Hatch and the machine built as a flat-tracker for California. Thus it had the all-alloy short stroke scrambles engine in a rigid frame with the earlier lighter teles. No front brake or mudguard was fitted but both wheels had alloy rims and fat tyres. The oil tank was mounted up by the rear wheel in the old toolbox position and the rider perched on a saddle.

With only 250 lb of weight and plenty of tree-stump pulling power the take off was pure sprint—full throttle, drop the clutch and spin the rear wheel. The power was up a touch on the stock engine for the flat-track unit had a central plug, 9:1 compression ratio and a GP carburettor on a long inlet tract.

Although this particular model was of 500 cc, in later years it was to be followed by a larger single built for the USA. This was the 18TCS/G80TCS Typhoon which had an all-alloy engine stretched out to 89 × 96 mm and 597 cc. Compression ratio was usually 8·7:1 but an alternative piston giving 12:1 was also available and peak power was developed at 5500 rpm. The cycle parts were as the scrambles CS models with open exhaust, no lights, short dualseat, alloy mudguards and competition tyres. A 600 cc flat tracker was also built and smaller trials models destined for the USA were labelled the model 16MCT although these seem to be rare birds and would have been less suited to American style desert racing and similar events.

Aside from these more special builds the road singles for 1958 were given AC electrics which brought a good few alterations, including a change to a cast aluminium primary chaincase. The scrambles and trials machines continued, however, with magneto and pressed steel case. On the road models the alternator rotor was bolted to the end of the crankshaft, while the stator was located in the outer half of the chaincase. The controlling rectifier went under the seat and the ignition coil under the tank.

The timing side was altered with a new and much smaller outer case to support the camshaft ends and carry the contact points. The cam for their control was attached to and driven by the inlet cam and the whole enclosed by a simple outer cover. Without the forward magneto the whole appearance was much changed.

The only other changes of note were to the twin pilot lights, which were dropped, to the rear dampers which were shortened, and to the finish. In this the wheels became all chrome plated without painted centres and painted tank panels were offered as an option. The scrambles machines were given a new seat, wider mudguards, a slimmer oil tank and, for the American market, the option of a smaller diameter but wider front tyre. The lighting set that had always been available for the competition models was made quickly detachable, while the frame of the trials model was made lighter and ground clearance increased a good deal to a claimed 10 in.

In May 1958 the machine colour was brightened up a little from the black and gold or silver, although this continued to be used as standard. The option offered for AJS was blue for mudguards, tanks and toolbox with silver panels, while the Matchless had silver guards and petrol

1963 Matchless road single with new front hub, normal Girlings, 18 in. rims, restyled oil tank and kneegrip recesses on a G80

1962 AJS 16 showing the older features including silencer and mudguards which were to change for the next year

Final version of the 350cc trials AJS, the 16C of 1963–64 with pad saddle but still much as its predecessors

tank with red oil tank, toolbox and tank panels.

1959 saw little change to the road models with just deeper section mudguards appearing but the trials model received another frame and a needed reduction in weight. The new frame gave a shorter wheelbase and was fitted with long inclined Girlings. The fork they controlled had no bridge but one arm was fixed to the pivot spindle and the other was secured to it by a cotter pin. Further weight was saved by the subframe, a smaller oil tank and the fitment of 5·5 in. brakes in offset hubs. For both road and competition models bright finishes were available in blue or red.

For that year the model designations were altered, with the 16MS, 16MC, 16MCS, 18S, G3LS, G3LC, G3LCS and G80S becoming the 16, 16C, 16CS, 18, G3, G3C, G3CS and G80, which helped a little but not much. At the end of the year the 350 cc scrambler was discontinued.

1960 brought new frames for the singles with duplex down tubes and full cradle under the engine. The gearbox ratios were closed up a touch and the 500 cylinder head was modified on the inside and in the ports and thus needed a new piston. The headlamp shell was made smaller but continued to carry the speedometer, while a two level dualseat was adopted.

The trials 350 had the rear mudguard support strengthened and the fork pivot improved. The scrambles 500 was further changed with the oil tank moved to the left to make way for a big GP carburettor, which carried an air filter in the old tank place. When the model was ordered in road trim, as was possible, it was fitted with an alternator and the battery went on the right under the air filter.

At last the company ban on press road tests was partially lifted and *Motor Cycling* had a G3 with the duplex frame on loan. It was not a test in the full sense with tables of performance figures, but the text spoke of 75 mph obtained by laying on the tank, about par for overweight 350s of that era. In fact it was very similar to what the mid-1930s G3 would do, for the extra power of the postwar machine was counter-balanced by the added weight it had to tow along. Handling and comfort were good as were the brakes,

Road AJS model 16 or 18 in 1963, the last year of the all AMC machine

but the lighting was below par and the horn feeble. The two-level dualseat was praised by both rider and passenger.

1961 brought few changes, although the oil pump drive was improved by strengthening the gear teeth, and the inlet guide located with a circlip as the exhaust had been for some while. The mudguards were shortened a little and the tank badges enlarged, but that was it and production just ran on.

Production, in fact of a rather overweight and staid line of models that were beginning to lose touch with the market. There the accent was on 250s with a sporting performance and big twins, with the number of riders seeking a quiet, reliable plodding single, growing smaller as time passed by. Even the colours remained the same, just reversed on the petrol tank when the two-tone option was specified, and this attempt to jazz up what was basically a quarter-of-a-century old design was rather out of place. The customer for the heavyweight single was much more likely to prefer the traditional black with the discreet gold or silver lining. Or to show a preference for olive green, if the customer was the Dutch Army who bought 300 Matchless 350s early in 1961.

In the middle of that year came news of a plan to move the AMC plant to Sheerness on the Isle of Sheppey. The Plumstead site may have had investment in its machine shop but had remained in an area that was well out of town and with its own special traffic problems. Perhaps to make sure it did not move out of reach, the staff payroll was stolen in the following month!

The move to Sheerness was finally called off late in the year when it was realized more fully that there would not be the required pool of skilled labour available. Perhaps the full cost of the new factory and the downturn in trading conditions were more real reasons, for labour supply is one of the most basic of criteria in site selection.

In 1961 AMC fortunes were on the wane with a loss replacing their 1960 profit and considerable rumblings from the shareholders as to the way the group was run. At the same time the tariff protection that had existed since the end of the war disappeared and the scooter and the Mini

1964 AJS 16 or 18 with revised engine and Norton forks and hubs

were eating into the transport market.

Travel was changing in the UK with the M1 open from London to Birmingham and sufficient affluence to make a £500 Mini look very attractive alongside a £300 big twin motorcycle. It may not have been as fast but the phenomenal roadholding made it fun to drive and, of course, it carried four and their luggage. It was to be another ten years or more before affluence had moved on enough for the bike to be a second, and often more convenient, vehicle.

Meanwhile there was little attraction to motorcycle cruising as the motorway and dual roads became boring and the machines were not really fast enough for riders to do long trips quickly; 95 or the ton down the bypass was one thing, but a steady 85 for 250 miles something else altogether.

Despite the problems there were changes for 1962 with names for all the models, bigger tank badges, and a revized road 350 engine. This had dimensions of 74 × 81 mm and a compression ratio up to 8·5 : 1. As with the competition short stroke engines, the barrel had the push rod tunnels cast-in but remained in iron. It had bigger valves, carburettor and exhaust pipe and power was up to 23 bhp at 6200 rpm. The petrol tank was larger at over 4 gallons and located on a pair of expanding rubber bushes at the front on the underside and a pad at the rear.

Otherwise the machine was as the old long stroke, which was dropped in road form but continued as the trials 16C and G3C. The new model 16 was accompanied by the inevitable G3, and both by sports versions with downswept bars and chrome plated mudguards and chainguard. Model numbers of these were 16S and G3S.

Detail changes were the addition of a breather tower in the oil tank, roll-on feet on the centre stand, stronger kickstart spring, louder horn, a battery change and a key for the ignition instead of a knob on the switch. The trials 350 had a narrower but deeper petrol tank.

The new tank badges were large zinc alloy, chrome plated, pressure die-castings. The AJS one had the letters set in an oval surrounded by a panel with horizontal ribs, while the Matchless flying M was flanked above and below by pronounced bars. In either case the tanks retained kneegrips aft of the badges.

The names for the models were not to prove too popular, and for the heavyweight singles were Sceptre (16) and Mercury (G3), Sceptre Sports (16S) and Mercury Sports (G3S), Experts (16C) and Maestro (G3C), Statesman (18) and Major (G80), and Southerner (18CS), Marksman (G80CS) and Typhoon (G80TCS).

The Motor Cycle had a Statesman on test in March and a confirmed most of the findings of their opposition with regard to handling, braking and the continued fitment of a poor horn. Top speed with the wind up the rider's tail was 87 mph and, as with the 350, this compared well with a pre-war 83 mph. The model 18 did all that the rider expected in the manner of the big English single and an appealing way of travel it was too with the engine turning over in a slow but forceful way aided by the big flywheels. Heavy wheels, low compression ratio and not too many revs all combined with a high gear to give a very special type of motorcycling.

And this was confirmed by a test of a Matchless G3 Mercury, which retained the restful quality of the single even with its reduced stroke. A later test with a Garrard single-seat sidecar attached showed how these qualities enabled the 350 to pull the added weight with just a gearing reduction. 60 mph was reached by the outfit

The Matchless G3 or G80 in 1964 showing the Norton hubs, the same machine was also offered as a Norton by changing badges

and its handling was sporting making it a pleasure to use.

Late in the year the sports version of the new 350 was dropped but its chrome plated guards were made available as an option for the standard model. For 1963 there was a new front hub with fewer cooling fins but wider linings and it turned on ball races, not the taper rollers used for so long.

The height of the machines was reduced and their appearance altered by a whole series of measures. The subframe and rear fork were new and the rear units inclined Girlings with normal ends, the AMC clevis having finally left the singles. 18 inch rims were fitted along with new mudguards and both oil tank and toolbox restyled more to curves. The dualseat was narrower and the kneegrips set in tank recesses to reduce width at this vital point. A new silencer appeared with tapered section at each end and no tailpipe, and the stop light switch was in direct contact with the brake pedal and also acted as its height stop. A full chaincase was available as an option and a pair of zig-zag lines were added to the tank finish.

For the competition man the 500 scrambler received the new front hub and the works air cleaner, while the trials 350 was left alone.

During late 1962 AMC had moved the Norton production line to Plumstead where it began operations early in 1963. In 1964 the effect of producing all the models in one place, and of desperate standardisation moves to cut costs and improve sales, became clearly visible.

The existing road models and the trials 350 all had their engines replaced by units based on the scrambles motor and its 85·5 mm stroke. Bores were 72 and 86 mm and compression ratios 9·0 and 7·3 for the road and 7·0 for the trials engine. Push rod tunnels were integral with the cylinder and all engines had the head sleeve nuts screwed to long crankcase studs.

Inside went a steel connecting rod, single row alloy caged big end bearing as used in the camshaft road racer, steel flywheels and a timing side roller plus plain bush to replace the old flanged main. Lubrication was by a Norton gear pump which replaced the old reciprocating plunger design and made for another common component. It was driven in Norton fashion by a worm nut

The 1965 AJS model 18 with diamond shaped tank badge, its change for that year

Matchless G85CS in 1966 with all alloy engine in welded frame with machined front hub and conical rear

that also held the timing pinion in place. The oiling system was altered with a direct feed into the end of the crankshaft to the sides of the big end rollers and the rocker lubrication taken from the scavenge line so the pipe was less intrusive.

On the outside the changes to the road models were also directed at standardisation, for the frame was modified to accept Norton Roadholder forks and Norton hubs front and rear. The front brake thus became 8 in. diameter and the customer had the option of the special sidecar fork with reduced trail.

The competition models were less affected but the 500 was fitted with the Norton oil pump and the 350 with a short rigid seat with fibreglass base, revised sub-frame and shorter rear Girlings.

Team preparing for the 1966 ISDT with Mick Andrews leaning over the saddle. He retired but John Lewis and Peter Gaunt both won golds

Not much else was to be altered. Late in 1964 the trials 350 was dropped, victim of the many two strokes that were so much easier for most to ride and the change for 1965 was the adoption of a diamond-shaped badge for the AJS models.

At the same time the two road models were offered with Norton badges screwed to the tank which incensed followers of all three marques but indicated how desperate and how out of touch the once great firm had become.

The road models remained unchanged for 1966 but the scrambles derivative was replaced by one with a new frame and sold as a Matchless only, the G85CS. This used the all-alloy engine as before with central plug that allowed a 12:1 compression ratio to be specified.

It was housed in a welded, duplex frame that carried the rear fork between the tubes so that it was properly supported at the ends instead of desperately clutching at a centre pivot as in the past. At the front went lightweight forks which carried the AMC hub with all the fins machined off. At the rear went the magnesium-alloy conical hub from the road racer.

The air filter went behind the right side racing plate and the oil tank was fitted between the engine plates above the gearbox. Fabricated footrests were attached at three points with a clamp right across the frame and competition tyres fitted. A protection plate went in front of the engine and the exhaust pipe curled over the gearbox and inside the frame tube. Dry weight was 291 lb and power 41 bhp at 6500 rpm so it went well but, of course, took a strong rider to get the best from it.

The same engine with a 12·5:1 ratio, special cams and much reduced fins was also offered for speedway use, as the G85CSS. It had the magneto bolted directly to the timing chest in order that the ignition would not be disturbed when the engine was taken out of the frame. Twin float chambers for the alcohol fuel were fitted to the prototype.

In fact the G85CS was a near copy of the machine the Rickman brothers, Derek and Don, had been building since 1962. They had been successful in scrambles in the 1950s but by 1958 sought something better than was available off the shelf. The result they called 'Metisse', French

for 'mongrel', and used a Triumph engine, BSA frame and Norton forks. It worked well and by 1962 the brothers were building their own frames and began to use the Matchless engine, when Triumph stopped supplying.

The result was typical Rickman with a very light, very strong frame, beautifully finished and carrying parts designed for the job and reflecting all the brothers' experience.

During 1966 the firm's financial position went from bad to worse and production of the road singles came to a half. To the end they retained the same features of reliability and economy coupled with adequate if unexciting performance and good handling. The brakes had always been a little marginal, due to the weight they had to stop, and the electrics gave meaning to the term 'Prince of Darkness', coined by riders for Joseph Lucas. The cylinder looked lonely once the magneto went, and the rounded styling was not to everyone's taste, but as basic transport the singles rang the bell and the superb finish continued nearly to the end.

The Rickman Metisse using the G85CS engine in either 500 or 600 cc sizes

The company was taken over by Manganese Bronze in September 1966 and took the name Norton-Matchless. Its range comprized twins and one single, the G85CS scrambler, which received one change to improve the oil pump output. Its red petrol tank was made from fibreglass but this was often changed for an alloy Lyta unit which was part painted, part polished, and lined to set off the silver frame finish very well.

Production continued in a small way into 1969 when the last of the big singles left Plumstead. The company was now part of Norton-Villiers who moved to a new factory near Andover, and in 1971 the old works was closed for good and scheduled for demolition. By then the Matchless name, at least, was becoming a memory.

3 Lightweight singles

Late in the 1950s AMC decided to return to the quarter-litre class with a new model. They had built 250s in pre-war days and needed a smaller model to supplement their range of traditional singles and postwar twins. Most newcomers to motorcycling started on small machines and firms found that brand loyalty could take them on to buy the larger model after a year or two. In addition there was talk of legislation restricting learners to small machines and AMC needed a model to fit this need and supplement the two strokes built by their James and Francis-Barnet subsidiaries. Without a small four stroke they had nothing to offer against the small BSA, Triumph and Enfield marques.

Their answer was a clean-lined model which incorporated much of their single cylinder practice with some fresh thinking. The result looked like unit construction, although it was not, and in time became known as the lightweight model. In fact, at 325 lb, it was far from light but the name stuck as an easy way of referring to the machine as distinct from the larger singles.

The engine of the new model was based on dimensions of 69·85 × 64·85 mm which gave a 248·5 cc capacity. The actual crankshaft throw was 32·385 mm but the cylinder was offset 0·25 in. forward of the crankshaft to give a *désaxé* effect to reduce piston slap and this increased the piston stroke by a few thou.

The bottom half followed AMC single practice with a built up crankshaft turning in two ball races on the drive side and a plain bush on the timing. The big end had two rows of caged rollers. As was normal, the roller track was a sleeve in a nickel-chromium case-hardening steel pressed on to the pin which was then pressed into the cast iron flywheels and secured by nuts. The mainshafts were simply pressed and keyed into the wheels.

The connecting rod was in steel with a hardened sleeve pressed into the big-end eye and a bush for the small-end. The rod was ribbed round the big-end. The piston was wire-wound and had a shallow dome with valve cutaways to give a compression ratio of 7·8:1. It was retained by a bored gudgeon pin held by circlips and ran in a well finned iron barrel that was deeply spigotted into the crankcase and had the push rod tunnel cast in. To suit the lay of the rods the tunnel was of a figure eight cross-section and this section had a twist in it like a slow helix.

The reason for this was the line of the cylinder head which was skewed round 21·25 degrees to bring the exhaust to the right. The head itself was in aluminium alloy with the valve seats cast-in. Head and barrel were held down by four long sleeve nuts screwed to long studs fitted to the crankcase and the valves were restrained by hairpin springs. They slid in pressed-in guides located by a circlip on each and above them went a rocker box assembly copied from the larger singles. Thus it carried built up rockers with live spindles turning in a pair of bushes and had the usual side cover held by three nuts. No valve lifter was fitted but the rocker ends were grooved to help lubrication and the push rods had adjustors at their top ends.

The timing gear was of the simplest with a pinion keyed to the crankshaft meshed with a gear on a shaft carrying the two valve cams on its inboard end and the ignition advance and its cam at the outer. Above the cams went a pair of trailing followers to move the push rods which reached them via two separate holes in the top of the crankcase. Both camshaft and follower

pivot shaft were supported in the crankcase wall and by a small outer cover with the first turning in bushes.

Below the timing chest went the usual AMC plunger pump worm driven from the crankshaft through a slot cut in the main bearing bush. The system was dry sump so the pump had two diameters for supply and return. Less usual was the siting of the oil tank in the crankcase as in the Enfield. The oil sat in a space formed by the timing side crankcase, outside the inner wall and L-shaped, below and in front of the crankshaft. The space so formed was enclosed and sealed off by a lid which was not flat but formed to give it stiffness and to increase the tank capacity.

The oil was pumped to the big-end and the rockers from where it drained over the timing gear and into the crankcase. There it was collected by the scavenge pump and sent through an internal fabric filter housed in the left crankcase half before returning to the oil tank. The

Left **John Surtees and Cyril Quantrill inspect a cut-away G2 engine unit in John's showrooms at West Wickham in 1958**

Below **Exploded drawing of 250 cc engine unit with drive side case over the page. Note oil tank casting and simple valve gear**

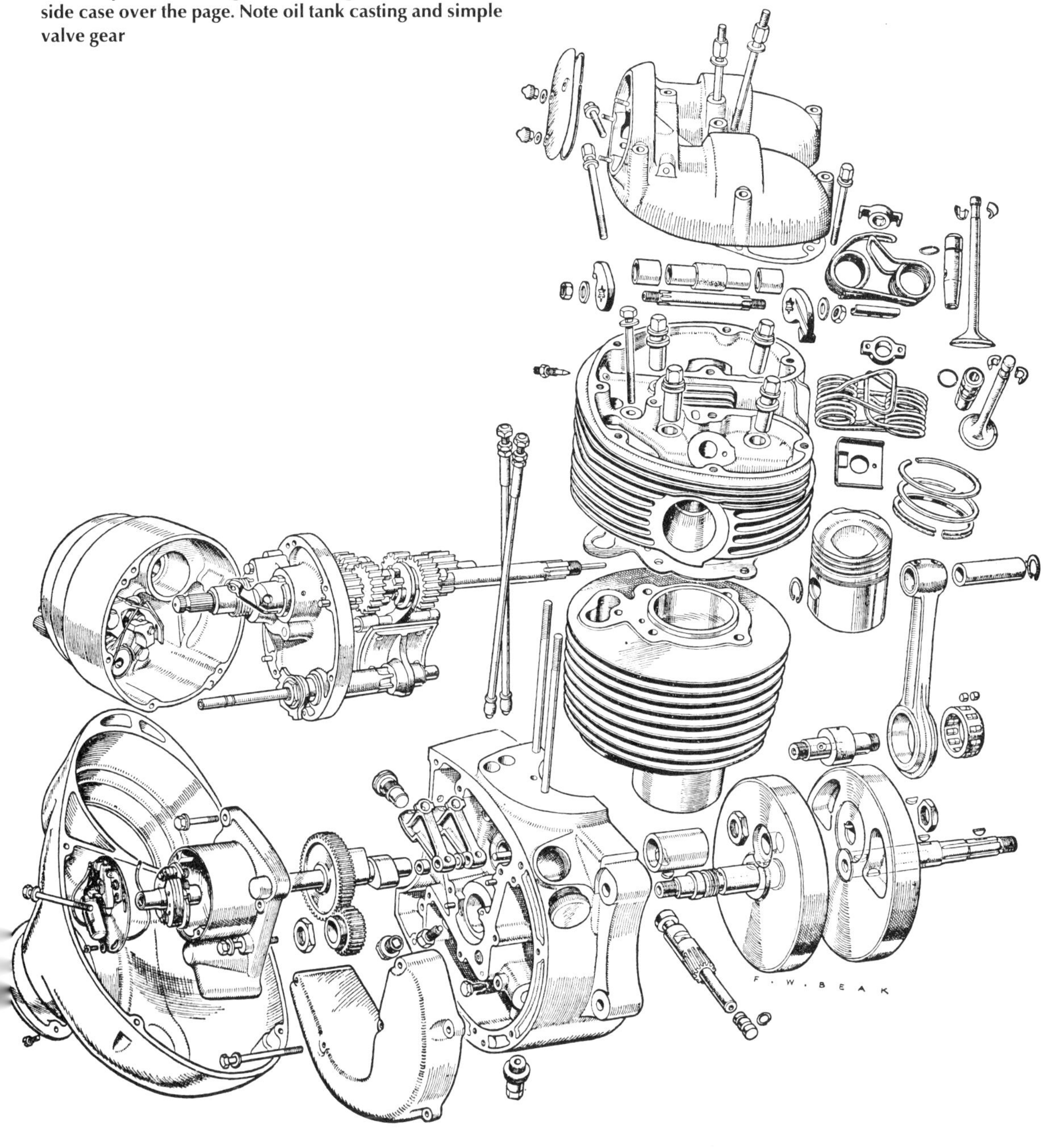

tank cap was a larger round screw in the top of the crankcase just ahead of the cylinder.

The engine had a timed breather built into the drive side mainshaft. This was part drilled from its inner end and ported to a sleeve keyed to it. This revolved in a ring fitted between the two main bearings, and a hole in this vented to the outside world.

The crankcase was split on the vertical centre line and had the gearbox in a separate housing strapped to it. The housing was cylindrical but the mainshaft off-centre so that rotation of the shell varied the primary chain tension without recourse to slippers or jockeys. That aside, the crankcase halves were conventional but the outer cover on the right and both inner and

Above **The gearbox which when installed has the gears at the top far above the oil level if this falls**

Below **Drive side of engine unit showing how the gearbox shell was clamped and the chain adjusted**

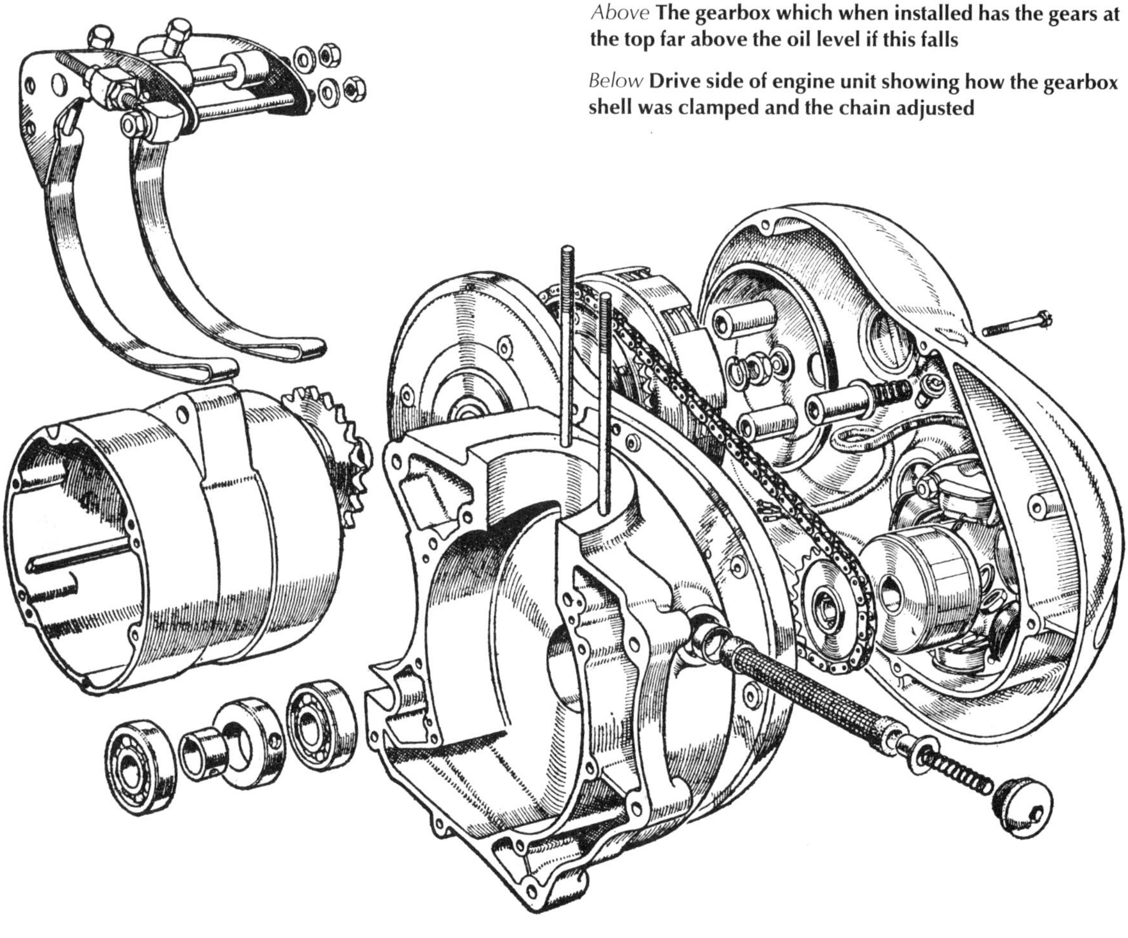

outer halves of the chaincase ran the full length of the complete engine and gearbox unit.

Ignition was by coil with the points accessible under a small plate set in the right outer cover and the generator went on the left. The rotor was keyed to the crankshaft outboard of the sprocket and the stator was located in the outer chaincase. The carburettor was an Amal Monobloc set at a downdraught angle with an insulation block between it and the head.

The primary drive was by single strand chain to a Norton style clutch with built-in shock absorber. Three insert plates and three springs were used and a simple lever lifted the pressure plate which had a central adjustor screw.

The gearbox was of normal English type with the layshaft set behind the mainshaft and the barrel quadrant selector plate and change mechanism at the bottom. A round plate went on the right to support the shafts and a round end cover went outboard of this to enclose the mechanism. A small plate gave access to the clutch cable end and the end cover sat in a hole in the engine outer cover. It could thus rotate within this when the chain was adjusted.

Two problems came with this gearbox, the first an appetite for gearchange springs and, of more potential concern, a need for three pints of oil. This second need arose from the cylindrical

The Matchless version of the AMC 250 cc single, only colour and badges distinguished it from the AJS

nature of the shell and the position of the gears and shafts stuck right at the top like stalactites in a cavern roof. As a good few owners were to find out, it took the full quantity of oil to give a level that the gears could dip into and any shortage meant they ran dry and soon wore out.

The actual chain adjustment was by a drawbolt above the gearbox and this and the clamp bolts were hidden under a small cover. On the outside of the box went a folding kickstarter and a gear indicator.

The engine unit went into a composite frame of which the main part was tubular and comprised top, down and seat tubes brazed into lugs. Under the engine the tubes were joined by a channel steel pressing which was itself boxed in under the gearbox. The rear subframe was bolted on and the rear fork had the pivot pin attached to the right leg and held by a cotter to the left. Girling units controlled the movement and at the front went hydraulically damped telescopic forks.

Hubs were ribbed and full width with six inch brakes and tyres were 3·25 × 17 in. front and rear. The mudguards were very deep and close fitting with the front one supported by a bridge and a tubular stay to the rear. The rear guard was styled to the dualseat and carried a boxed-in number plate, while the final drive chain was protected by guards or enclosed if the optional chaincase was specified. Below the seat on the right went the tools, battery, rectifier and tyre pump, while a similar cover on the left hid the horn and provided space for an optional air filter. A centre stand was provided and the finish was to the usual high AMC standard in black and blue for AJS and red for Matchless, the colour extending to flashes on each side of the engine.

Model designations were 14 and G2 and a quick early spin showed that they were good for just over 70 mph with brisk acceleration and good brakes. But then, having at last been allowed to ride an AMC test bike the magazine was hardly likely to verbally run it over sales director Jock West's toes before they had one for a full test.

The new machine was destined for export only at first but came on to the home market in June 1958 following a March release. It had detail changes only for 1959 but was joined by a scram-

The lightweight AJS model 14 in 1959 with ribbed dualseat

bles version typed the 14CS or G2CS. This had a 10:1 compression ratio and modified flywheels, while the extra power called for better steel for some of the gearbox parts. The frame had a heavier gauge down tube and sub-frame modified to allow the fitting of 19 in. wheels. To compensate for this extra long Girlings were fitted and at the front went stronger forks. Tyres were 3·00 and 3·50 in. competition and alloy mudguards were used. A shorter, thinner dualseat was fitted and an open exhaust pipe. Offset hubs went into the wheels.

It looked quite smart but weighed 90 lb more than a Greeves Hawkstone which was £10 cheaper, so it was not surprising that it did not catch on too well. One model was sold for road racing and was modified by the works with alloy rims, clip-ons, rearsets, rev-counter, TT carburettor and reverse cone megaphone, but it was just a once only job.

1960 brought a new model of greater capacity to offer a substitute for the overweight, heavyweight 350. Dimensions of 72 × 85·5 mm were used and the new machine copied the 250 in nearly all respects. The engine had a valve lifter added to the rocker box and the flywheels were altered in shape and width. Viewed from the side they were in the form of a quadrant with a radius round the crankpin and remained in cast iron. The crankshaft turned in a pair of ball races on the drive side and a bush on the timing as the 250 but that model had the inner drive side main changed to a roller bearing as failures had occurred. The 350 barrel had an extra three fins as it was longer and the piston was flat topped with a chrome plated top ring and gave a 7·5:1 compression ratio.

On the outside the light 350 had Teledraulics at the front end, 18 in. wheels and a three point mounting for the petrol tank as used on the 250. For both machines the tank capacity was $3\frac{1}{4}$ gallons and a roll-on centre stand and two level dualseat were adopted. On the scrambler the gearbox ratios were revised and bottom gear raised, while the finish of the road models could be enhanced by fitting optional chrome plated tank panels.

The first of the new 350s was borrowed by *The Motor Cycle* for a quick trip to Wales and proved able to cruise at close to 70 mph and return a

Matchless G2 in 1961 with altered seat but otherwise little changed and still with full chaincase

50 mph average on give-and-take roads. The roll-on stand proved excellent but the exhaust was rather noisy, although the engine itself was quiet enough.

The transmission was smooth and gear change light, although there was rather a large gap between third and top. The primary chain was a duplex one not the single strand originally specified, and the clutch had an extra plate behind the sprocket which removed any trace of snatch. It was a comfortable machine to ride.

For 1961 there were a few detail changes to the gearbox, the engine breather to stop the sleeve rattling as it sounded like the big end failing, larger tank badges and full chaincase as standard. For the scrambler there was a stronger crankpin and simple coil ignition with a Varley dry electrolite battery in place of the earlier

1961 model 14 with air filter connected to carburettor and revised headlamp shell mountings

Matchless G2S of 1961 with low level bars, chainguard and more chrome plating than on the standard model

AJS version of the sports model, the 14S, in 1961

troublesome energy transfer system.

At the end of the year a sports model was introduced which was reputed to have more power and was brightened up with chrome plated mudguards, chainguard and petrol tank. It also had semi-drop bars but was otherwise as the stock machine. For 1962 the bars were made shorter and all the light-weights fitted with a longer kickstart lever. On the 350 only the breather was improved and the inner roller main bearing fitted.

All the models were given names which were Sapphire (14) and Monitor (G2), Sapphire Sports (14S) and Monitor Sports (G2S), Scorpion (14CS) and Messenger (G2CS), and Senator (8) and Matador (G5). They also had some colour changes with all blue or red finishes with white mudguards being one option and white tank flashes, gold lined, ran forward from the kneegrips.

In May 1962 two 'super-sports' models of the Sapphire and Monitor were introduced with the type letters CSR tacked on to the model number. In AMC parlance these stood for Competition, Sprung or Sports and Roadster, but back in 1958 when they had first been used for one of the twins they had instantly become Coffee Shop Racer and as this they stuck.

The CSR models were in keeping with the trends of the times to provide more sporting 250s to cater to the desires of the learner who was then legally restricted to that capacity when solo in the UK. It meant in time that they far exceeded a staid 350 in performance but at the expense of tractable behaviour and an easy to use spread of power.

To get the performance the engine was given a bigger carburettor and inlet valve, longer inlet tract, higher compression ratio, stronger valve springs, stiffer connecting rod and crankpin, and steel flywheels. The gearing was raised, full width alloy British Hub drums fitted, the front with an air scoop in the backplate, the forks from the

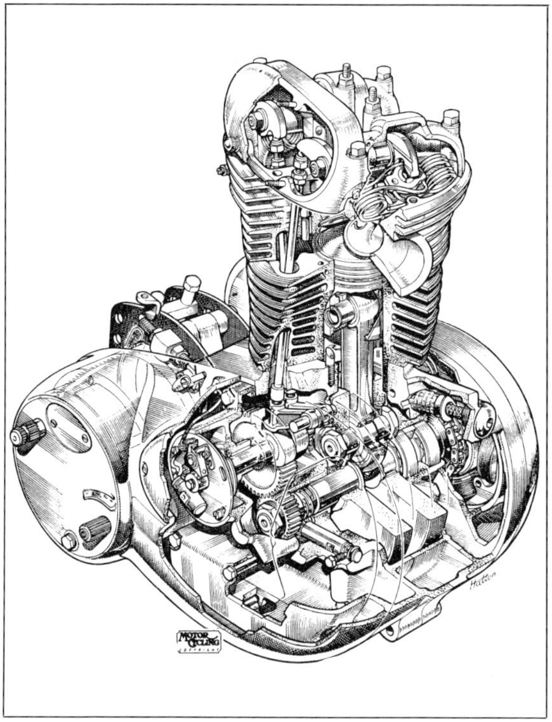

Above **Line drawing of the 250 cc Lightweight engine unit used by the models 14 and G2**

Below **The competition 250, the Matchless G2CS in 1961 when coil ignition replaced the energy transfer**

The AJS model 14S in 1962 with revised tank finish

The standard model 14 in 1962

Matchless G2 in 1962, little changed from 1958 launch

The coffee shop racer model 14CSR as sold from 1962 to 1965 with its own style of tank decor

scrambler used, and the bars taken from the sports model.

The finish was similar to the latter with chrome plated mudguards and chainguard but in addition there were plated panels on the tank sides, the barrel was painted silver, the fin edges of the head polished and the rocker cover polished. As on the latest scramblers, the timing cover and primary chaincase were polished and without the coloured flash.

On test it proved capable of 75 mph at its best and behaved well on the road. The exhaust note

The Matchless G2CSR in 1962 with polished chaincase and timing side cover

1965 AJS model 14 CSR. Coil valve springs, new silencer, fake front brake air scoop and Sapphire Ninety name

was rather loud as was the horn but the front brake had a tendency to fade, possibly because the slots in the air scoop had not been carried through so no air could enter that way. The handling was good and the riding position gave a slight forward lean which suited the machine's abilities.

Later in the year the 350 cc model and the sports and scrambles 250s were dropped from the range so only the standard and super-sports CSR went forward into 1963 and neither had any changes. The standard model only continued to the middle of the year and then that too was dropped to just leave the super-sports.

1964 saw no changes aside from the adoption of polychromatic blue for the AJS, but 1965 brought several. One at least was unexpected for it concerned the valve springs which were changed to coils. In addition the compression ratio was raised to 9.5:1 and the gear ratios closed up. A new and more efficient silencer without any tailpipe was fitted higher and more closely tucked in and new names taken, these being Sapphire Ninety and Monitor Ninety.

The improvements took the top speed to 83 mph on test without loss of tractability and in this case the brakes did not fade, although the air scoop was still only a dummy.

There were only a couple of changes for 1966 when the mudguards became polished alloy and the exhaust pipe was given a different bend to have a semi-sweptback line.

By this time the company was in dire trouble so it was not surprising that a reader survey carried out by *Motor Cycle* reported only average to good finish and poor spares and service backup. The horn was considered dreadful and the electrics none too good with tales of blown bulbs and boiled batteries. Reliability was nothing special either and, of course, by then more and more riders had become used to Japanese machines and were more critical.

In the end the CSR models were swept away on the tide of AMC's affairs and the firm decided to concentrate on big twins, so the 250 was dropped in the middle of 1966 although still in the price list in October, no doubt to clear stocks.

4 Twins

AMC need a twin in their range. Following the Triumph lead in 1937 BSA and Ariel had been quick to bring models out just after the war, and were followed in 1948 by Norton and Royal Enfield.

The Plumstead twin was announced late in 1948 for export only, so home customers could only look with envy at the models shown at Earls Court that year. As usual there were two, the AJS model 20 and the Matchless G9, and these used many common parts. Close examination revealed more variation than usual between the two marques, aside from the expected tank and timing case badges.

The heart of the machine was the new engine which had the basic layout of the English parallel twin with pistons moving together dictated by the magneto, then considered mandatory. In many other respects the AMC twin was unusual, and in one it was unique. Unlike all its contemporaries it had a third, central, main bearing between the two crank throws. It also had separate heads and barrels and gear-driven camshafts fore and aft.

Engine dimensions were 66 × 72·8 mm which gave a capacity of 498 cc and the crankshaft was a one-piece iron casting complete with massive flywheels formed as the inboard crank webs either side of the centre main. While some questioned the use of a centre main, preferring to let the crank be free to whip and whirl, AMC stuck to their design and it did have its advantages.

Exploded line drawing of the AMC twin engine with its unique centre main. Separate heads and barrels, gear drive to camshafts and electrics, gear oil pumps and alloy rods

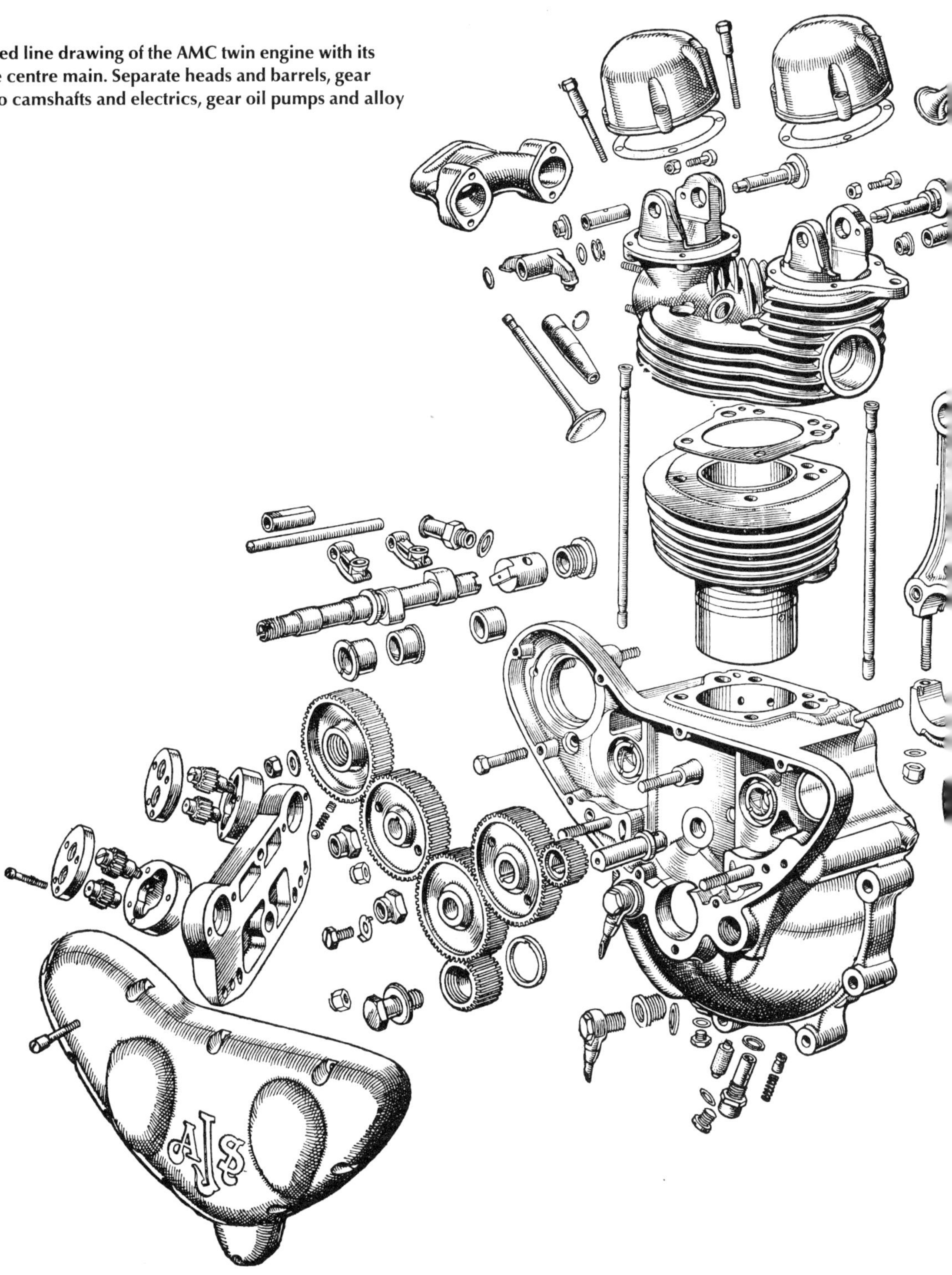

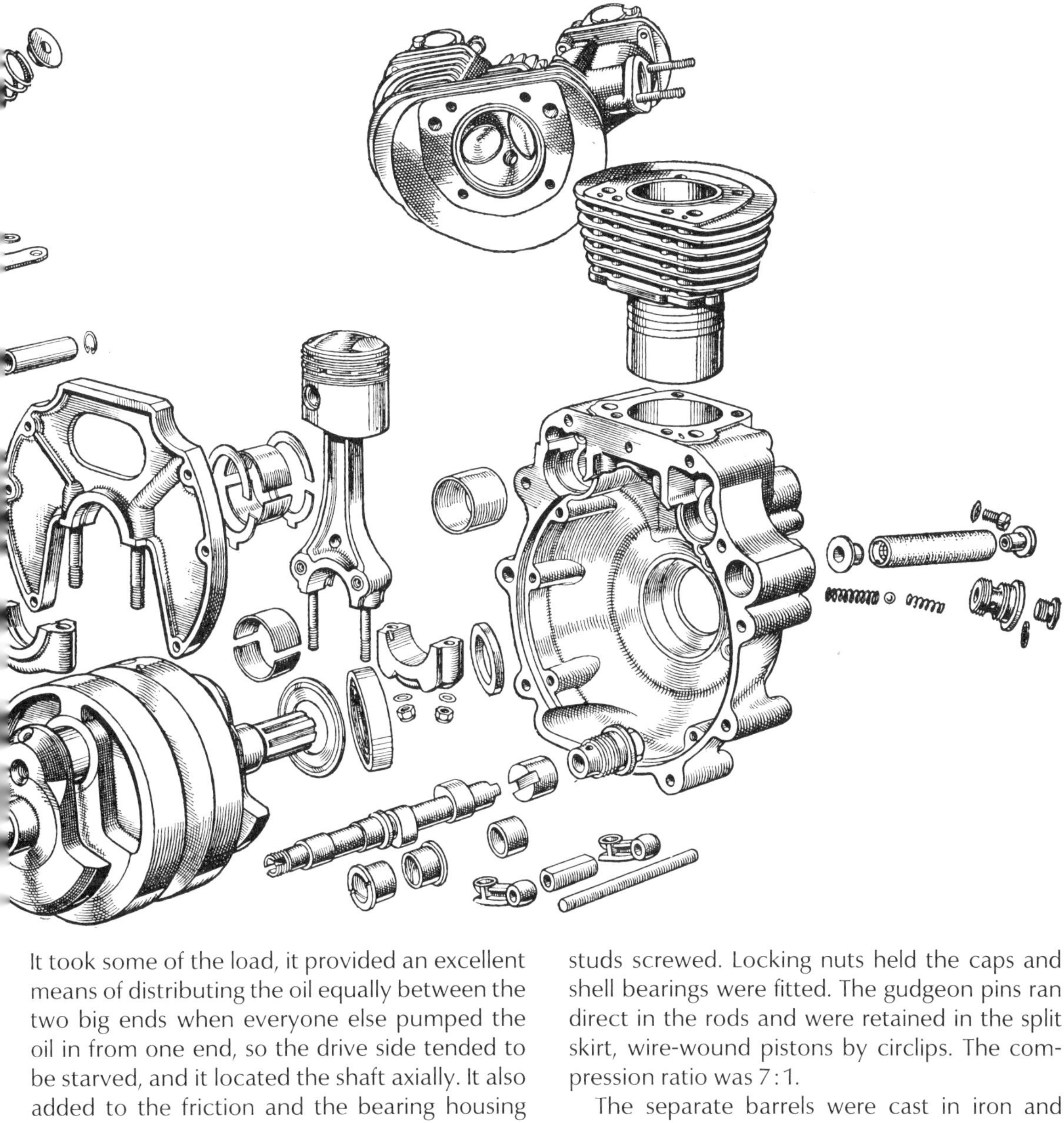

It took some of the load, it provided an excellent means of distributing the oil equally between the two big ends when everyone else pumped the oil in from one end, so the drive side tended to be starved, and it located the shaft axially. It also added to the friction and the bearing housing and its location was perhaps not as rigid as it needed to be.

The one-piece crank meant split big ends and the rods were forged in Hiduminium RR56. The caps were located on studs and these held in the rod by cross trunions, round bars that fitted into holes running across the rod into which the studs screwed. Locking nuts held the caps and shell bearings were fitted. The gudgeon pins ran direct in the rods and were retained in the split skirt, wire-wound pistons by circlips. The compression ratio was 7:1.

The separate barrels were cast in iron and deeply spigoted into the crankcase. Their spacing was such that each was well supported and the crankcase, although vertically split on its centre line, had adequate material on the inner sides of the spigots.

The cylinders spigoted up into the light alloy heads and a gasket was also employed. Each head was held by four dome nuts screwed to long studs fitted to the crankcase and had shrunk-in valve seats. Integral with each head were posts for the inlet and exhaust rockers above the individual valve wells. The exhaust pipes were a push fit into the port, while the two inlets were joined by a cast aluminium manifold which carried the single, flange mounted, type 6 Amal carburettor with float chamber on the right.

The rockers had ball inner and pad outer ends and were bushed to oscillate on fixed spindles. The spindles were eccentric to their supports and their rotation varied the valve clearance, which when set was locked by clamping the inner end of the spindles with a nut and bolt. The valves worked in guides located by circlips and were restrained by duplex coil springs and collars with split collets. Each rocker assembly was concealed by a domed cover held down by four bolts. The head fins between the rocker boxes were placed diagonally to encourage air flow across the combustion chambers, and the plugs were angled outwards between the valves.

The four push rods ran down through head and barrel to contact cam followers that trailed on the inlet side but led on the exhaust. The camshafts were two in number placed fore and aft of the cylinders and ran in three bronze bushes, one in the left case and two in the right. They were driven by spur gears from a pinion keyed to the end of the crankshaft, via an idler, to gears keyed to their ends. Behind the inlet and ahead of the exhaust sat small cross rods and these carried the cam followers, with pads on their undersides and cups on top for the push rods which were in aluminium alloy with steel ends.

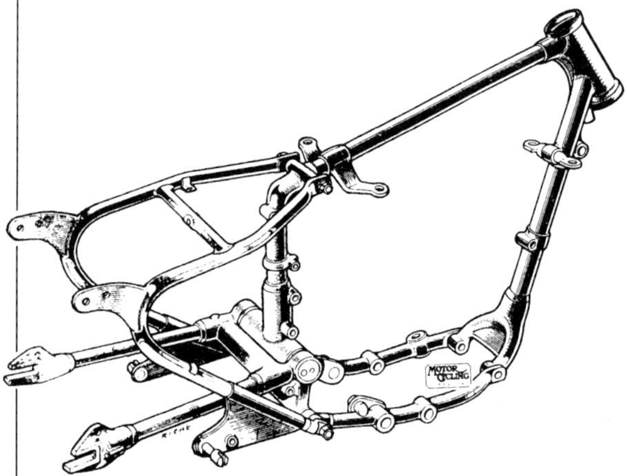

The swinging fork frame introduced for 1956 but still with single downtube

The two halves of the crankcase used the separate centre main panel as a spigot between them and this was bolted to the left side. It was cutaway on the underside so could be assembled to the crankshaft with the bearing shells and clamped to it by a single cap. On either side went a split thrust washer. The outer ends of the crankshaft were supported in a roller bearing on each side.

On the right, timing, side the gear chest was carried fore and aft to drive the electrics. These comprised the dynamo clamped to the front of the crankcase and driven by a small pinion meshed with the exhaust gear, and the magneto driven in like manner from the inlet. Manual advance was used.

Lubrication was by twin gear pumps both housed in a plate bolted onto the timing side of the crankcase. This plate also supported the outer end of the fixed spindle the timing idler turned on, and each pump was driven by a slot in the end of a camshaft. The pumps could be interchanged but correctly the exhaust camshaft drove the supply and the inlet the return, which had a greater capacity achieved simply with wider pump gears.

Each pump comprised a front and back plate with a body between them containing the two gears. The upper gear engaged the camshaft and was also slotted across its outer end to enable it to be turned by a screwdriver to engage with the driving shaft. The whole timing chest was enclosed by a single cover and this was one item that varied between the two marques. The AJS

Above **Graham Walker on a French trip with a G9 and sidecar**

Below **The 1957 model 30, the 600 cc AJS version of the twin**

cover was fairly slim so had bulges in it to accommodate the oil pumps with the make letters between them, while the Matchless cover was smoother with just a slight recess carrying the flying 'M' symbol.

The lubrication system was dry sump with an external tank connected by a pair of pipes and banjo fittings to the right side of the crankcase below the timing cover and either side of the crankshaft line. There were no other external oil pipes as the supply was through drillings. From the feed pump, oil was passed through a felt filter housed in a horizontal chamber in the crankcase just below the dynamo. From there most of it went to the central main and thence to the two big ends. The spillage from there looked after the roller mains, small ends and piston skirts, while a direct feed went to the walls of the cylinders.

Oilways also served the camshafts and at the left end of the exhaust and driven from it by a tongue and slot was a rotary distribution valve. This sent oil alternately to the valve rockers and to sumps in the camshaft tunnels into which the cams could dip as they turned. By using this device the upstairs region received its oil supply in a pulse rather than at a continuous high pressure.

In the cylinder head the oil supply was further metered by the use of brass plugs with a flat on them and the oil then reached the rocker spindles. It drained down the push rod tunnels to the

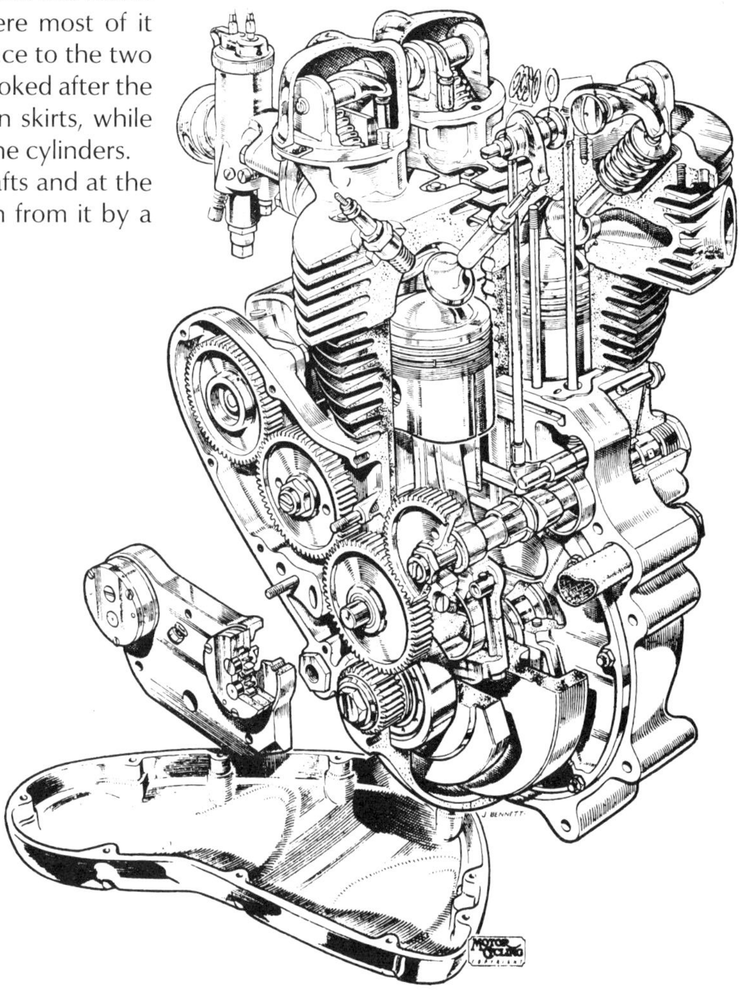

Line drawing of the 600 cc twin engine

The G11CS in 1958, a trail 600 with siamezed exhaust and tucked in silencer

camshaft sump, looking after the cam followers on the way, and then into the crankcase, from where it was scavenged. To ensure that this pump was kept primed, a metered bleed was taken from the feed pump.

The inlet camshaft also had something to drive at its left end and in this case it was a timed breather whose outlet directed oil mist at the rear chain. Both breather and oil valve were accessible by removing a screwed plug in the crankcase so could be readily serviced. A further facility was a plug in the non-return valve that held the filter in place. This could be removed and a gauge substituted to enable the pressure to be checked.

The remainder of the machine had much in common with the springer singles so the transmission comprised a cam-type shock absorber on the engine mainshaft connected with a single strand chain to a Burman CP gearbox. The normal pressed steel chaincase was used complete with its usual oil leak problems but without provision for the dynamo drive.

The frame and cycle parts were very much as used for the singles with swinging fork rear suspension and Teledraulics at the front. Thus all the features brought in that season for the single went onto the twin, where applicable. Items that were different were the megaphone-style silencers fitted to the Matchless, the dualseat supplied as standard to that model, and the petrol tanks which differed. The AJS had one with a 4 gallon capacity as against the 3 gallons of the Matchless, but both were chrome plated, the AJS with silver lines and blue pinstripes around black panels and the Matchless in red and silver.

For the rest it was twin toolboxes tucked into the corners of the subframe with the oil tank on the right and battery on the left in front of them, horn mounted under the front of the tank, centre stand, front stand, pillion footrest on frame extensions, a pillion pad for the AJS and Lucas lighting equipment.

At that time only the Enfield Twin had a swinging fork frame, the others used plungers, and the AMC twins looked very smart and modern. The Matchless with its dualseat, megaphones and bright finish was possibly the preferred choice, but for a while this was academic for home buyers. In addition to their type numbers the models were also given names, the AJS being the Springtwin and the Matchless the Super Clubman.

It was not until late summer in 1949 that a few twins reached the home market to be quickly snapped up by eager buyers. They proved to be very nice machines on the whole, although some had rather more than their share of the traditional English oil leak and the brakes were never more than adequate and really needed another inch on their diameter. For all that they went well, handled nicely, while the rear candlesticks kept their damping oil, and were comfortable to ride. This was due not only to the seating but also the easy, tractable engine that helped the rider rather than made him work hard at putting up a good average.

1950 brought little change but the twins received the ribbed mudguards and five-spring clutch common to the singles, while the AJS had the offset type silencer fitted. Curiously the Matchless cost nearly £3 more than the AJS. One single-model change that did not have to be incorporated was the long torque arm for the front brake which the twins had from the start.

In 1951 rather more twins reached the home market and again these had many of the single's changes. Thus they had jampots at the rear, modified forks at the front with the forged steel crown, revised chaincase seal, tidier controls and centre stand with longer legs. The frame was altered around the seat tube to make provision for an air filter, and the magneto cut-out, which had been on the handlebars, was moved to the contact breaker cover. The AJS tank received the oval metal badges and the Matchless dualseat was covered in vynide instead of the leather used before.

The sole twins-only change for 1952 was to the crankcase breather. In place of the camshaft

The 500 cc twin, the AJS model 20, in 1958 with cast chaincase but still fitted with dynamo and magneto

Above **Nice outfit pulling away from the kerb. Siamezed exhausts, single downtube and full width hubs**

driven timed unit went a spring loaded flap valve set in the drive end of the crankshaft which was drilled through to suit. This directed the mist into the chaincase where it either added to the oil level or leaked away.

Otherwise it was as earlier years with all the single changes including the B52 gearbox, primary case access cap, alloy backplate for the front hub, iron top crown, underslung pilot lamp, colour coded wiring, positive earth, flexibly mounted dynamo regulator, and die-cast light alloy tank badges. The finish, as dictated by regulations, was much reduced in chrome plating, with the rims Argenized and the tanks in lined black. The overall gearing was dropped by a change in engine sprocket from 21 to 20 teeth.

Early in the year the curious pillion seat, linked at its forward end to the saddle, was announced for the Springtwin but was superseded by the adoption for 1953 of a dualseat. Just about all the detail changes of the singles also applied to the twins but special to them were modified cam followers and rocker covers only held by two bolts.

Also announced for 1953 was a racing kit for the twins following the successful showing of

Below **The CSR model in the 1958–59 period when it was built in G9 and G12 forms**

them in racing form in the Manx Grand Prix. The kit comprised camshaft, twin carburettors, high compression pistons and rear-sets with the options of rev-counter and megaphones. This activity was quickly superseded by the appearance of the G45 racing twin, which used a modified

Making notes on a 1959 standard twin, either a G9 or G11; interesting 'kit car' in the background

G9 engine in a set of cycle parts from the AJS 350 cc racer, the 7R, which had been in production since 1948.

The changes for 1954 were as on the singles

The standard model G9 in 1959

1959 model 20 deluxe with two tone tank finish

with the twins having the full-width light alloy front hub, straight spokes, twin pilot lights, flared mudguards, oil tank changes, new prop stand spring, flexible fuel lines and the clutch cover on the outer chaincase. The tank badges became plastic and for the first time both marques shared a common petrol tank of 3·75 gallons, also fitted on the 500 single. The twins' price also became the same at a nice round £240.

1955 continued the pattern with many detail changes, including a qd full width rear hub, dished front hub, barrel – contour cooling fins on both hubs, larger fork tubes, a headlamp shell lengthened to take the instruments, simplified oil

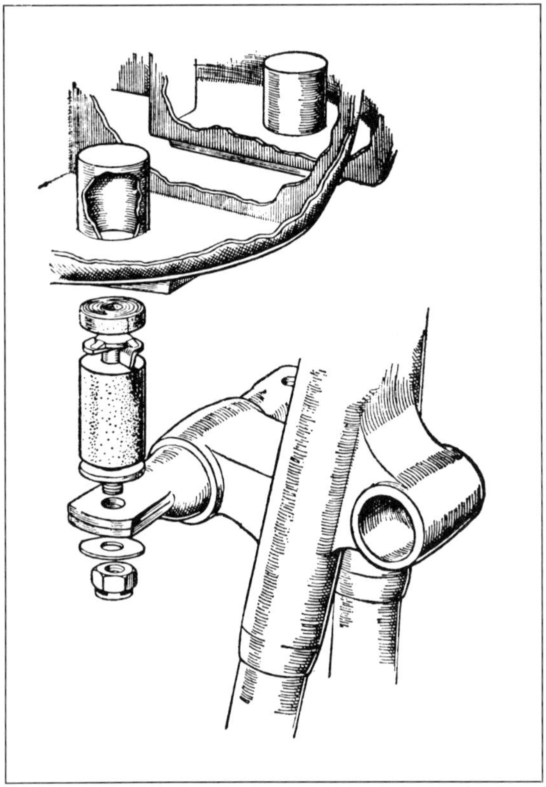

Above **The 1961 tank mounting with rubber bush which expanded to grip the tank tube as the lower nut was tightened**

Below **The 1961 AJS 31CSR with chrome plated tank sides, siamezed exhaust and short dualseat**

tank and battery mounting, new front mudguard, rear reflector, Amal Monobloc and a new silencer shape for the AJS. Internally the rocker arms were grooved to carry oil to the push rod cups and a shallower cap nut fitted over the filter.

The AMC twins had managed with their 498 cc for some years, but from abroad the cry was always for more cubes to give easier high speed cruising and brisker acceleration. This had first been met by stretching the twin to 550 cc around 1954 and this became the model G9B for the USA. For 1956 AMC met this demand with two new models, the AJS 30 and Matchless G11. In essence these had the standard engine bored out to 72 mm to make the capacity 593 cc. At the same time compression ratios were raised with the 500 up to 7·8:1 and the 600 adopting 7·5:1.

Both twins received all the new 1956 cycle features with the new frame, styled oil tank and toolbox, longer seat, and front brake with cam lever at the top, as the most noticeable. Less obvious was an outer panel over the oil tank spaced from it to prevent the pillion passenger touching the tank itself, which became hot on the twins. There was also a move by the horn to under the seat which was neat but not so audible, the grouping of the control cables for neatness, the deletion of the front stand and changes to the rear brake, whose adjuster moved to the front end of the brake rod. The forks were altered in detail at the top of the legs, the AJS badge became a little bigger and the primary chain adjustor went between the engine plates under a snap-on cover. To distinguish the new 600 it had a chrome plated petrol tank painted and lined to give the appearance of side panels.

The twins changed over to the AMC gearbox during 1956 along with the other models and for 1957, like them, gained Girlings with clevis ends to control the rear end and ribbed sides to the oil tank cover and toolbox lid. Inside there were modified cams and bigger valves for the 600. Chrome tank panels became standard so the tanks could be painted without any plating problems and colours were black for the 500 but AJS blue or Matchless red for the 600.

The standard models had some changes in 1958 with the fitment of the cast alloy primary chaincase, but altered with a small dome around the crankshaft end as the dynamo was retained so no alternator was fitted. Thus the case only had to clear the sprocket as the shock absorber had transferred to the clutch body when the AMC box came into use. The rear units were altered to reduce the seat height and the twin pilot lamps went, as did the paint on the centres of the wheel rims which became all chrome plated except for the model 30 which has blue centres, silver lined. There were two further models of the 600 in 1958, these being the CS and the CSR. The first of these were sports scramblers evolved mainly from needs in the USA. They used the 600 engine running on an 8·5:1 compression ratio fitted into the scrambles frame with the full width hubs. A siamezed exhaust system was fitted with the single silencer on the right and fatter section tyres capped with alloy mudguards. The lights were quickly detachable and used the old type headlamp shell with the switch in the back of it, while the speedometer was separately mounted on the fork crown. To complete the picture high handlebars, the 2 gallon competition tank and the competition dualseat were fitted. As options the customer could have the standard tank and road tyres fitted, but these remained in the CS sections.

AJS model 31 de luxe of 1961 with better seat and more comforts than on the more sporting versions

The AJS model 20 in 1961 in two tone livery

The CSR models were announced in January 1958 to offer a high speed road model by combining the most suitable points of the standard and the CS machines. The effect was to produce this model with the standard tank and road tyres. It kept the high compression engine and siamezed exhaust in the scrambles frame with alloy mudguards and competition dualseat, but had the standard handlebars. The quickly detachable lights were fitted and as standard the machines were supplied in AJS Mediterranean blue or Matchless red for the petrol and oil tanks and the toolbox. The tank sides were fitted with chrome plated panels and the front fork covers and rear unit shrouds finished in the same way.

Early in 1958 *The Motor Cycle* co-operated with AMC in a high speed test to put 100 miles into the hour with a fully equipped road model. The machine was the Matchless Sports Twin, the rider Vic Willoughby, and the venue the MIRA high speed track. For the run a gearbox sprocket with an extra tooth was fitted, the handlebars turned upside down and a pad added on the tank and to the rear of the seat. The pillion rests were lowered to aid rider comfort, and the twist-grip friction tightened up to hold the throttle fully open. It was a hard, cold ride for Vic but the Matchless covered the distance comfortably, although it ran low on fuel for the last lap or two and missed a couple of times. Afterwards it was refuelled and ridden back to London and a later inspection revealed a generally clean internal condition aside from a slight pick-up on one piston.

From the middle of the year colour options were introduced to brighten the models in either blue or red on the same lines as for the singles.

These options were extended for the 1959 models to include two-tone finishes, while the range itself was considerably altered. The 600 cc machines were all replaced by a series of larger capacity with a 650 cc engine as first used for 1958 US models. In both 500 and 650 sizes four models were offered, these being standard, de-luxe, scrambles CS and Sports Twin CSR while type designations were 31 and G12.

The new engine was much as the earlier ones and the capacity was achieved by lengthening the stroke to 79·3 mm which gave 646 cc. The barrel became larger and had one more fin, while inside went 600 pistons and rods. The sports 500s followed the lead of their larger cousins with a higher compression ratio and siamezed exhaust systems. Ratios were 8·5:1 for these models but 7·5:1 for the standard and de-luxe 650, while the 500 was at 8:1. The one other distinguishing feature of the standard models was the fitting of an alternator to the end of the crankshaft plus the necessary outer chaincase with bigger bulge. The electrics of these models were altered to suit, exactly as on the singles, and a distributor added in the original magneto position to direct the sparks from the coil. The other three versions all kept their magnetos and lighting equipment continued to be offered as an option for the scramblers.

On the chassis side the standard and de-luxe models used the frame with vertical rear units, while the CS and CSR had the scrambles type with them more inclined. All except the CS had a new 4·25 gallon petrol tank with centre welded seam, while the scrambler continued with its more meagre two gallons. It and the CSR were fitted with alloy mudguards while the others had the new deep section front used by the heavy-weight singles.

The smaller versions of the CS and CSR models did not last for long, which was hardly surprising. Customers seeking urge on- or off-road went for capacity, more horses and the 650, while buyers of the 500 would seek the de-luxe to gild the lily. So for 1960 there was just one 500 road model but the four 650s continued, albeit not without problems which indicated that the basic design

Matchless G12 de luxe from 1960 or 1961, still with megaphone silencers

The 1961 Matchless G12CSR, the sporting coffee shop racer with 650 cc of punch

The 1961 G9 with two tone tank option so could be standard or de luxe model

had been overstretched and if driven hard would object.

The main change for 1960, as on the singles, was to the full cradle duplex frame. Also common was the three point tank mounting, although the fixing details varied, closer gearbox ratios, reduced size of headlamp shell, small bodied battery and two level dualseat. The engines had a new design of cylinder head giving the same compression ratios with reduced valve angles. The head steady lug was made thicker and a horizontal fin added on the underside of which went three small fins laid diagonally to assist air flow. Two rate valve springs were adopted.

The 500 and the standard 650 kept their coil ignition and alternators but the de luxe and CSR retained the older magneto and dynamo. The CS was supplied with magneto only as standard with the optional lighting equipment still to be had on demand.

About this time a significant internal change began to be incorporated into the engine, this being a change of crankshaft material to nodular iron. The centre main had not proved to be the answer to the inherent balance problem of the parallel twin and consequent vibration, in fact it seemed to fall between two stools. Twins were often happy and nicer to ride if the crank was free to flex a little as the vibration would then be patchy and could be avoided. The AMC solution lacked the really rigid support needed to do a worthwhile job so the crank could still flex a little but in a restrained manner so it was there all the time. With more capacity, power and revs

Matchless standard G9 in 1961 in listed standard finish rather than one of the many options

it began to object but, where other machines had a steel forging or bolted structure that could flex, the AMC was cast and just snapped.

So new machines began to be built with the better nodular iron crankshaft and broken ones repaired with the new part.

Not many people seemed to want a 650 cc scrambler so this model was dropped for 1961 leaving an all roadster range, although the big twin remained available in enduro trim for the American market. This was effectively the CS model fitted with dynamo and lights and complete with high bars, toolbox and short competition seat.

The remaining models received oiling system changes, restyled mudguards and larger tank badges. A variety of finishes was again offered along with the standard black with the AJS colour birch grey and the Matchless cardinal red or, for export, Hades red. The two-tone finish for the tank was reversed so the grey or red was applied to the top and the blue or arctic white below.

Motor Cycling produced a road test of the Matchless G12CSR when it managed 108 mph at MIRA. The acceleration was as one would expect, really good especially from 80 mph onwards when most machines tended to tail off. Fuel disappeared at a rate on the preferred side of 50 mpg and the handling and gearchange both assisted rapid progress over any roads. The seat was comfortable but too short for two, and the brakes rather marginal for the weight and speed of the machine. The lights were reported as ad-

A 1962 Matchless G12 with new tank badges

The 1962 Hurricane or model 31CSR as it was better known, in this case minus kneegrips

equate but again the horn failed to impress.

Near the end of the year the 500 twin was withdrawn bringing its long run to an end and the 650 models were reduced to two only, the standard and the CSR. In effect the de-luxe could still be bought by ordering the standard with the appropriate options.

It was machine name time for 1962 with the twins the Swift (31) and Majestic (G12), and Hurricane (31CSR) and Monarch (G12CSR), but never was the sports twin known by anything other than its initials, CSR. Changes were mainly detail as for the singles with a stronger kickstarter spring, roll-on stand, a return to the 1959 style battery, a new horn, new tank mountings, new badges and a removable ignition key where coil ignition was fitted. The CSR models lost their dynamos, took to alternators and changed to the standard road frame and hence a revised exhaust system.

Special to the standard twins was an increase in fork spring rating to that of the CSR and a breather tower for the oil tank which the sports model already had. The new tank mounting was an attempt to combat the vibration, whose effect on the tanks was simple—they split! One magazine writer went through over a dozen on his staff bike and, while the 1962 system was a better attempt to isolate the tank from the vibes, the problem was still there. The new badges on the outside were die-cast zinc alloy with chrome plating but hardly matched the dignified air of the standard model.

In the middle of 1962 a new option was made available for the CSR models, this being a fibreglass headlamp cowl. It carried a small plastic screen and was coloured blue or red to match the marque it was fitted to. In it were mounted speedometer, rev-counter, ammeter and light switch on the top panel and a Lucas light unit at the front with a car-type beam adjustment using three screws. It was also available minus the rev-counter.

At the same time came news of two more options to boost the power of the CSR, the first being pistons giving a compression ratio of 10·25:1 and the second, twin carburettors. Which must have done wonders for the crankshaft.

In the main the changes for 1963 applied to the standard models only and mirrored the singles. Thus the seat height was reduced with a change to 18 in. rims and a new subframe, Girlings with standard eye ends were fitted, the seat made narrower, the mudguard section changed, the oil tank and toolbox made more rounded and the slimmer front hub with wider shoes and only five fins fitted.

Both models received the new silencer without tailpipe, a new petrol tank with recesses for the kneegrips and wider oil pump gears that pushed the output up.

The next year, 1964, saw the road range feel the effect of standardisation, the presence of the Norton twin in the Plumstead factory, and the pressing need to cut costs due to the firm's financial problems. The main change was to Norton hubs and forks with the adaption of the alloy, full width units of 8 and 7 in. diameter. The forks were the Roadholders and to fit these the frame had to be slightly modified. The sidecar forks with reduced trail were also available and in either case the legs were spread to allow a 4 in. tyre to be fitted if required.

Right **Rider's eye view of the 1964 Hurricane showing manual advance and tank zig-zag decor**

Below **1962 Matchless G12CSR**

Below **1962 AJS model 31**

The CSR was given the 18 in. wheels, altered subframe and rounded oil tank and toolbox, as fitted to the standard model the year before, and also had its gearing changed. Its mudguards became chrome plated steel and on both models 12 volt electrics were adopted and twin sets of points fitted to the standard machine, while the CSR stuck to its magneto.

Late in 1964 came a move to more cubic capacity using a 750 cc Norton Atlas engine. This followed earlier ideas of stretching the existing AMC unit to the extent which had resulted in

The Matchless G12CSR in 1964 with Norton forks and hubs

the 750 cc G15 back in 1962. Such machines of this size that were built followed the lines of the G12 of that year and all were destined for export.

The next sign of the effects of standardisation at Plumstead was a Norton twin in a CSR frame with Norton forks built up for road and enduro use. This was seen in prototype form in the autumn of 1963 and from this work came the detail changes that allowed the Roadholders to be fitted to the range for 1964.

The final move was to adopt the Atlas for 1965 which gave the models 33 and G15. The Norton

1965 AJS model 31 with new oil tank shape

1965 AJS model 31CSR with hotter engine and chrome plated tank sides

The 1965 G15CSR with Norton engine, AMC gearbox, Norton forks and hubs all in an AMC frame with lovely sweptback pipes

engine went back as long as the AMC and was just as well stretched, old and rather overdeveloped. In the form used it had twin carburettors, magneto ignition and a rev-counter. For the rest the machine was as the standard 650, but, as it had Norton forks and hubs, who the customers were supposed to be only AMC knew. Norton fans would buy the Atlas as a true Bracebridge Street design with its featherbed frame, while AMC men preferred AMC engines even if only of 650 cc. To them the Norton cycle parts were bad enough without an engine as well.

For the AJS there was a new diamond shape tank badge for 1965 while the model finish followed the lines of earlier years in blue or red depending on the marque, with black frame and forks plus chrome plated mudguards.

In October 1964 came a sports version of the 750 under the Matchless label. It was the G15CSR and came with all the goodies desired by the cafe racer set already fitted. The standard bars were low and flat but lower ones were available, rear-sets were fitted along with a reversed gear pedal and shortened brake pedal, the gearbox cam-plate was reversed to get back to a one-up-three-down change and the footrests folded up to let the folding kickstart swing down. Unlike the G12CSR, which continued with siamezed pipes, the 750 had twin exhausts which were well swept back in best road racing style. The front forks had gaiters and the rear units lacked lower covers. Light alloy mudguards were fitted and chrome plating applied to the tank sides, head-lamp shell, chainguard and instrument panel

that carried rev-counter and speedometer side by side with the lights switch between them. The tank top, the oil tank and the toolbox were in cherry red and the sports model also had narrower section tyres than the standard one.

During 1965 the big sports Matchless was joined by an AJS version, the 33CSR, finished in blue, and for 1966 both had their gearing raised a little, as did the sports 650s. Reflecting the hard times the firm was on the colours remained for the finishes but with less variation from model to model. In the middle of the year the 650 was dropped so finally bringing the AMC twin to its end. Only the Norton powered models remained in their AMC frames.

The firm ran into 1967 as Norton-Matchless but still with the two AJS models in the lists. The Norton engine had some changes made to its lubrication system and the CSR models reverted

The G15CS also built as the Norton N15 by changing the badges

to 19 in. wheels, but otherwise it was business as before. The standard AJS came with high-rise bars but the flatter type fitted to the Matchless could be supplied if required.

In the middle of 1967 the AJS models were dropped but the Matchless pair continued with a further version, the G15CS introduced that spring. This was a model on the lines of the earlier CS type and fitted with a small tank and trail bike tyres. It ran on into 1968 with the CSR and the road model, which became the G15MkII fitted with capacitor ignition, and this system went onto the CSR as well.

All three straggled on until 1969 but then they went the same way as the AMC singles, to bring the line to a close.

5 Porcupine and 7R, G45 and G50

AJS were heavily involved in road racing from their early days onwards, while Matchless had little to do with the hard stuff after 1914. Thus, although they had won three TTs by then, few Matchboxes were seen in the TT in the Twenties and they all retired.

In contrast AJS began that heady era with four TT wins and were runners most years in the 1930s. By the end of that decade they had a blown four of 500 cc in action and only Gilera could match that, for the other Italian exotica of that period may have been built but were not to be seen at the classics.

During the second war AJS gave thought to the way to go and the first result was a new engine with three cylinders, laid horizontally and supercharged, a little on the lines of the 1940 Guzzi 500. This gave a much more rigid engine structure design than the vee-4 with its separate cylinders and involved camshaft drive.

This unit was designed by Harry Collier, but in those war years the family suffered two bereavements—the first when Bert Collier was killed in a road crash in 1941, and in 1944 when Harry died. Thus the firm lost two good engineers and no more was heard of the triple.

In its place came a twin, also designed to be supercharged, and with the cylinders laid flat to the ground. Joe Craig had a hand in the engine for he was at AMC during those years before returning to Norton late in 1946.

The two cylinders were selected at a time when blowers were still allowed and the thinking

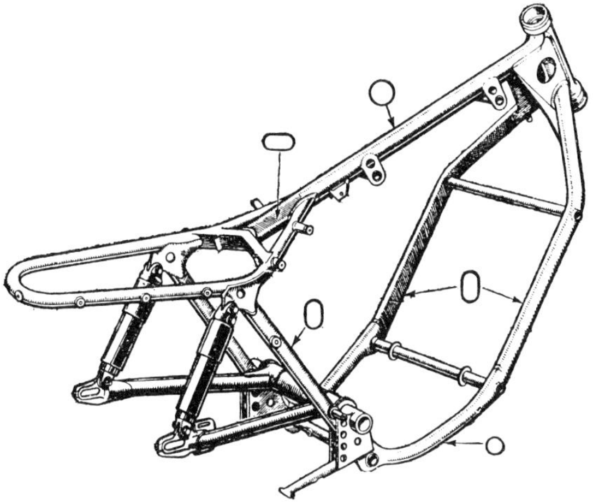

Above **The Porcupine frame and its oval sections**

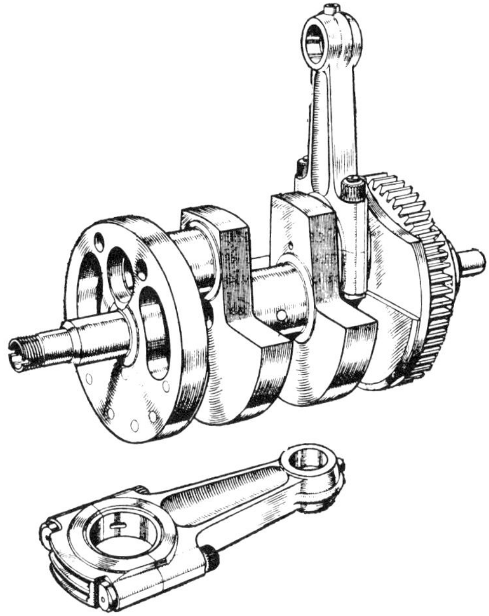

Above **Porcupine crankshaft and connecting rod**

Below **The Porcupine engine with all its spines and fins, outside clutch**

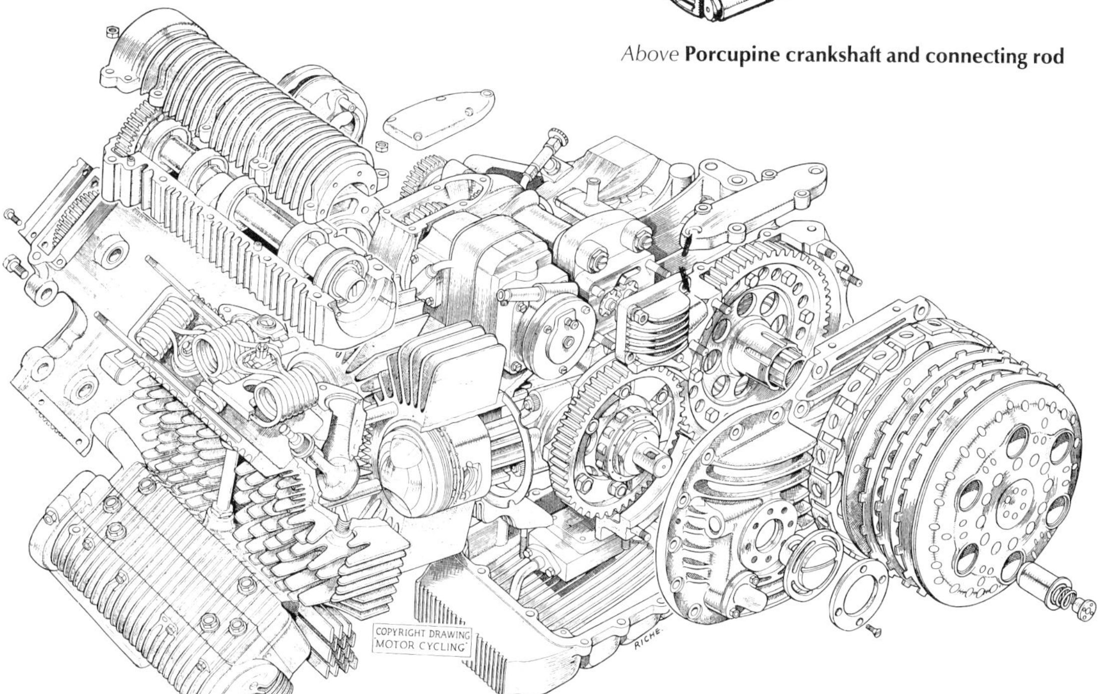

was that a compact, air-cooled twin would be better than a transverse four which would demand water cooling. Their experiences pre-war had shown that the cooling of a blown engine was no easy task and this was borne out not only by the Gilera but also by then current car racing practice.

The twin would be light, well tucked in and with the weight low down, all factors in enabling its power to be used to the best. The alternative of plenty of bhp and not much handling had been well impressed on all who had seen Rusk hold the four on the road by sheer strength, and this lesson on how not to go racing had been taken to heart.

So a supercharged engine with two forward-facing cylinders presenting their heads to the air was laid out and, at the end of 1946, came the ban on blowers. So the cylinder head was revised to raise the compression ratio but retained its rather wide valve angle around 90 degrees.

The new machine was entered as an AJS and purely as a factory machine, there was never any intention of marketing replicas. With the head change brought about by the alteration in the rules, they did not have too much time for changes as two machines were entered for the Senior TT to be ridden by Les Graham and Jock West. In the end they were so rushed that they went to the Island with their only trial a quick dash down the Rochester bypass.

The twin cylinder engine was of unit construction with gear primary drive and gear driven twin

Jock West on the Porcupine getting away at the 1947 Senior TT

Right **Late 1948 AJS advert showing the first 7R to promote the name and the show at Earls Court**

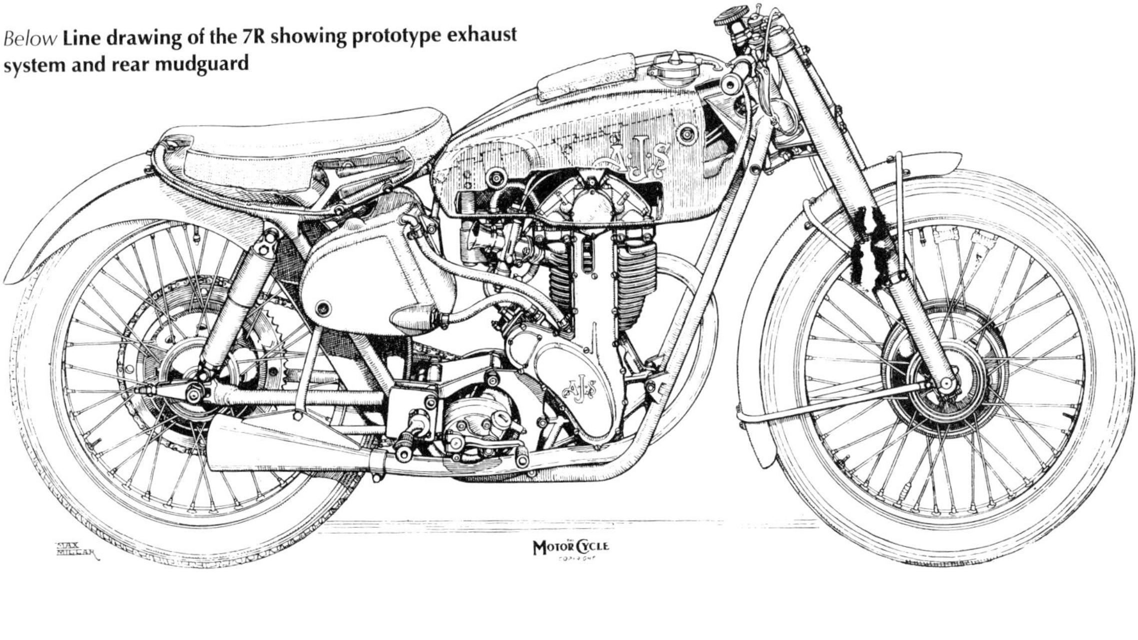

Below **Line drawing of the 7R showing prototype exhaust system and rear mudguard**

MOTOR CYCLING
November 18, 1948
A·J·S
The Race-bred
STAND 69
EARLS COURT
Motor cycle

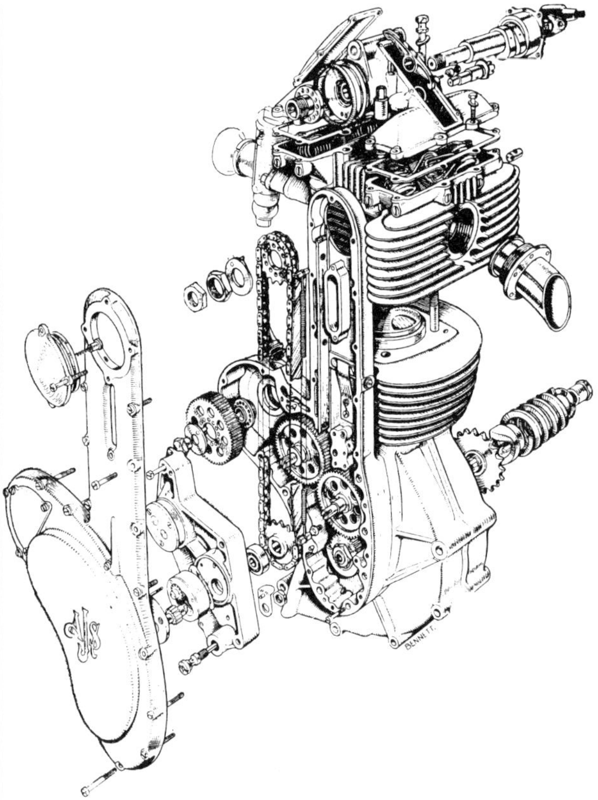

Left **Line drawing of the 7R engine showing general construction**

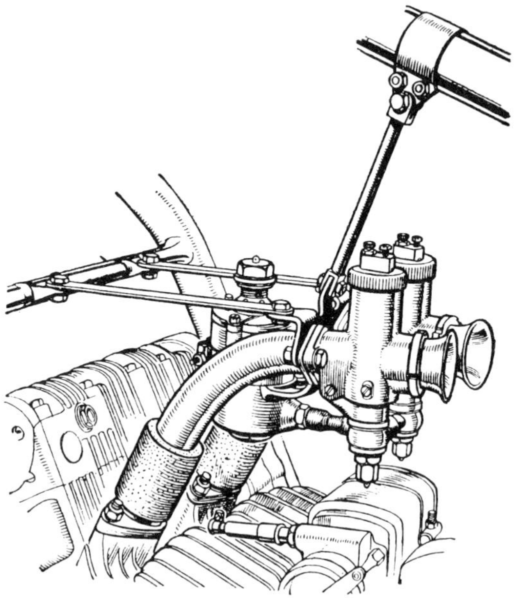

Below **The carburettor arrangements for the 1948 Porcupine, quite a change from the down-draught layout of 1947**

overhead camshafts. Its dimensions were 68 × 68·5 mm so the capacity was 497 cc and the heart of the engine was the one-piece crankshaft with three main bearings forged in steel and machined from the billet. The big end journals and the centre main were nitrided for the indium flash shell bearings, while caged rollers were used at each end. The centre main located the shaft and the webs either side of it were in bob-weight form. Both outer webs were circular, the timing side hollowed away and the driveside, on the left, with the primary gear attached directly to it. Thus the main bearing on that side was located outboard of the drive and the crankshaft ran backwards as the gear was directly meshed with the clutch on the direct gearbox.

The crankshaft was carefully balanced in the normal manner but in addition the factor could be varied in the frame. This was done with weights set in the inner webs behind Allen screw plugs. Access to these was by removing the crankcase sump.

The connecting rods were forged RR56 light alloy and unbushed at the small ends. The big end was split with the cap located by close fitting diameters on the bolts and these had their heads locked to the cap recess by a flat. They were secured by splined nuts on special washers which sat in countersunk recesses in the rod, the use of the spline allowing a smaller clearance for the special key employed to tighten them.

Each piston ran on a case hardened gudgeon pin which was internally taper ground and retained by round wire circlips. The pistons were

Les Graham in the 1949 Senior TT he should have won

forged with a full skirt and domed crown into which valve clearance pockets were machined. Each carried one scraper and two thin compression rings and ran in its own separate cylinder. These were aluminium alloy castings with shrunk-in iron liners which spigoted deeply into the crankcase to some $1\frac{3}{4}$ in. The depth of spigot was such that they had to be machined to clear the flywheels and slotted to clear the rods. The cylinder fins were radial and above, below and on the left of the bore some 2 in. long, but between the cylinders and on the right, they were shallower. Each barrel sat on a washer between it and the crankcase.

It was the cylinder head that gave the model its name. Early descriptions referred to its cooling fins as 'hedgehog' or 'spike', for they were lengthy, interrupted, and pointed forward. Before long the term 'Porcupine' was coined and adopted for all time.

The two heads were cast as one complete with the wells for the valve springs but the camboxes were kept separate and bolted to it. With its mass of fragile spike fins it was indeed like a porcupine and a very good example of the art of skilled casting in light alloy. Each barrel spigoted into its respective combustion chamber and was sealed with a simple gasket.

The valves were all in KE965 and the exhausts were sodium-cooled. Valve guides were in bronze and a press fit in the head with the lower

20 OCTOBER 1949 SIXPENCE
LONDON SHOW GUIDE
THE
MOTOR CYCLE
AJS
32
Quality Motor Cycles
with the Race-bred Reputation
STAND Nº 37

valve spring plates located to them. Hairpin springs were used with each pair overlapped under a retaining collar with a plain hole in its centre. Into this went a second collar with a flange reduced to eight segments overlapping the first. This inner collar was secured to the valve by split collets.

Each cambox was split along its centre line and the two halves sat on eight studs fitted to the head. The two halves were well finned to assist cooling and clamped onto the five roller bearings, each with a split alloy cage, which supported the camshaft. This was turned from a forging and the shaft was hollow to reduce weight and inertia. The bearings were positioned either side of each cam and behind the drive gear with the rollers running directly on the tracks machined in the shaft. The bottom half of the housing carried alloy guides for hollow tappets with pressed-in, hardened contact pads, and shims under the pad head allowed the valve clearances to be set, although it was a tedius job.

Each cylinder was retained on four studs screwed into the crankcase and a total of eight nuts, some of splined form, held the head in place to make a solid, rigid structure. Each plug was angled out to the side and inlet and exhaust positioned top and bottom. The cylinder axis was not quite parallel to the ground but tilted up a little at the front.

The massive crankcase was cast in magnesium alloy and the choice of unit construction was forced on the design by the need to save space. The gearbox was, however, kept in its own separate chamber with its own oil. The case was open on the left at the front to allow the crankshaft complete with centre main housing to be inserted. Behind this it was closed off with a wall to seal the gearbox and outboard of the drive gears was a one-piece cover. This carried the outer race for the left main and a second race in which the gearbox drive pinion rotated. The clutch went outside the cover so ran dry in the

Left **The year they won the 500 cc championship but not mentioned in this showtime advert from late in the year**

Below **The 1949 7R minus its racing plates but equipped with massive megaphone**

air and the cover was well finned and carried a breather housing which located to a timed port on the end of the crankshaft.

On the right the crankcase had a round door with the right main outer race in the case and a separate end cover for the gearbox, which was assembled from that side. Underneath went a sump ribbed on both inside and outside, while the case itself was ribbed on the front underside.

The timing chest went on the right and the right crankcase door was formed as part of it. The chest ran from the crankcase forward and then branched into a Y to join to the two camboxes and also to bolt to the side of the head. It comprised three parts, the main casting, an outrigger plate and an outer cover. The gears that carried the drive ran on roller bearings on spindles held between the main casting and the outrigger plate which was bolted to it. Thus the cover was unstressed.

The gear train involved a total of eight pinions, the first of which was fixed to the crankshaft. This drove up and a little forward to a much larger gear, the first of three of various sizes all of which were drilled full of lightening holes and balanced. The front and largest was at the junction of the Y and drove each cambox via an intermediate. Each camshaft gear was attached to its shaft by a peg and hole vernier to allow the timing to be set or altered, and access to the fixing nut was

Below **The Porcupine used in the 1950 Senior TT by Ted Frend**

Right **Bill Doran at May Hill, Ramsey, in the 1951 Senior in which he finished second**

68

by means of a small cover on the end of the cambox.

The first large idler, driven by the crankshaft pinion, also meshed with a third gear above it and this drove a cross shaft and the main oil pump. The pump was of the twin gear type and a separate unit on the left only concerned with supply. A skew gear cut on the drive cross shaft meshed with another which drove a shaft running down to a scavenge pump located in the sump complete with small pick-up pipe and filter. Behind the supply pump went a filter unit bolted to the top of the gearbox casting on what were intended as the blower mountings and the main supply went through this and then to the centre main and on to the big ends.

A secondary supply was taken from the pump to the cam boxes and supplied via metering jets to the cam flanks. The oil in the inlet cambox drained to the exhaust one via a connecting pipe and was scavenged back to the tank by a third pump fitted to the end of the exhaust camshaft. The system was dry sump with an external tank, and the return pipe had a bleed-off with an adjustor to feed the rear chain. It did this by taking the oil to a jet set within a groove cut into the gearbox sprocket. From this holes were drilled outwards into the hollows between the sprocket teeth so that the oil was centrifuged onto the rollers.

The oil pump drive shaft carried a third gear between the others and this meshed with the magneto gear in front of it, the pair sitting within a bulge in the crankcase casting above the en-

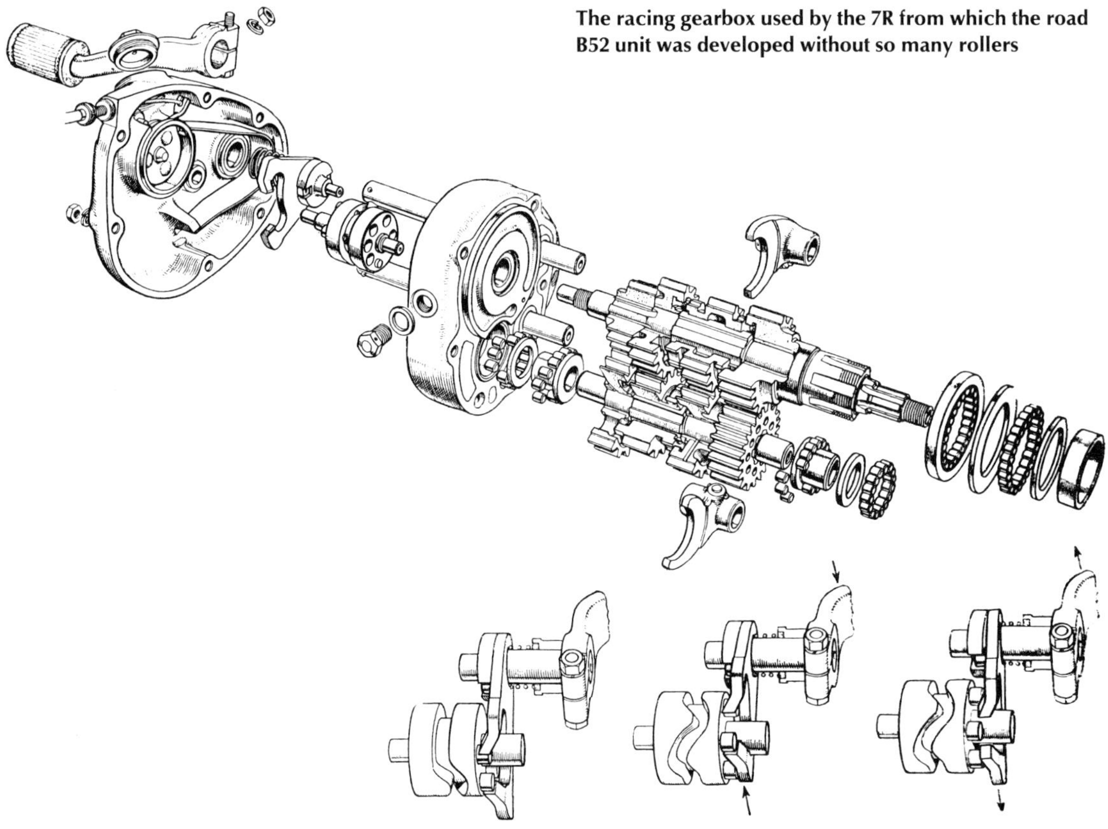

The racing gearbox used by the 7R from which the road B52 unit was developed without so many rollers

Above **Rod Coleman at Kate's Cottage on the E95 in the 1952 Senior TT in which he was fourth**

gine. A top cover enabled assembly to take place, while a side cap gave access to a peg and hole vernier for setting the timing. The magneto was a racing BTH mounted onto the crank case with manual advance.

The carburettors were twin racing Amals mounted to act in downdraught with the single float chamber between them. The assembly was attached to the engine by short rubber inlet tracts which allowed it to be easily removed and also provided a degree of flexibility in the mounting.

Like the exhaust, the end of the inlet camshaft was given a job to do and had the rev-counter drive taken from it. The exhaust system com-

Below **Porcupine in 1951 guise with under engine oil tank but fitted with spike cylinder head. Leaning on works van**

prised a pipe with plain megaphone for each cylinder.

The engine drove the gearbox with a pair of spur gears and the clutch ran in the air on the left. The gearbox was of conventional English form with four speeds and mainshaft above layshaft, but although the output sprocket was concentric with the input it was on the opposite, right, side to give a cross-over drive. The box employed roller bearings for the layshaft, free rollers for the inner sleeve gear mainshaft bearing and needle rollers for the free gears, so turned over very easily. Gear selection was by two selectors and a flat, round camplate located in the back of the box on a separate plate with the positive stop mechanism.

The clutch had six springs and its lift mechanism was a simple lever with hardened adjustor screw. This moved a ball thrust race and this a long push rod with mushroom at the lift mechanism end. The lift lever pivoted in a small block bolted to the gearbox outer cover and this carried an outrigger ball race for the gearbox mainshaft. The cover was bolted to the box end plate which carried the sleeve gear and layshaft bearings, and the clutch lever was enclosed by a small outer lid so it and the cable end were kept out of sight. The gear lever was on the right as normal.

The chain driven three valve 7R in its 1953 frame with vertical seat tubes

Many of the alloy castings which went to make up the engine were in Elektron, including the main crankcase, and this all helped to keep the weight of the unit to a minimum. It went into an all-welded frame with swinging fork rear suspension in an era when forged lugs and plungers were the norm. The frame had a single top tube and duplex down tubes of oval section which ran under the engine in round section and then turned up, again in oval form, to the tops of the rear units. At this point they joined the seat loop which ran into the top tube, while this was extended back, in oval section, to a bridge that joined it again to the seat loop. The steering head was well braced and cross tubes were used just below it and under the engine.

In fact the latter was the front engine mounting with lugs formed in the lower front of the crankcase being clamped to the cross tube. At the rear the frame was bolted to the back of the gearbox and a cross tube acted as bearing for the rear fork. The tube was housed in short bushes welded to the frame tubes and the bolts that held it also secured the footrests which could be adjusted a small amount.

The rear fork had the wheel spindle held in slots by a splined and flat sided distance piece and a nut, adjustment being by draw screws in clevis pieces that bridged the fork ends. The rear units also had clevis ends top and bottom and were described as oleo-pneumatic and as similar in design to the Teledraulics fitted at the front, the damping of which had been revamped.

Both wheels had massive magnesium alloy conical hubs with cooling fins and were laced into Dunlop light alloy rims with straight spokes. Tyre sizes were 3·00 × 27 front and 3·50 × 27 rear, while both brakes had twin leading shoes. Each

Exploded line drawing of the works 7R3B engine based on the stock 350 but with shaft drive to the camshafts. Complex assembly and never raced in this form

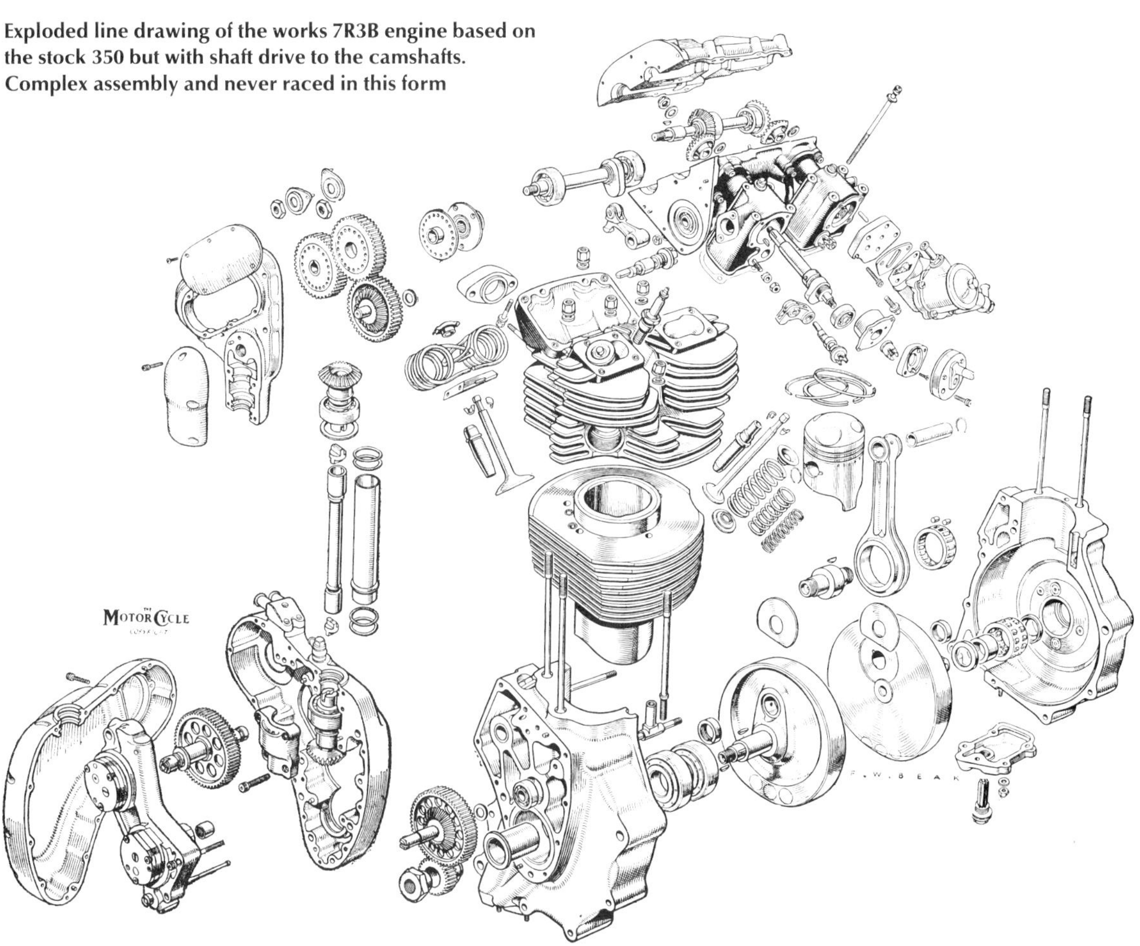

shoe had its own pivot in the backplate and was moved by a cam which acted against a roller mounted in the shoe. Pull off springs connected cam and shoe to return both and the cams were connected by an external, adjustable link rod. Inside the brake a bracing plate was bolted to the two shoe pivots and to the backplate. The rear brake, as the front, was cable operated with an adjuster at the pedal end positioned so that it could be operated by the rider while in motion.

The front brake adjuster was halfway down the left front fork and the story is told that during the Swiss Grand Prix in 1949 Les Graham had the adjuster lock nut come loose and while battling with Gileras had to re-set the adjuster as and when he could. This was at Berne and the only available place on the circuit was through the start and finish area so the word went to Gilera that winning the Swiss was something you did with your left hand on the forks. They tried it at Monza and then asked Les, who explained his odd crouch in that race.

Both wheels had mudguards and the rider a racing seat in the modern sense, not a saddle and pad as was then normal. The petrol tank looked massive but had a big tunnel in its underside to direct air to the oil tank. Capacity was six gallons and the tank was internally baffled.

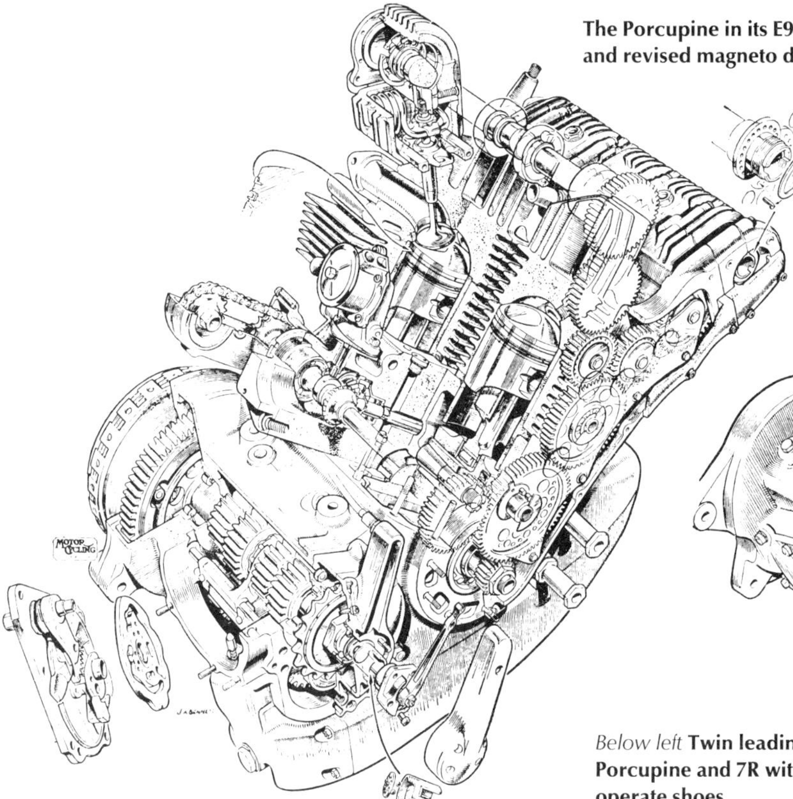

The Porcupine in its E95 form with inclined cylinders and revised magneto drive but otherwise much as before

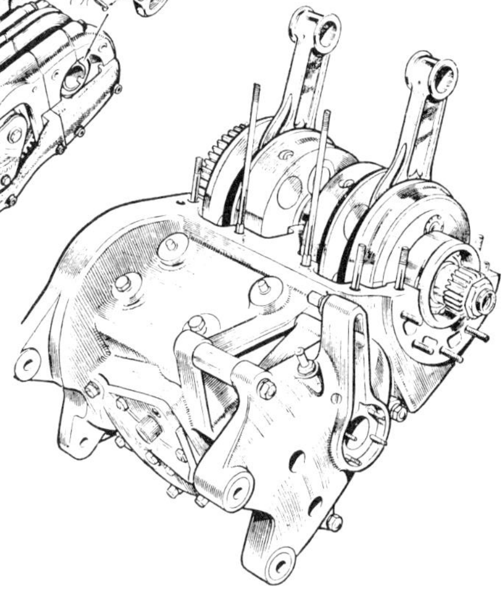

Below left **Twin leading shoe front brake used both by the Porcupine and 7R with internal cams and rollers to operate shoes**

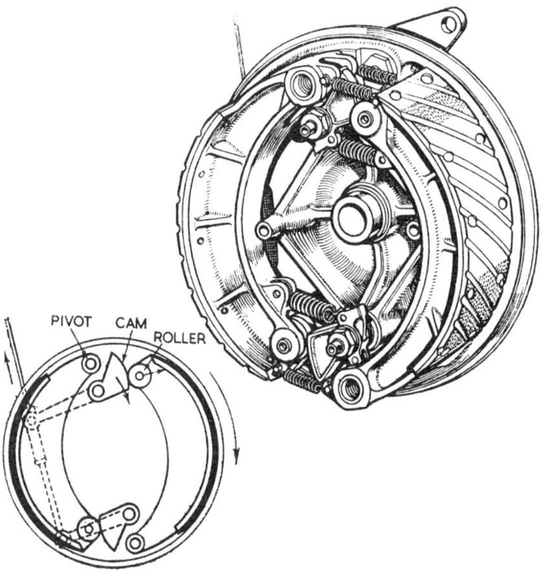

The oil tank held 12 pints and was of wrap-round form with the filler cap on the left to suit the TT pits as they were then used. It had two large cooling tubes run through it from front to rear and, like the petrol tank, was in light alloy. It was finished with aluminium paint which contrasted with the cooling holes, for matt black would have been better technically if not aesthetically.

The complete machine was finished off with racing number plates, rev-counter and narrow, fairly flat, light alloy handlebars. This last exercise in weight reduction gave Jock West some exciting moments in TT practice for the right end snapped off. The machines weighed in at 370 and 373 lb carrying 12 pints of oil and 6 gallons of petrol, so dry were around 310 lb.

When analysed the Porcupine's debut in the TT was very good, much better than the 9th and

14th places that Les and Jock finished in would indicate. Graham came off on the second lap but restarted to remain on the leaderboard, until his chain came adrift at Governor's Bridge on the final lap so he had to push in. He had ridden much of the race with an injured hand so his first lap was his fastest.

Jock West, who finally came home last, was even more unfortunate for, after a very slow start when the engine failed to fire, he suffered severe clutch slip for the first lap and took nearly an hour and a half to struggle round to the pits where adjustments were made. Once he was able to use the undoubted power of the twin he really set to work and his fourth lap was only three seconds longer than the fastest lap of the race.

He had less joy in the Dutch where his was the sole AJS and retired, and due to this non-

Left **Jock West having a canter on the final E95 with pannier fuel tank**

Below **The 1954 7R, sleeker than in 1948 but still fitted with AMC rear units**

started in the Belgium the following week. However, matters improved in Ulster where West was third and Ted Frend fifth, while Graham retired. West's model ran with plain pipes without megaphones on that occasion and the clutch plate and plug problems that had beset the team at the TT were now behind them.

The Porcupine was a works machine only but in February 1948 it was joined by a production 350 cc single for sale to private owners as well as for use by the factory team. This was the 7R with a format much more in the pre-war AJS tradition with a chain driven single overhead camshaft engine and separate four-speed gearbox.

AJS had a long history of camshaft singles but the new model was a completely fresh design by Phil Walker. The engine was a straightforward single intended to be reliable, easy to work on in the field, durable and thus well suited to the private owner of perhaps limited financial and technical levels. It could, and was, capable of being worked on in a grass paddock, although this was never recommended, and like all racing engines it responded to careful assembly and carburation setting.

The engine was of traditional English single form with vertically split crankcase and timing side on the right. It was based on dimensions of 74 × 81 mm which gave a capacity of 348 cc and the crankshaft was built up with round steel flywheels, drilled for balance. Both mainshafts and crankpin were pressed into place and secured with castellated nuts. The crankpin followed AMC practice with a separate hardened sleeve pressed onto a toughened pin and the big end bearing was a single row of rollers running within an alloy cage. The connecting rod was a steel

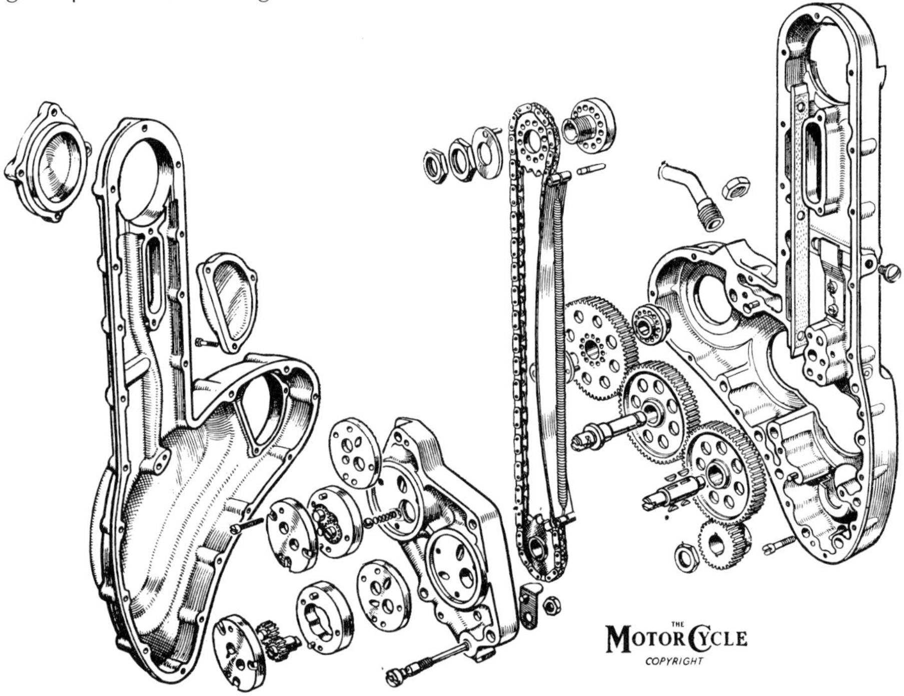

forging and webbed round both eyes for strength with lightness, the small end carrying a phosphor bronze bush. The piston was forged and secured by a hollow gudgeon pin retained by circlips.

The crankshaft was supported by a ballrace on the timing side but on the left, drive side, went a two-row caged roller with a further single row roller outboard of that. The left mainshaft was hollow and carried the engine breather which exhausted onto the primary chain.

The crankcase was massive and heavily ribbed externally to give maximum support to the mains, barrel and mountings. It was cast in magnesium alloy as were the camshaft drive inner and outer halves plus the cambox, and for corrosion protection all these parts were given a coat of special gold coloured paint that was to characterize them for many years and give a chromate finish.

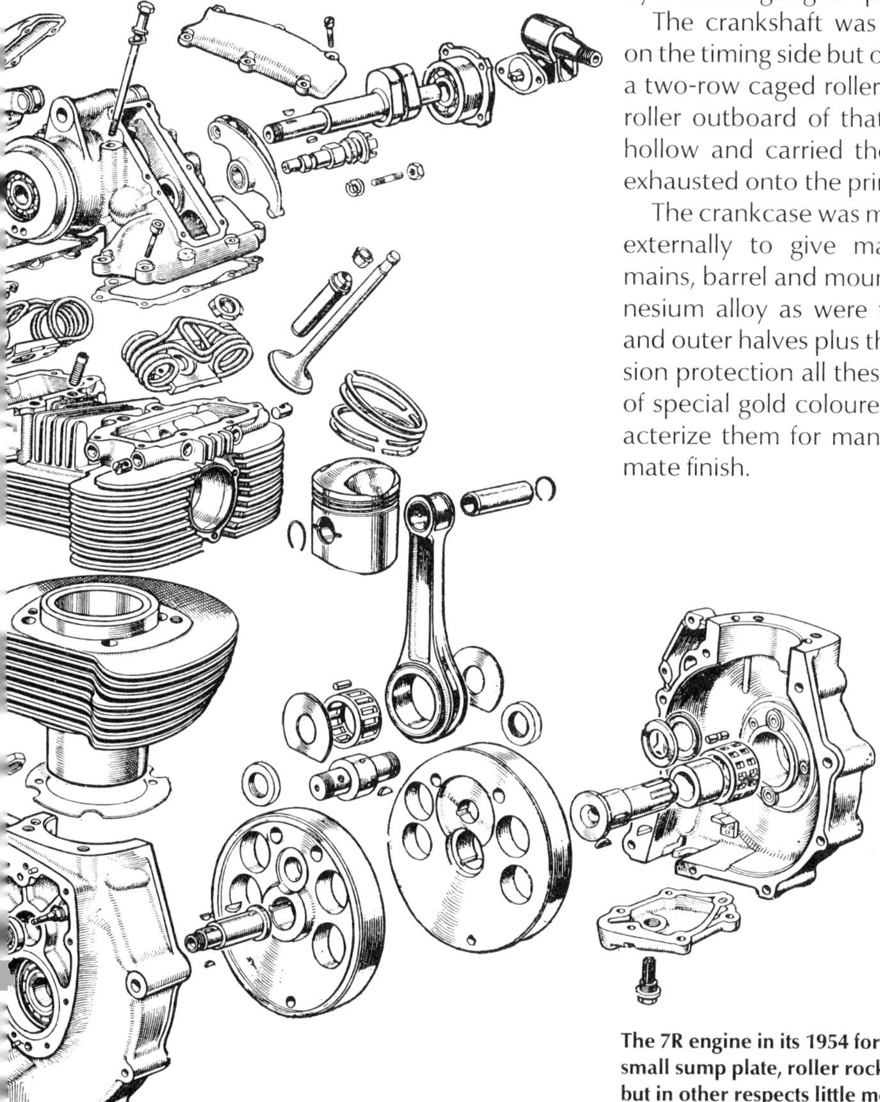

The 7R engine in its 1954 form with pressed in mainshafts, small sump plate, roller rockers and narrower valve angle but in other respects little modified

On top of the crankcase went the cylinder in aluminium alloy with a shrunk-in iron liner. This was very deeply spigoted down into the case and also up into the head. The piston within it carried one scraper and two compression rings.

The cylinder head was also in aluminium alloy and no more complex than that used on the ohv singles. It was a massive casting well finned on all four sides with the fins cleared away for the cam drive. At the front, in the centre, went the exhaust port which was threaded to take a pipe ring-nut and this was always wire locked to a hole drilled in one fin. At the rear went the inlet flange for the TT Amal carburettor which was offset to the right with a remote float chamber to its left near the centre line of the machine.

The top of the head had inlet and exhaust valve wells and between them diagonal fins to direct the air from left to right. To assist the flow the upper section of the cam-drive covers had a slot cast through it. The tops of the valve wells stood just above the fins so could be easily machined parallel to the underside of the head, while the whole structure was of compact form so unlikely to be damaged during workshop handling. In each valve well went a pressed-in shouldered guide with the valve controlled by hairpin springs retained by a carrier and cotters. Head and barrel were held down by four special long nuts screwed onto long studs fitted into the crankcase top.

Onto the cylinder head went the one-piece cam and rocker box cast in magnesium alloy. It fitted over the two valve wells, completely sealing them, with the camshaft positioned directly over the centre line of the engine. It was held down by four long bolts which screwed into the tops of the cylinder head nuts and a further twelve short bolts which screwed into trunnions. These were short lengths of bar, cross drilled and threaded, which went into horizontal holes in the cylinder head sides near the top and spaced around the valve wells. One end was slotted in line with the thread to assist assembly and this method abolished fears of stripping a thread in a pricey part. It also allowed the cambox to be slid sideways away from the cam drive to which it was spigoted and hence both it and the head could be quickly removed at a circuit if the valves needed a touch between practice and the race.

The camshaft ran in two ball races, the right in the casting and the left in a small end housing that allowed the shaft to be assembled and also carried the rev-counter drive gearbox. The camshaft end was slotted to drive this and its other end was of parallel form with two keys at 90 degrees. Onto the shaft went a vernier coupling and this had a peg and hole arrangement to vary and set the valve timing. The cams were formed as part of the shaft.

The rockers had radiused followers and oscillated on plain bushes on eccentric mounting pins which provided the means of setting the valve clearance. No valve caps were used and each rocker was enclosed by a separate cover plate held by six screws.

The drive to the camshaft was by gear and chain with a pinion on the end of the crankshaft secured by two keys and a nut. This meshed with a larger gear which was keyed to a shaft alongside the lower sprocket, each with two keys. An endless chain connected the upper and lower sprockets with a rubbing strip on the rear, drive side, and a Weller tensioner on the slack. This tensioner comprised a spring steel blade with rolled ends, the upper located to the housing. Between the ends went a long tension spring whose purpose was to force the strip into an arc against the chain and thus keep it under control.

To further assist this the tensioner itself was damped with a friction device which worked in a slot cut in the back housing and was loaded by a flat spring. The camshaft drive was enclosed by a two-part case that ran up the side of the engine and the cam chain was tensioned by peel-off gaskets between head and cambox. The case inner bolted to the timing side of the crank-

Above **Derek Ennett winning the 350 cc class in the North West 200 on his 7R**

Below **This is the early production G45 of 1953–55 which differed from the prototype in respect of tanks, gearchange and rev-counter drive**

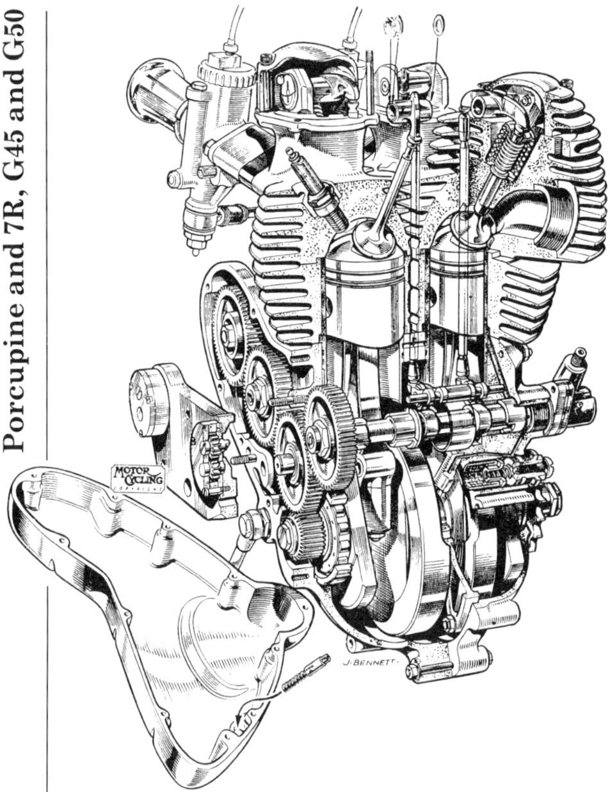

Line drawing of the G45 engine with its finned exhaust rocker covers and twin carburettors

case and located to the camshaft bearing housing of the cambox. It was enclosed by an outer cover which in turn carried an access cover for the vernier drive at its top and secured by four screws.

Lower down an inner member in magnesium alloy carried the timing side bearings, the oil pumps and the oil feeds within the cam drive cover. The camshaft drive spindle was supported by two ball races, one in the inner member and the other in the crankcase. Above and behind this went an intermediate gear whose spindle ran in bronze bushes and this in turn drove the magneto gear.

The magneto itself was a racing Lucas and the final gear incorporated another peg-and-hole vernier to assist timing setting. Access to this one was by a small cover held by three screws to the outer cam drive cover. The magneto itself was bolted to a flat surface provided on the rear of the crankcase halves.

The oil pumps were as on the twin, then as yet to come, being gear types in round housings. They bolted to the outside of the inner member and were driven by tongue and slot by the camshaft drive and intermediate gear spindles. The first of these turned the scavenge and the second the supply pumps.

The lubrication system was dry sump with an

The Junior TT winner of 1954 with pannier tank, ridden by Rod Coleman. Tank hole is to pass air to carburettor region

external oil tank, and the only pipes were those which ran from the tank to the engine connections set in the timing chest behind the barrel. The main oil feed was to the big end via a quill set in the inner member, while a subsidiary feed went to the camshaft and hence to the working faces of the cams.

The engine carried a cam-type shock absorber and drove to a four-speed close ratio Burman gearbox with stubby direct gear pedal. The clutch was a dry multi-plate type and the box was carried in alloy plates and pivoted at the top

Half a world from home four G45s line up in New Zealand. Note studded front tyre on left machine

for primary chain adjustment.

The frame owed much to that of the twin and was all welded with swinging fork rear suspension controlled by angled rear units. As with the twin, oval section tubing was used with a dualseat supported by the subframe and attached to a single top tube. Triangular engine steadies were bolted to this and the top lug of the cambox, while twin frame loops ran under the engine and gearbox to bend up to the upper rear unit fixings. At the front went the Teledraulic forks with shrouds as on the twin.

The brakes were massive twin leading shoe devices in conical hubs as on the works twins and the backplates were restrained by a torque arm at the rear and twin bolts at the front. Hubs were in magnesium alloy and spoked into high tensile steel rims, although light alloy ones were available as an option. Tyre sizes were 3·00 × 21 in. front and 3·25 × 20 in. rear.

Rear wheel adjustment was by draw bolts with left and right hand threads which moved the spindle relative to the fixed nuts at the ends of the forks. These were closed and the draw bolts threaded into them and U-shaped pieces that pulled or pushed the spindle. It was a fiddle to assemble for there were distance pieces and col-

A. R. Clark sits on his G45 on the start line at Crystal Palace at a 1956 meeting

lars on the spindle, but once in position chain adjustment was very easy. The snag was that gearing changes were done on the rear sprocket so the wheel had to come out again.

The mudguards were in light alloy and neatly fixed. The front had a pair of short stays either side of the fork leg plus a rear stay, while early line drawings show the rear wheel encased by a well valanced mudguard. In practice this became the same narrow section as used at the front supported by a long stay running back from the top unit mountings. The valanced guard managed without this and would have avoided a 7R problem that remained for years—a habit of the rear tyre throwing stones down the carburettor bellmouth unless the owner took precautions to stop them with sponge and sheet.

The oil tank was a wrap-round with the filler on the left, and the idea was to put the sides out in the wind to cool them. In practice they made the riding position uncomfortable and became so hot in a long race they could burn the rider's legs despite the heavy leather boots worn in that era. The petrol tank was of nearly five gallons capacity and, like the oil container, made from light alloy. Both were held by bolts which went through the sides of the tank into lugs on the frame and were rubber mounted. Those bolts did not go in easily and once home were hidden from sight by rubber bungs on each side. Wing nut filler caps were fitted to both tanks and the petrol one had a rubber chin pad stuck to its top.

A friction steering damper was fitted and the handlebars fixed to the top fork crown. Footrests were as on the twin with a cup at the inner end which fitted onto a boss with a cross bolt to secure. As the rest was off-centre to the cup which was drilled for a variety of positions of bolt, its rotation gave a choice of footrest placement.

An early drawing shows the exhaust pipe run-

Derek Ennett jumps Ballaugh Bridge with his G45 on his way to 6th place in the 1956 Senior TT

Above **Alan Shepherd descending Bray Hill on the way to winning the 1958 Junior MGP**

Below **The 1957 version of the 7R with revised dimensions, reversed cone megaphone and Girlings**

ning out between the duplex down tubes and then back between them just below the timing cover, back over the right tube under the engine, under the gearbox end cover to a horizontal megaphone. This had a long strengthening rib which bolted to a frame stay. In fact the pipe ran outside the frame at the front to a simply enormous megaphone which was tilted up and out.

The 7R was announced as the Junior but within a month became known as the 'Boy Racer', a nickname that was to stick to it for all its days. It was reliable but not as fast as the KTT or the Manx and had to be kept on the boil to make it perform well. The power came in around 5500 rpm and it peaked at 7000, which did not give a very wide power band for a 350 with four-speed gearbox.

Early in the year Jock West gave the machine an airing at Brands Hatch, this of course when it was a one-mile grass track where riders climbed Paddock bend. The machine ran in full road racing trim, even to a ribbed front tyre, and only did a few laps.

The first production 7R went to Fergus Anderson who rode it at Pau that Easter and held a close second for most of the race before being

Earls Court 1958 with the Matchless G50 on show and raising plenty of interest

forced out with clutch trouble. By the time the TT came round the first batch was complete and delivered so that a good few private owners were AJS mounted in the Junior with four riding their 350 cc machines in the Senior.

The works also ran 7Rs in the Junior and fitted them with 3.00 in. section rear tyres to help them along, but to no real avail for they finished some way down the field with Maurice Cann on a private one ahead in fifth position. Ten finishers were on the 7R that year, while the Manx and KTT mustered five apiece.

Line drawing of the G50 engine, much as the 7R but with external oil drains from the head

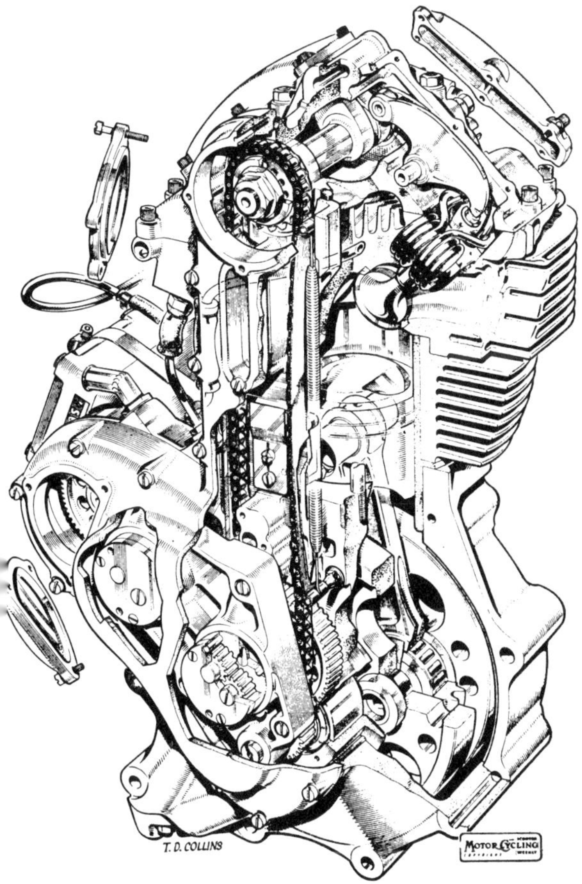

The firm's real efforts went into the twin and for the TT it had a number of changes from the 1947 models. A new rear hub was fitted with the backplate held by an alloy torque arm instead of the two bolts used before and the brake pedal was simplified. A smaller rear sprocket was fitted as the soupdish of 1947 gave the rear chain a hard time, and this was eased by having more reduction in the primary gears.

The frame was given gussets to stiffen up the top rear unit mounting points and the megaphone supports, while the seat was made shorter. The engine received a new finned oil cooler turned from solid alloy bar, anodized and dyed black, while the oil tank was given the same finish to improve heat dissipation. A new Lucas racing magneto was fitted and the inlet tracts completely changed. In place of the vertical mixing chambers went curved steel tubes which were joined to inlet stubs with short lengths of rubber hose. The tubes carried the chambers in their normal horizontal position with the float chamber between and ahead of them. The float chamber was changed to a top feed and it and the two mixing ones were joined to a single bracket which was fixed to the frame by one tube running up to the top tube and a pair running forward to the frame cross-member.

In terms of intake efficiency it was a step backwards and brought about by the carburation problems inherent with the tunnel effect of the petrol tank above the intakes and the nature of the TT carburettor. This was designed to accept not more than 15 degrees of downdraught and any increase caused problems with the pilot system flooding. At one time I had one set at 45 degrees and it was super-sensitive to float height, but for straight down it needed to be modified.

For reasons of pride or stubbornness, AJS persisted with this arrangement even when a racing Dell'Orto became available that was designed for the 250 cc racing Guzzi. Just as they persisted with their own suspension units long after every private owner had switched to Girlings. The AMC

The 7R in 1960 with cable rear brake and a number of other small improvements

ones worked passably well for a while but never stayed constant for long so the machines became harder and harder to hold as races progressed.

It was suggested that AJS would not use an Italian carburettor for patriotic reasons, but this overlooked the reason for entering races which was to win them. Such logic was not to stop the Italian multis happily running on English tyres with their Lodge plugs fired by a Lucas magneto.

The final changes to the twins for 1948 were brazed-on pivots for the handlebar controls and the trial of a 3·25 in. section rear tyre in practice. This was found to be too narrow so the 3·50 was fitted for the race. In this Les Graham lay second for a while and in the lead briefly but retired, as did the other machines. In Europe matters again improved with West 3rd in Holland and 2nd in Belgium, where Graham set the lap record and they both finished in the 350 cc event.

In Ulster they had problems with water on the plugs for it rained as it only can in Ireland, but despite stops Graham was 3rd and there was no doubt that the twins were competitive with the Grand Prix field. Late in the year they attacked and broke world records with the twin and during the winter Fergus Anderson took some Australian records using his 7R.

For 1949 not a lot happened to the works machines, but they won their one world championship for make and rider, Les Graham, with Bill Doran fourth in the 500 cc list. Reg Armstrong took third in the 350 class so all in it was a good year, except at the TT. There Doran stopped with gearbox trouble when in the lead he had held for most of the Junior race with only 12 miles to go. In the Senior, Les Graham had his magneto armature shear at Hilberry when well ahead on the last lap. He pushed in to 10th behind his team-mates. A sad ending to a brilliant ride by a most popular sportsman.

The machines were little altered for that year with the 7R gaining a magnetic sump plug. On the Porcupine the most noticeable change was to the carburettor layout, for the mixing chambers were mounted at an angle on much shorter inlet tracts. The assembly of mixing and float chambers was supported in a new manner

Bob McIntyre's 7R with special frame and other details

which incorporated rubber mountings on which the front of the petrol tank sat. Internally the clutch gear was altered to incorporate a shock absorber with three coil springs between the two working parts.

For 1950 the machines were modified to a greater extent and for Porcupine and 7R the front hub was strengthened by bolting the iron drum to the magnesium alloy hub shell. The oil tanks were made slimmer and the petrol tanks given knee recesses to enable the rider to tuck away more. On the works models a trial fairing was fitted in most races.

The Porcupine had its compression ratio raised a little to take advantage of the improvement in fuel quality that occurred that season, but this increase was limited by the inherent layout of the combustion chamber. AJS were finding that wide valve angles and a classical hemisphere design were alright for a blown engine running on a lowish ratio, but inhibited the use of the ratios that were becoming normal. It is a curious reflection on the company outlook that they did not take the relatively easy step of redesigning the head to narrow the valve angle and adopt downdraught carburettors to give the best inlet tract shape and flow. Strange, for they had thought at one time of casting the head in silver to obtain a heat conductivity three times greater than aluminium. In this design the valve seats were silver soldered in place and the head was for the blown engine.

The idea got to the point of a visit to Hatton Garden but then the snags appeared, not least of which was a cost of £350 per casting (in 1946) but with an agreement to buy back machining scrap and any unwanted heads. It was also necessary to alloy the silver with copper to get the necessary strength and to enable the intricate sections to be cast. This dropped the conductivity to not much more than aluminium, so rather removing the point of the exercise, while the head would have been more than three times as heavy as the final Y alloy one.

Back to 1950, and the inlet tracts were altered yet again to try to get clean carburation. This time they splayed out to quite a degree and each tract had a pair of ribs along its top. The carburettors themselves were the experimental GP type and they were fed by twin float chambers, each mounted on to a front downtube with a clamp bracket. In their new position the carburettors were much more accessible than with earlier layouts. For the cycle parts there was little change other than the points common with the 350, but cooling flutes were added on the left side-plate of the rear hub and the handlebars were mounted further back and made narrower.

The 7R received a good few changes for 1950. Inside the engine the compression ratio went up to 8.85:1 in conjunction with a slightly reduced valve angle, from 80 to 79 degrees, larger inlet valve, smaller valve stems and collet spring retainers. The bottom half was stiffened up in various ways, the first being an increase in crankpin diameter of the part pressed into the flywheels. The timing side shaft lost its inner nut and gained a flange so was pressed into place

Fred Neville going out to practice on the G50 for the 1961 Senior MGP, sadly he died in a crash when leading the Junior on his 7R

through the flywheel to which it gave better support. The flywheels themselves were reduced in diameter and the timing side bearing changed to a roller race.

The scraper ring of the piston was changed to a pair of tapered rings in a single groove and woe betide anyone who assembled even one upside down! One 7R was stripped and rebuilt ten times in one week in an attempt to cure oiling up problems before it was spotted that the ring was the wrong way up because the mark had rubbed off. Fortunately in those times testing could be done by stuffing a road silencer up the megaphone and adjourning to the local bypass. Cured, the 7R went to Scarboro' and faded at the first corner in practice—plug lead off, so the rider breathed again.

Further engine changes were to the oil pumps which became made in three parts, an increase in oil supply to the cambox, and the addition of a small finned sump to the underside of the crankcase. This held a gauze filter in place which protected the pick-up feed to the scavenge pump.

Primary chain lubrication was by the same method used for the final drive on the Porcupine. A timing valve was built into the magneto idler pinion shaft which allowed crankcase pressure to take oil via a needle adjuster to a boss round the mainshaft. Holes in the boss let the oil drip into a groove turned in the inner face of the sprocket and from this reservoir radial holes took the oil out to the sprocket teeth and chain rollers. In practice this was not to work too well and was soon abandoned.

Power was up by 2 bhp and was transmitted to a new Burman gearbox, the 7R 50, via a modified clutch. This had a complete drum in place of the older slotted type and the drive was obtained by spot welding tongues to the inner surface to turn the the five clutch plates clamped to their inner mates by five springs.

The gearbox was conventional English in design and layout with a direct acting gear pedal moving the selector cam and thus the selectors on their shafts. The case was in magnesium alloy and the layshaft turned in double roller bearings at each end. The clutch was lifted by a three-ball ramp mechanism installed in the outer end cover.

Externally, aside from the narrower oil tank, the new model was easily recognized by the exhaust pipe which curled back inside the right downtube to sweep past the timing cover instead of below it. Both pipe and megaphone were shorter.

During the year the Porcupine was run with a 10 in. front brake, and the works 7R with a much larger carburettor bellmouth trumpet.

1951 brought some extensive revision to the Porcupine which lost its spikes and gained a head. For convenience the new heads were made separate with horizontal fins over the combustion chamber. By the TT one machine had

American visitors to Earls Court in 1963 admire Colin Seeley's immaculate G50 outfit

this new design as a one-piece head but still without the traditional quills. The main oil pump was set into the base of the crankcase and the oil tank became a long boat-shaped casting which bolted to the underside of the engine and carried eight pints of oil. It ran back under the gearbox with a filler tube near the front on the left side.

The carburettors were revised yet again with a single central float chamber with integral extensions to each side to support the two mixing chambers. These had horizontal jets and the whole assembly was suspended from the frame top tube and connected by curved inlet tracts and short rubber hoses to the engine.

The frame wheelbase was reduced by an inch and jampots fitted to the rear end. It was still to be some time before AMC were to admit that maybe Girling did know best about dampers. The units fitted had alloy spring boxes as part of a weight reduction exercise. The forks were made an inch shorter with an alloy top crown and fabricated, two part, sheet steel lower one. No upper fork shrouds were fitted and swan-neck clip-ons were used for the first time.

At the rear end, the mudguard was lengthened to suit revised racing regulations and its support triangulated. The seat was made shorter and its rear hump was built to carry two spare plugs with a zip fastener to secure the pockets. Wheel sizes front and rear came down to 19 in. with 3·00 front and 3·50 in. rear sections.

The works 7R had many of the changes made to the 500 twin, including the shorter wheelbase, revised forks, new seat, clip-ons, 19 in. wheels and jampots. The engine was moved forward in the frame which gave the exhaust pipe a problem to turn clear of the frame, and the crankcase was made narrower. The valve angle was narrowed to 74 degrees and the inlet downdraught increased to 12 degrees, which reduced the depth of the combustion chamber. The inlet offset remained at 20 degrees. No engine shaft shock absorber was fitted so the chain line came

Alan Shepherd on his G50 at the Belgium GP in 1963 where he finished 3rd; he took second spot in the 500 cc world title that year

in and both chains were lubricated by a simple feed with metering jet and tap.

The production models had engines based on the 1950 works unit so had that camshaft and their compression ratio raised to 9·4:1. The oil feed to the camshaft was improved. On the outside went jampots, a more extensive primary chain guard and a jet metered oil supply for the primary chain, the sprocket feed being discontinued.

That year AMC were involved with the Clubman's TT and that event saw ten twins in the Senior. These had engines that were standard aside from port polishing and careful assembly

Ron Chandler practising for the 1964 Manx GP on his G50

and which ran on open pipes and without an air cleaner. The lights were removed and alloy mudguards fitted. As the AJS tank was larger than the Matchless the six models of that marque had a saddle and pad in place of the usual dualseat to allow the larger receptacle to be carried. It had the flying 'M' badge attached to the sides.

There were also six 350 cc singles, two with iron engines and four all alloy. Preparation was as with the twins plus TT carburettors. Like the twins they had rearsets and reversed gear pedal but neither model was really competitive and 7th by a twin was their best result.

A few months later another Matchless was to create a furore and start a new model line. The occasion was the Manx Grand Prix and the machine the prototype of what was to become the G45 twin. In essence it was a hybrid constructed from a 7R chassis and a modified 500 cc Super Clubman engine. It was an experimental unit with well finned alloy heads and barrels on a G9 crankcase. One of the most noticeable features was the way the head fins continued all the way up the exhaust rocker boxes. A single TT Amal was fitted and short exhaust pipes with megaphones. A rev-counter drive was taken from the magneto gear with the right-angle gearbox bolted to the outside of timing cover.

For the rest the model was works 7R with the forks as used by the team at the TT, clip-ons and a large tank carrying the flying 'M' transfer. Wheels and brakes were as the works used so the G45 was on 19 in. rims from the start. It made a promising debut, for Robin Sherry finished fourth after laying third for a while.

At the classics the firm had little success, although Doran won in Holland on the 350 but it was Geoff Duke and Norton's year. For private runners it was a different matter for the 7R continued to carry its riders to good places and many wins in international events. It was certainly fulfilling the designers' aims for once set up it would run well for meeting after meeting with minimal attention, a very important factor for circus runners in those days of many meetings and slow vans to travel the miles between them.

In 1952 both the Porcupine and the works 7R were drastically altered, the first with a new frame and engine angle, and the second with a three-valve cylinder head.

The Porcupine lost all claim to its early sobriquet as the new engine had the cylinders inclined at 45 degrees with conventional axial fins. The cylinder heads had transverse fins across the top of the combustion chamber bent into a vee to clear the plugs. These were central but masked and fired the mixture through slots. In most other respects the engine unit was as before with the crankshaft, gearbox and oil pumps unchanged, the timing cover modified to suit the new cylinder angle and the sump retained under the crankcase but brought up in front of it as well.

One item that did change was the magneto which became the rotating magnet type mounted to slope back behind the cylinders. Its drive was modified to a cross-shaft driven by the timing gears with a chain on the left up to the instrument.

The carburettors fitted to short, nearly straight inlet tracts and were GPs with large intake trumpets. Both were fed from a single top-feed float chamber suspended by a rod from a flexible mounting attached to the left frame tube. This rod allowed the float height to be easily set or altered.

An air duct took cold air over the heads to the region of the bellmouths when the machine first appeared in TT practice, but by the race the float chamber had moved to the right, the duct gone and baffles added around the carburettors to deflect the heated cooling air away from them. On the exhaust side the pipes were fitted with reverse cone megaphones.

The frames were new with a shorter wheelbase of 54.5 in. and had a touch of the featherbed in the headstock area with tank rails and downtubes crossing over in that region. The rails ran straight back from the bottom of the headstock to vertical seat tubes and on to the tops of the inclined rear units. The down tubes ran from the top of the headstock to the front of the crankcase to which they were attached by two bolts on each side. They were cross-braced just above the cylinder head. The seat tubes were braced by a diagonal tube and ran down to the rear fork pivot and to the rear of the gearbox, to which they were fastened by two more pairs of bolts.

The rear unit sub-frame and the seat were braced by a pair of small tubes and the main frame had a tube on each side running from the junction of the tank rail and seat tube, down and forward to pick up on the crankcase just below the back of the barrels. Each of these tubes was bolted in place with an adjustable clevis end at the top. Rear suspension was by jampots.

A completely new rear hub was used with the drum on the left remote from the sprocket. The drum was shrunk in the magnesium alloy casting and the sprocket mounting drum braced to the brake with cross bolts and distance pieces. The sprocket itself was in alloy and held on a ring of studs with nuts.

The rear mudguard was mounted from the rear fork so unsprung and rear chain oil was kept in the seat stay. A 6·5 gallon fuel tank was fitted, held down on rubber mountings by a long strap running back from a pivot at the headstock to two retaining tension springs just in front of the seat. Tyres were as 1951 and a head fairing was tried but not used in the TT. The gearchange lever was across the frame and a rather lengthy tube with a knob on the end, but the change was light and fast enough.

There was one further AMC twin in that Senior TT ridden by Ernie Ring which had the Matchless engine in the 7R frame and went well until the rider crashed.

The changes to the works 7R mainly concerned the cylinder head and valve gear. The new head had three valves, one inlet and two exhaust, and three camshafts so was nicknamed the 'triple-knocker'. It was built in two forms and the first was typed the 7R3A and used in the TT. The design was by H. J. (Ike) Hatch who had been responsible for the pre-war Excelsior Mechanical Marvel radial four-valve engine. In the AJS head the inlet laid back on the centre line but the exhausts splayed out radially as well as being inclined forward. Each valve was opened by its own camshaft with a roller follower under the cam on an eccentric pin for adjustment of the clearance. The inlet camshaft lay across the head in normal fashion but the two exhausts ran fore and aft at a down-pointing angle to match the valves. The link between the three shafts involved a layshaft positioned ahead of and above the inlet camshaft and gear driven from it by spurs on the right. This shaft carried two bevel gears and each of these was meshed with a bevel on the aft end of an exhaust camshaft. Each of the three camshafts turned in a pair of ball races, one by the cam and one behind the drive gear, while the layshaft used three races fitted close to its three gears.

The first engine type had the inlet camshaft chain driven from a sprocket mounted on a jackshaft in the crankcase just as in the stock motor. Thus the whole of the lower timing gear, magneto drive and oil pumps could be left alone, and the one change was to the upper part of the casing which enclosed the chain. This was laid back to run direct to the inlet and gave the engine an odd appearance. To accommodate it the cylinder fins on that side were machined away and they were also removed a little on each front corner to clear the exhaust pipes.

The cylinder head was rather more complex than standard and had revised stud fixings, as the normal front ones would have run into the ports. They were moved round and back and a fifth stud added on the front centre line. It was attached to the crankcase by a trunnion into which it screwed and which located into the case on each side. The head had one inlet and two

exhaust valve wells with their upper surfaces angled forward and at different levels. Into them went the inlet valve with its twin, interlocked hairpin springs and the two exhausts each with triple coil springs.

The cambox bolted down on to the valve wells and was itself split into four parts. The inlet section had a cover on its rear upper side and this joint line passed through the centres of the inlet camshaft and the layshaft to clamp on to the various bearings they ran on. It also had the inlet cam follower fitted to it. On to its front, lower face were bolted two exhaust camshaft housings and these also seated on to the cylinder head over the exhaust wells. Each one carried one camshaft on its two bearings and a cam follower. From the front of the right one the rev-counter drive was taken and in later years the left one was used to drive a mechanical petrol pump using a pin follower and an end nut in the form of a face cam.

Colin Seeley in full flight on his Matchless-Watsonian outfit

Between the exhaust wells went the plug which was inclined forward a little, a flange at the rear carried the carburettor and the exhaust pipes were secured by flange nuts which screwed into the head. Each one carried a small megaphone.

For the rest, the engine dimensions were 75·5 × 78 mm and a very short rod was used, so short that the sides of the piston had to be cut away to clear the flywheels. Otherwise it was as before but with the crankcase in aluminium alloy.

Initially this engine went into a 7R frame, but by the TT a new design was in use. This had a single top tube which was joined and braced to duplex vertical seat tubes which ran down to support the rear fork pivot and on under the gearbox and engine to turn up to the base of the headstock. Forks, rear units and tank mounting were as on the twin and the remote rear hub was also used but reversed to suit the chain line.

The gearbox was modified internally with the bearings being changed. The sleeve gear was supported in two roller bearings, the mainshaft in it by a pair of needle races in the sleeve and the clutch drum on two rows of rollers.

The triple knocker engine was raced in this form but suffered during development from the fixed cam chain centres. This meant that any alteration to the normal 10:1 compression ratio called for a new piston rather than a skim from the base of the barrel. In 1954 Hatch removed this restriction by designing the 7R3B which had the camshafts driven by a vertical shaft and bevels just as the Norton and Velocette opposition used. Thus at one point the firm had racing ohc engines with drives by chain, shaft or gear train, the three normal methods.

The revised engine needed few changes to add the new camdrive which was to improve the cylinder cooling by offering less obstruction to the air flow than the more massive chaincase. The drive shaft was positioned on the cylinder axis and had Oldham couplings at each end. These connected to bevel gears each of which ran in a needle race and a ball bearing, and the lower gear meshed with a mate coupled to the normal 7R intermediate spur gear driven by the crankshaft pinion. This pair was supported by a ball race in the crankcase and a needle race in the oil pump housing, which continued to act as an outrigger support and as mounting for the two pumps.

The normal timing case was cut off at crankcase level and the shaft tube clamped by the outer case cover, its centre being on the split line. The bearings themselves were held by a small half clamp under the cover.

At the top end the main cambox casting was modified to provide a bearing housing below and forward of the layshaft. The gear on the right end of this that drove the inlet camshaft was meshed with another on a jackshaft running in that bearing and coupled to a bevel. This bevel meshed with that at the top of the vertical shaft.

The three spur gears were enclosed by a casting that bolted to the side of the main cambox and its lid, and in turn this had two outer covers. The upper was simply an access plate that enabled the fitters to reach the peg and hole verniers between gears and shafts, but the lower acted as a clamp for the upper bevel bearings and the top end of the vertical shaft tube.

The three-valve engine was often run alongside the two-valve but showed little advantage. It had to be driven harder to get the performance which made it less easy to get the best from and it was a difficult engine to work on. Only the A type was raced in anger, the shaft one not receiving any development after being built in the middle of 1954, so only just available for 1955. It was then to fall victim of group policies.

Returning to 1952, when the three-valve engine made its debut, the stock 7R received little attention as the firm must have been at full stretch with the changes to the works models.

A sideline interest at the TT that year was a special built by Bob Collier for Bill Storr to ride. This used a 1949 7R engine laid well forward to reduce height and frontal area. The special frame employed a massive 8·5 in. diameter ball bearing as a head race, trailing link forks with bonded rubber suspension medium, and the same medium for the rear fork. The rider adopted a semi-prone position and his feet were alongside the back of the rear tyre.

It was a very enterprising try but it failed to make the line at the TT yet was run in practice at the Belgium and then forbidden to start. Later in the year it did run at Silverstone, in mid-field.

Late in 1952 came the next step in the G45 story when Derek Farrant won the Manx GP riding the prototype and leading from the start to finish. As before, the machine was a 7R down to the tyre sizes, fitted with the modified twin engine.

There was something of a controversy over the appearance of a works prototype in what was essentially considered to be an amateur event. There had been murmurs in 1951 but in 1952 the offending machine committed the error of winning and, in addition, other 1951 works models were lent to selected runners. Against this, it was by no means unusual for prototypes to run in the event.

However, by October Matchless calmed the situation by announcing that a small batch of twins would be built for the 1953 season and these would be firmly based on the prototype which had thus done its job.

The G45 engine followed the standard G9 design closely with few changes. The iron crankshaft was used, although a steel one was tried but it had no shock absorber on its end. One item that did change was the camshaft, and the followers had needle bearings for their rollers and moved alloy push rods with steel ends. The pistons had solid skirts and gave a compression ratio of 9·4:1, while the barrels were alloy muffs with iron liners. The heads were more deeply finned than standard and the fins were carried up the exhaust rocker covers. All the covers were non-standard and in magnesium alloy and under them went straight line rockers. Triple valve springs were fitted.

Ron Chandler down at Brands Hatch in 1966 running in his AJS

The engine had twin GP carburettors fed by a central float chamber, a racing Lucas magneto, and a rev-counter driven by the magneto gear. The cycle parts were 7R but with a 5·5 gallon tank bearing the Matchless flying M in silver.

For 1953 the standard 7R had a good few modifications based on the work done with the 1951 works engine. The valve angle was reduced to 74 degrees and more downdraught given to the inlet. In the bottom half there were a number of changes to stiffen things up. The big end rollers were narrowed a little and the crankpin nuts changed to a plain round section with an attached hexagon. This allowed them to be done up properly after which the hexagon part was cut off. Removal entailed splitting the round portion away and two new nuts, but overall it was a better system.

As the castellated nut that secured the drive side mainshaft in the flywheel was difficult to really tighten and rather thick, it went, and the shaft became as the timing side with a press fit in the wheel with a shoulder on the inside. As this was again narrower than the nut the effective support was increased and the outer nut on the shaft helped to hold everything together.

The drive side main was changed to a two-row caged roller and the outer sleeve was flanged so it could be secured to the crankcase wall. Upstairs the rockers gained roller followers so the effective radius was halved, and externally a shorter exhaust pipe and megaphone were fitted. The pipe fixing was changed to a clamping collar secured by three screws which went into the head, but could be awkward when the rider was in a hurry and the engine hot.

The crankcase lost its external ribs and the engine went into a new, narrower frame with shorter forks. The shock absorber went into the clutch and chain lubricant in the top frame tube from where it was fed to the primary by pipe and the final drive sprocket by jet, in the same manner as the Porcupine.

The rear engine plates were replaced by a forged alloy bridge which linked the engine, gearbox and frame together and stiffened the assembly a good deal. A remote gearchange was fitted and the primary chainguard extended all the way round the chain.

Wheels reduced to 19 in. with the twin leading shoe brake retained at the front but a single used at the rear. The petrol tank was supported on rubber mountings, the front ones clamped to the down tubes and adjustable, and held down by a strap. The seat was made shorter but the jampots remained.

By the time the TT came round the G45 had a steel crankshaft with shrunk-on flywheels, the rev-counter driven from the exhaust camshaft and was in the new set of 7R cycle parts. Aside from the silver lining, the only variation was in tyre section, with the twin half a section wider, and petrol tank capacity as the engine top intruded less into it than on the single.

The Porcupine was by then termed the E95, a type number first used in 1952 and applied to the sloping engines. For 1953 the carburettor angle was increased from 25 to 49 degrees so the engine finally had some slight downdraught. Separate cylinder heads were fitted and on one the spike fins once again appeared by dint of saw cuts through those cast. A return spring was added to the gear pedal to counterbalance its weight and the whole unit went into a new frame. This was much as in 1952 but extended under the power unit to a full duplex with single round section top tube.

The 7R3A was little changed from 1952 but some engines were run with a 30 degree downdraught instead of the usual 15 degrees for the inlet. The frame was much as the new standard one except that the main tube from the fork pivot to the top of the rear units was brought forward as a vertical member and a light subframe added to it, so in that respect it was to the 1952 format.

1954 brought the final development stage to both the E95 and the works 7R3A, and in this

Paddy Driver with Tom Kirby on the left receives the Wills Trophy at Thruxton in 1965. Disc front brake on the G50

guise they became the Mark 2 variants. The changes were all to reduce height and improve wind penetration but without the adoption of streamlining.

This was done by lowering the headstock and shortening the forks to pull the front end down and by fitting a lower seat at the rear. Tank top height was drastically lowered and the new tanks deepened down nearly to wheel spindle level. To do this the sides were extended so that the result was really two pannier tanks with a bridge at the top but carefully mounted, to isolate them, and braced to prevent the walls from panting in and out.

The tank was shaped to act as streamlining by running the sides out to the width across the rider's knees and then providing recesses for his lower legs to tuck into. Despite the apparent size, the capacity remained around 6 gallons due to the large tunnel through the centre. The tanks were not the same as each underside was tailored to suit the engine it had to clear, and the 7R tank had a tunnel through each side to direct cool air into the region of the carburettor intake. At the rear of the tank was a header tank which was open to the main one at the top so it could overflow in either direction.

All this change placed the petrol taps at the base of the main tank well below the carburettor so a mechanical pump had to be added to the system, driven by the left exhaust camshaft on the 7R and by the magneto drive shaft on the twin.

On the 7R a normal float chamber was fitted and supplied from the header tank so all the pump did was to transfer fuel from main to header which overflowed back when full. The twin was more complicated; it had an extra chamber, the spill tank, which was located low down behind the gearbox and set in the centre of this was a normal float chamber supplied by the main tank. Its outlet connected to the spill tank and it kept the level around the mid-point. From the spill tank the fuel was lifted by the pump to the header tank and from there it went to a pair of weirs on each side of each carburettor. Their function was to maintain a steady fluid level within the mixing chambers regardless of the loads the machine was subject to or the effects of vibration. Surplus fuel fell over the weir and drained back to the spill tank, which was vented to atmosphere.

The one snag with these schemes was the need to prime the header tank before the engine would start. It could be done by pushing the machine a long way, but the mechanics soon learnt that it was quicker and easier to stand the machine vertically on its back wheel. This became an accepted feature of paddock life.

There were few other changes but on the 7R

the chain oiling was altered so the feed supplied the final drive sprocket as before and both sides of the rollers of the primary chain. This was done with metering jets in the feed pipes with pins in them to limit the flow. The 7R oil tank was also made slimmer.

The production models had some changes and the G45 cylinder head was cast in Y alloy with more substantial rocker posts. The rockers gained an oil hole and a groove to improve the lubrication of the push rod cups, and the valve springs were modified. The exhaust valve heads were made slightly convex instead of flat and the cam follower rollers turned on more, but smaller, diameter needles. The crankshaft became a steel forging which replaced the machined from solid 1953 type but without any significant dimensional change, and the mains were locked to their housings in the crankcase.

Both the 7R and G45 had the primary chainguard altered by the addition of a drain pipe in the base to remove any accumulation of oil, and had ventilation holes drilled in the front part. They both had the gear change linkage modified a little and on the 7R the drive side main bearing was altered to reduce wear.

All the work paid off for Rod Coleman won the Junior TT and was second in Ulster with the twin. It was a swansong for the twin and the triple knocker for early in 1955 AMC announced that they no longer intended to compete with specialised racing machines but would run a works team using standard G45 and 7R models. These would, however, have modifications incorporated in them for trial before they were used in

Metisse with Matchless engine being built by the Rickman brothers to their normal very high standards

the production versions. Thus the Porcupine and the three-valve 7R, in either form, went onto the shelf and the race meeting support was reduced to the TT, Ulster and selected international events.

Sadly Ike Hatch had died in 1954 and in his place Jack Williams was appointed Chief Engineer. Over the years he was to gradually increase the power of the 7R despite a mandate that gave him very limited finances and restricted the areas he could work in.

There were virtually no changes to the production racers for 1955, although the twin oil feed for the primary chain was adopted by both models.

1956 brought the many detail changes resulting from the works' use of the standard models and a change of engine dimensions for the 7R to 75·5 × 78 mm and 349 cc. That engine also had the flywheels reduced in diameter, a piston with just a single Dykes ring, and a scraper and port changes which together added some 3 bhp to the output which rose to 38 bhp at 7200 rpm. Externally, reverse cone megaphones went on both machines along with a new tank shape with knee cut-aways, a narrower oil tank, clip-ons, works-type footrests and foot controls, a positive stop twistgrip to ease the load on the cable nipple, rotating magnet magnetos, magnetic rev-counter, revised rear suspension units and larger brake air scoops. The end covers for the wheel hubs were slotted to draw air through the brakes. The frame was made narrower across the footrest mounting and the gear pedal operated directly.

The great days were over for at the end of the year came an announcement that AMC would no longer enter a works team in racing events. While sad, it did not stop the steady flow of production racers leaving Plumstead, and for the private owner this was the main thing.

The other major improvement for 1957 was the adoption of Girling units at the rear end which saved owners the chore of changing them as soon as they received their new machine. It was also a year when vibration began to become more apparent on the single which was now running at a higher engine speed. Jack Williams wanted to track the cause using borrowed electronic equipment, but he was not allowed to as this meant calling in outside assistance, which ran contrary to company policy.

To solve the problem he had to resort to track tests and in the end these showed that at 7300 rpm the frame resonated in time with the engine. The effects centred on the bridge casting over the gearbox, so this area was modified and the problem cured.

Before this happened the 7R reputation received a boost from an unexpected quarter—

Colin Seeley with a G50 special and the Fath engined four, both in his own frame and cycle parts

'Ah-so, how to make machine handle.' The Bob McIntyre special when ridden by Jack Findlay

the world of moto-cross. Bill Nilsson from Sweden decided to turn one into a scrambler and started from a 1954 model.

The engine was enlarged in both directions to 80 × 96 mm which increased the capacity to 483 cc and a flat top Mahle piston fitted. A TT carburettor was used but of the usual 7R size, and the valves remained standard. This proved to work well and the engine turned out plenty of power low down with just the right characteristics to suit the circuits. The standard cycle parts were used but most were modified a little in one way or another. A BSA gearbox was fitted and adapted to take the Burman clutch, and a small BSA tank was used.

At the start of the season the sceptics said it would not work, by August Nilsson had won the World Moto-Cross Championship.

After 1957 there were no more G45 twins as they failed to keep pace with the developments of the opposition, but 1958 brought a new Matchless contender in the 500 cc class, the G50. This was in essence a bored out 7R and a model that could have been built as far back as 1948, just as prewar there had been 350 and 500 cammy Ajays.

There were a number of changes introduced on the 7R that year and most went onto the G50 as well for the chassis was identical. The most noticeable was the adoption of the racing AMC gearbox which was also fitted to the Manx Norton with slight alteration to the width of the fixing lugs. The box had a shorter mainshaft than the standard unit so the clutch and chain were brought in and the layshaft was shorter thanks to the absence of a kickstarter, and had ball races at each end. A cam lever clutch mechanism was fitted, although hardly everyone's choice, and the outer cover was shaped to accommodate the exhaust pipe and allow it to tuck well in.

The box was supported by a bolt across the frame beneath it and upper plates that bridged the back of the engine to the seat tube. A remote linkage was shown, but a reversed gear pedal used in the end, and the clutch was the three-spring type.

In other areas the rear units had their upper mountings moved back so the units were nearly vertical, the seat and its rear hump were made lower and the front number plate made into a fibreglass moulding which incorporated the mountings for screen and rev-counter. The chain lubrication was amended to feed the final drive by drip, as the old method was not practical with the new gearbox shell.

For the 7R engine there was an increase in downdraught angle to 14·5 degrees, inlet port modifications and an increase in tract length achieved by making the carburettor heat insulating plate into a distance block. The float chamber mounting changed from pillar to rubber diaphragm and internally the exhaust cam lift was increased and made longer, the piston modified

Tom Arter with the Arter-Matchless raced by Peter Williams in 1973 to 2nd place in the Senior TT at an average over 100 mph

to give a squish effect and the ignition backed off a little thanks to the better breathing. The engine breather was altered to a timed outlet still in the drive side mainshaft.

There was just the one G50 in the 1958 TT and it was ridden by Jack Ahearn. It pulled a very high gear and ran easily up to 6800 rpm, where it pushed out 49 bhp on a 10:1 compression ratio. It looked just like a 7R apart from some extra oil pipes which connected the crankcase and cylinder head. These were used in lieu of the usual internal drillways through the cylinder as the larger bore of 90 mm would have run into them.

For 1959 the two singles were built and both had a narrower rear frame with the exhaust pipe tucked in more, modified front forks, a fairing lug on the headstock and a fibreglass seat pan with hump extended back as a tail and mudguard. The 7R had a larger carburettor, new big end cage and raised compression ratio, while the gearbox internals were modified to correct one or two faults that had shown up in use during the previous season.

There was no question of the machines competing at classic level, but they continued to uphold the 7R tradition of giving the private owner a good ride with minimum problems.

1960 brought more changes to both machines. The cornering clearance was increased by a number of measures and thus the frame lower tubes were raised, the footrests narrowed, the rear fork narrowed, and the timing cover and gearbox end cover modified to tuck the exhaust pipe in even more. The oil tank was cutaway around the carburettor to ensure that air could reach it, and the fuel tank lowered an inch, while its knee recesses and the seat hump were taken forward an inch. The twistgrip action was made quicker, the steering damper knob changed to a wing nut, and the rear brake operation altered to a full cable in place of the old type inner wire that acted as a rod.

On the inside went a new inlet cam with more lift, port modifications and a finer vernier for the magneto so the timing could be set more accurately. The clutch centre was altered to take an internal abutment washer, and the holding nut was locked by a washer on a D-shaped extension of the gearbox mainshaft and held onto this by an outer circlip. On the G50 only a larger inlet valve was fitted.

Mike Hailwood rode an odd hybrid at that time with a G50 engine fitted into a featherbed frame with a Harold Daniell five-speed gearbox. An interesting combination, but for the TT he reverted to a 500 Manx although he did use a 7R in the Junior.

At the 1960 Manx GP a special 7R appeared with another variation on the rear engine plates but any testing was minimal as the engine tightened in the first few miles.

About that time some special frames began to be built to take the AMC single as riders sought for an advantage over their rivals. One such machine was for Bob McIntyre with frame tubes that could hardly be shorter for one pair ran from headstock to rear fork pivot, another forward from there at crankshaft level to the third, front downtube, pair. Very compact indeed.

Another, which was built late in 1961, was the work of John Surtees and Ken Sprayson of Reynolds and was much on the lines of the later Rickman Metisse with Norton front fork and Oldani brake. Like the McIntyre machine, it was fitted with a 7R engine.

The 1961 changes were again to details only and mainly affected the cycle parts so were common to both models. The forks were fitted with multirate springs and gaiters, while improved and matched Girlings went on the back end. The front brake had a bigger air scoop and the oil tank a smaller filler cap, while the timing cover was revised some more to allow the exhaust pipe to follow a better curve, which in turn moved the megaphone back a trifle.

For the 7R only the gearbox was made to run slower by increasing the size of the output sprocket and decreasing that of the engine one, in each case by one tooth. Compression ratio went up to 12:1 and tyre sizes were made common with the G50. Power was 41·5 bhp at 7800 rpm and that of the 500 was 51 bhp at 7200 rpm.

That year Jack Williams also designed a new fairing for the two machines which was made and sold by Fi-glass in Kent and suited all the racing singles back to 1954.

1962 saw the AMC racing singles reach their final form. There were a few alterations, some to squeeze the last ounce out of the engine and to this end a shim was added under the barrel to enable the squish clearance to be accurately set. The good breathing allowed the ignition timing to be retarded and engine breathing reverted to a flap valve in the end of the hollow drive shaft. The chain line was pulled in and forged big end cages adopted.

Externally, the gearbox mounting was changed to a pair of all embracing plates on the lines first seen at the 1960 Manx, the gear pedal became light alloy and the tank strap rubber. On the 7R the carburettor was flexibly mounted and both models fitted with the Amal flat matchbox float chamber. The brake linings were changed and lost their traditional diagonal cross saw cuts. In their place went two liners on each shoe with a small gap between them for dust collection.

Far more dramatic was the announcement of the G50CSR model in February. It was proposed to build twenty-five of these for the USA so they could run in the classic 200-mile race at Daytona. To meet the regulations they had to be supplied with lights and generator in road form.

AMC did this by fitting the G50 engine into CSR cycle parts. The engine was supplied with a $1\frac{3}{8}$ in. GP carburettor and a stock AJS silencer but was to be listed with options which included

The Rickman Metisse on show at Earls Court in November 1966

a $1\frac{1}{2}$ in. GP, the normal size fitted to the road racer, and the megaphone.

The cycle parts were the heavyweight duplex frame with Teledraulics at the front and Girlings at the rear. Full width hubs were used and both wheels had 19 in. steel rims. The gearbox was the normal road AMC with kickstarter, and the machine was geared for 110 mph at 7000 rpm. The petrol tank was the small 2 gallon type and the oil tank mounted on the left to leave room for the carburettor. It did not have its usual outer panel and its normal place on the right was taken by a small 6 volt battery.

The electrics were provided by clamping a dynamo to the front of the crankcase and driving it by belt from a pulley mounted on the end of the crankshaft outboard of the sprocket. The belt was enclosed by a sheet steel cover fixed to that which went round the primary chain and kept that out of sight. The dynamo and its regulator were quickly detachable, as were the front and rear lamps.

Finish was in blue for the frame, forks and tanks, while the mudguards were polished and high American bars were fitted. Instruments were a 10,000 rpm rev-counter and 120 mph speedometer carried side by side on the top crown. The forks were gaitered and a dualseat fitted.

And that really brought the story to an end for early in 1963 AMC decided to stop building the camshaft single road racers in view of their financial problems. A few machines did emerge that year but then all was quiet until late 1965 when it was given out that a small batch of G50 engines had been built and ten sent to America.

During the 1960s the lack of new racing singles brought about a number of special frames which

Above **The Seeley Condor road version of the G50, perhaps the ultimate café racer single**

Left **The racing G50 Seeley with spine frame and disc brakes for both wheels**

used the existing engines. In most cases the aim was to reduce weight or improve handling to get the most out of what was available, and these activities were far removed from the titanic battles which took place in the classics during much of this time. Ultimately all these efforts were to be made null and void by the appearance of the TZ Yamaha in its various forms, but the machines received a new lease of life as vintage and classic racing took over around 1980.

It was no new thing to build a special frame for a 7R, for Geoff Monty had done this back in the early 1950s, but while production machines could be had few wished to go to all this trouble. Once the supply dried up the situation changed and early in 1966 the first of the results appeared built by Colin Seeley.

Seeley had raced a G50 propelled, immaculate sidecar outfit very successfully and his first specials had fully duplex frames. The top tubes ran to a point just above the rear fork pivot in a straight line once they had splayed out from the headstock and joined the down tubes, once these had run under the engine and gearbox. A subframe gave support to the seat and the rear units and special plates carried the power unit and transmission. Front and rear forks were Manx Norton and the front brake a double two leading shoe Eddie Robinson device of 8 in. diameter with floating cams. The exhaust system was carried at high level on the left at first, but this was later dropped.

A month later the Rickman brothers produced their road racing Metisse with a nickel plated frame of duplex form carrying a G50 engine and AMC gearbox but with Rickman forks and a disc front brake.

Late in 1966 the future of the racing spares became assured, despite the failure of AMC, when Seeley bought all the existing spares plus drawings, jigs, castings and the manufacturing rights. His purchase covered the AMC and Norton racing machines, but he in turn sold the Norton side to John Tickle to leave himself free to concentrate on the AMC models he was more associated with.

Early in 1967 another special frame appeared built for Tom Arter by Ken Sprayson, for Peter Williams to ride. In time this developed into the Arter-Matchless which pioneered cast alloy wheels and on which Peter went so very quickly at the TT.

The Seeley ran on with different versions of the frame, and the most interesting was the Mark 4 built from 1969. This had tubes running from the base of the headstock to the fork pivot and others from the top to the rear units. A pair of short tubes went from units to pivot and there were cross braces. The engine and gearbox were built into a unit and the whole assembly suspended in the frame. A long rangey exhaust system was fitted, finished in matt black, with tight fitting pipe and slow taper megaphone. A single disc went at the front.

It was light, it handled, and brought out the best in the AMC camshaft engines but by 1972 it had become obsolete for road racing, and expensive to boot.

As an aside, around 1970 Seeley built a roadgoing version called the 'Condor'. This followed the ideas of the G50CSR but used the Mark 4 frame with nickel plated finish, slimline forks and semi-open Girlings at the rear. The front brake was a massive duplex drum, while at the rear went a conical hub adapted to drive a speedometer. This instrument was mounted in a plate held by the left top fork nut and matched on the right by a rev-counter. Unlike the racers, this was driven from the right end of the camshaft.

A Concentric carburettor with massive bellmouth was fitted and the chrome plated exhaust pipe terminated in a slow taper silencer with reverse cone end. A dynamo was clamped to the front of the engine and a chaincase modified to suit the AMC gearbox and dynamo drive from the crankshaft end.

A stylish tank, a dualseat with tail-cum-mudguard and plenty of chrome made for an elegant machine but not one to many peoples taste. A very high performance single with racing cams muffed by a silencer can go well but the hazards of kick-starting a high compression single and the problems of keeping that engine up to the mark were such as to put off all but a handful of people.

It was a nice try, but few were built and with them the camshaft single came to its end.

6 Two-stroke finalé

The traditional AJS models vanished along with AMC in 1966 to leave their Matchless counterparts to stagger on for a short while before they too were terminated. The late 1960s were a period of change for the group, which became Norton Villiers and later NVT, but in 1967 the old AJS name was revived for a road racer far removed from the traditional Plumstead machine.

Among the staff of Villiers was Peter Inchley who had experience in depth of developing and racing two strokes. In 1966 he rode a special powered by a Villiers engine to a fine third place in the 250 cc TT, and the outcome was a new frame, the same engine and AJS on the tank for 1967. Unfortunately he retired that year through no fault of his own but from that work came two new AJS models late in 1967.

The first of these was the Double T Racer and was based closely on Inchley's 1967 machine. The frame of that model had been built by Ken Sprayson and had a 2·25 in. diameter tube backbone running from headstock to fork pivot. Twin loops ran under the engine, which was the 247 cc Villiers Starmaker with six-speed gearbox, and the complete production model took this name soon after its first appearance. The details followed racing convention of the time except that the 2·75 gallon petrol tank was supplemented by another of 1·25 gallon capacity located beneath the seat.

The second model was the Alamos scrambler, which again used the Starmaker engine but

Peter Inchley on the Starmaker powered Villiers Special

tuned to a lower level. A duplex frame fitted with telescopic front forks was used and the rear chain was adjusted by eccentrics at the fork pivot, unlike the racer which used snail cams at the wheel spindle. Only a four-speed gearbox was fitted and equipment was typical for the sport with a high level exhaust and high tensile wheel rims.

Just how well this machine could go was demonstrated by Malcolm Davis who won the British 250 cc title on it in 1968 with some good placings in world events also. He was less successful in the following year due to minor problems, but there was no doubt that the AJS was competitive.

1969 saw the launch of the Y4 scrambler and 37A-T trials models, the two earlier machines not really having got off the ground thanks to the general group troubles. The two new ones shared a similar frame although the wheelbase of the trials one was 4 in. shorter than the scrambler. Both were based on a massive tapered top tube and light duplex subframe and brace but, while the scrambler had twin down tubes, the trials model managed with one.

There were also differences in the make of front forks as the scrambler had AJS and the trials Metal Profiles, but both used Girlings at the rear. Brakes were respectively 5 in. and 6 in. diameter, the first in very light AJS hubs and the second in British Hub centres. Production had by this time moved to a new plant near Andover where the parts were assembled.

Early in 1970 came the Mark 2 model Y4 and an enlarged version, the Y5, of 368 cc. These were given the model name of Stormer and joined by similar machines typed Y40 and Y50 designed for and sold in the USA. All used a very similar two stroke engine with well ribbed crankcase, heavily finned alloy barrel, cast iron liner, and separate four-speed gearbox bolted to the rear of the crankcase. The clutch was clamped by a diaphragm spring and needle races used extensively in the transmission.

All four models followed the lines of the first Y4 and continued to use the eccentric rear fork pivot to adjust the rear chain. The models for the USA were fitted with a different air cleaner and the UK variant of the 250 had a close ratio gearbox, while the others used the alternative wide one. In fact this only affected the two lower

Dan Shorey inspects the two stroke AJS with its twin petrol tanks, one under the seat

gears but, in addition, the overall gearing varied on all four machines. Tyres, brakes and suspension were the same aside from heavier rate rear springs fitted to the 370 model, which was distinguished by a yellow tank, the 250s having red ones. All models had alloy mudguards as had been the norm from the start.

1971 brought a change in model numbers to Y41 and Y51 for the 247 cc and 368 cc machines. In addition they adopted common rear springs, altered gearing, and the option of wide or close ratio gearboxes. The compression ratio of the larger machine was reduced a little.

Late in the year the 370 was replaced by a larger version, the Stormer 410, which had a longer 74 mm stroke and 400 cc capacity but was otherwise the same machine down to the yellow tank. Various options were available including gearbox ratios together with rear springs, wide or narrow cylinder fin spacing, a silencer for the 410, heavier front fork springs, handlebar width and wheel rims in steel or high tensile aluminium.

The machine had been offered in kit form since 1969 but this method of avoiding purchase tax went with the introduction of VAT and this was one more nail in the AJS coffin. They continued on into 1973 but the trials and tribulations of what was left of the industry, the Meriden sit-in, the creation of NVT, the closure of BSA, and the considerable Government involvement were all matters taking place in realms far removed from the small AJS set-up. So development stopped and it seemed that the marque was doomed.

Then in stepped 'Fluff' Brown who bought all the two stroke spares and everything the compe-

Above **The FB-AJS Enduro model with lights and Villiers derived engine**
Top left **AJS model 37A-T of 1969 fitted with Villiers 37A engine**
Left **The 1970 250 cc Y4 moto-cross AJS**

tition shop had. He began to trade from small premises near Andover and before long found he was building complete machines which were sold under the FB-AJS label.

His range was created slowly and relied heavily on the inherited engine units, but in time he had 250 and 370 motors in various states of tune. These went to propel trail, enduro and moto-cross models all using similar cycle parts, well made and with quality components.

It was a successful formula for the engines pulled well so only needed the four gears and were easy to ride. Thanks to this they were very suitable for the average clubman and in many cases gave him a better day's sport than the Japanese models with their peaky power output and six-speed gearboxes that needed constant changing.

The front forks used on the moto-cross models gave a massive 12 in. of wheel movement and even the trail bike had 9 in. so the AJS was to the fore of suspension development from the start. In 1982 they went to mono-shock control for the rear, which gave 12·5 in. of movement with a remote reservoir for the unit which was linked to the fork by levers.

Alternative engines in 1982 were the 250 and 410 cc Rotax Bombardier units which meant swapping gear lever and rear brake over. This was, however, no new exercise for such an arrangement had been built by AJS before.

And so the AJS name continues, albeit on a machine far removed from that first built by the Stevens brothers, but with the same intent—to build quality.

7 Competition

The competition activities of the AMC group in postwar years might be considered to be at their height in the late 1940s when they were successful in both road racing and trials. In the 1950s the racing activities were soon tapered off, but in both trials and scrambles they continued to be successful with an emphasis on the great Scottish 6 Days events. They also played their part in the field of record-breaking using the racing models and in their last days were successful in the field of moto-cross with their two stroke powered models.

Curiously, nearly all this action took place with the AJS name on the tank, although the identical Matchless did come out on top on occasion. This facet dated from prewar days when the blown four was raced by Walter Rusk and Bob Foster, and earlier in unblown form by Harold Daniel and George Rowley but always as an AJS.

This was quite in order for Rowley for he was an AJS man from 1925 onwards and a remarkable all-rounder who was second in the 1928 Senior TT and rode for his country in the ISDT and for his firm in many a one-day trial. Postwar he looked after the AMC competition activities for a year or two until they were firmly established.

Because the various branches of the sport became more diversified postwar they are treated separately and only a brief outline of the high-lights among the many AMC successes noted. Alongside these performances by the fac-

Left **An AJS model 20 running in the MCC speed trials at Silverstone in 1952, the rider is J. R. Ballard**

Below **Paddy Driver on the G12CSR which led much of the 1964 Thruxton 500 until a rod went**

tory men the standard models were to be seen competing year round ridden by clubmen in local events, plonking up trials hills, flying off hill crests in scrambles, sliding round grass tracks and making up much of the 350 cc field at road races. They were also sprinted, hill-climbed and, one year, the Motorcyclist of the Year competition went to an AJS rider whose trials model made the obstacle course a little easier to cope with.

Road Racing

The highlights of the AJS racing efforts were the championships won by Les Graham and the factory in 1949, the year they were inaugurated, and Rod Coleman's Junior TT win in 1954.

By 1949 the Porcupine was well sorted out and really dominated the six classic 500 cc races. It won three of them, should have won the TT, was a close second in Holland and third at Monza. Any idea of an easy victory was scotched by the Gilera team which kept the pressure up throughout the season except at the TT, won by a Norton. In Europe Pagani won in Holland and Italy and only one point separated the two makes at the year's end.

For the riders title the fight was just as close with the first clash in Switzerland where Graham led Artesiani on a Gilera over the line followed by Daniel on his Norton and Pagani. In Holland Pagani won, but in Belgium it was Doran on the second AJS who led the field home with Pagani fifth and Graham not scoring, so down to third place in the points league behind the two Gilera men. In Ulster he put this right with Doran third and Pagani fourth, benefitting from his hard riding on the Clady circuit and the habitual Gilera dislike for it. This win effectively gave Graham the title for, regardless of the Monza result, noone could better his record, but Pagani tried hard and his Monza win brought him within one point of the AJS man who came off when fighting for the lead. Pagani had some consolation in his fine second place and the 125 cc championship he took that year.

AJS were less successful in the 350 cc class

Peter Williams en route to a class win at the 1964 Thruxton 500 on the 14CSR AJS

that year but Armstrong was second, although well behind the formidable Freddie Frith who won all five classics.

The Porcupine did not seem to adapt to the better fuel that became available in 1950 as well as the competition and they had limited success as the battle raged between Duke and Masetti on single and four; except at the Swiss held on the Geneva circuit where Graham had a field day and won both 350 and 500 cc events.

At the end of the year Graham went to MV and this left Doran and Armstrong to uphold the AJS flag. Doran won the 350 class in Holland and was second in the Senior TT, but the machines were slipping from their competitive position. 1952 brought a 500 cc win at Berne for Jack Brett but otherwise only leader board placings, while 1953 saw few of these.

1954 was better for it was the year AJS finished first and second in the Junior TT, while Pierre Monneret won the 350 cc class in the French. Elsewhere the Italian machines ruled the roost with only Norton making an occasional impression, and so it was to remain to the end of the decade and well beyond.

It was the 7R that provided the two pieces of classic news in the 1960s. In Ulster in 1960 Alan Shepherd hung onto the MV ridden by John Surtees for lap after lap but the cam chain let go and the world champion felt free to breathe again, while in 1961 the great Mike Hailwood had the gudgeon pin fail when leading the Junior TT with half a lap to go. That was the week he won three races.

In the Manx GP the 7R had a good run of success with Phil Heath finishing second in 1948, the model's first year. It won in 1950 and in 1951 and again in 1952 when Bob McIntyre was the victor and went on to finish second in the senior, riding the same 7R. And so over the years the 7R and later the G50 helped to keep racing alive by providing the private owner with his mount.

Records

The AJS involvement in records went back to 1929 when they made an abortive attempt on the world maximum but did take over a hundred others with Bert Denly doing the riding of machines prepared by Nigel Spring. After the war their first attack on records took place late in 1948 using a Porcupine ridden by Jock West, Georges Monneret and Les Graham at Montlhèry.

The machine was prepared with track handlebars and a slight rise in compression ratio to suit the petrol benzole it ran on, but was otherwise as raced without any streamlining. It circulated like clockwork and only the bumps and extreme cold bothered the riders, who were forced to call it a day after five hours due to fading light. In the bag were new records for 2, 3, 4 and 5 hours, 500 km and 500 miles in the 500, 750, and 1000 cc classes, a grand total of 18 figures all taken at speeds between 107 and 110 mph. The last lap by Les Graham was the fastest at 116·32 mph.

In 1950 they were back at Montlhèry with the Porcupine and moved the 2-hour and 500 km figures on some more to just over 115 mph. Encouraged they returned in 1951 with a 7R coupled to a Blacknell side car and captured 16 records in the 350 cc sidecar class plus the 2-hour solo record at over 109 mph. Many of the chair figures improved on those for larger machines so a further 20 records were taken, making 37 for that trip ranging up to 7 hours and 1000 km.

They made their last visit in 1952 when they brought a triple knocker 7R which was run without a front mudguard and with a small cowling to fair the tops of the fork legs into a small screen. Once again they were successful and 13 more records were taken including the prestigious one-hour at 115.66 mph. Apart from the 7-hours, all the records were taken at over 100 mph.

The 1951 record attempt at Montlhèry with either Doran or Monneret on the 350 sidecar

Trials

Many people rode AMC machines in trials but for the factory postwar two names stood out, those of Hugh Viney and Gordon Jackson. Both rode as AJS men along with Bob Manns, and on the Matchless side there was Artie Ratcliffe and Ted Usher.

Viney had ridden before the war and, like George Rowley, developed a technique of trickling through the sections and up hills aided by very low compression ratios, heavier than usual

The great Hugh Viney in typical style on his AJS

flywheels, perfect carburation and his own great riding skills. He joined AMC in 1947 and a few weeks later won the Scottish 6 Days at his first attempt, a feat then and since unheard of. He lost 6 marks on the Tuesday of that week and for the other five days the AJS plodded up hill after hill on its set and unvarying throttle opening. Artie Ratcliffe was second on his Matchless with the loss of 25 marks.

The next year was just the same and, although Hugh did drop 27 marks, his nearest competitor shed 39. He also rode in the ISDT and was a member of the British team that won the Trophy as well as winning a steady round of one-day national events.

No-one had won two Scottish events in succession before, although two riders had won twice pre-war, but in 1949 Viney went one better and made it three in a row, a feat that was not to be repeated until the 1970s. He also continued as a successful team member in the ISDT and went on to become team captain in 1953.

Viney was second in the Scottish in 1950 but even this gave AJS good publicity and, as Artie Ratcliffe won the event on a Matchless, AMC went home well pleased. They missed out for the next two years but Viney won for the fourth time in 1953 and Ratcliffe again in 1954.

The AJS team had a new member in 1952, Gordon Jackson, who helped them to many an award. In 1956 he won his first Scottish and, like Viney, went on to take three more in 1958, 1960 and 1961. His last victory was possibly the most famous for in the whole week he lost just one mark for a dab on Grey Mare's Ridge, and Peter Howdle was there to take the one picture that recorded it for MCN.

After that AMC began to fade in the highlands although they were second for three years, but their postwar record was truly outstanding with 10 victories in 15 years.

In national and trade events they had a good share of the honours over the same period although towards the end they, and everyone

Above **The famous Peter Howdle picture of Gordon Jackson losing his one mark on Grey Mare's Ridge in the 1961 Scottish**

Left **Artie Ratcliffe and his 350 cc Matchless late in 1947**

else, was having to give best to Sammy Miller and his Ariel.

The machines gradually evolved and always the works ones were a year or two ahead of production and further worked on to reduce weight and tuck in protruding parts. Jackson's machine was tried more than once with an engine speed magneto but this was never totally successful as it objected to the 8000 rpm it was sometimes called on to run at.

Scrambles

In the early 1950s AMC was represented by Geoff Ward on an AJS and Brian Stonebridge on a Matchless in most of the important scrambles. The machines they used were based on the production models but with internal factory modifications and future development. The cross they bore was the company policy that dictated the use of AMC rear units when everyone else fitted proprietary ones.

Despite this they were both very much front runners with Ward taking the ACU Star in 1951 and 1953, while in the European championship Auguste Mingels used a Matchless for most of 1953 when he took the title. Later, in 1956, Dave Curtis took a Matchless to second in the Star table in the face of very heavy BSA opposition, and in 1957 Nilsson won the world title using his special based on the 7R.

As the company fell on hard times so the competition activity shrunk, but this had no immediate effect on all the private owners who continued with the four strokes until gradually the lighter two stroke took over.

For AMC there was a brief revival when the

Bill Nilsson on his 7R engined moto-cross special which won the world title in 1957

Above **Auguste Mingels on his Matchless in the 1952 Moto-cross des Nations**

Left **Chris Horsfield sliding his Matchless with front wheel just clear of the ground**

Matchless engine was used by the Rickman brothers to power their Metisse scrambler. The very light, very strong duplex cradle frame gave the engine a new lease of life especially when opened up to 600 cc. The snag was that it was still a big machine for scrambling and not every one at club level had the Rickmans' ability, which was at world class. For most a Greeves was so much easier to pick up, and anyway production had to stop when the engine supply dried up.

While it was on offer, the Matchless Metisse gave precise steering, an engine with real punch from its first turn, and a proven gearbox. With the superb Rickman detailing and finish it made a handsome ending to a long line of competition singles.

Appendix

Specifications

Model	16M/G3L	16MS/G3LS **1**	18/G80	18S/G80S **2**
Year from	**1945**	**1949**	**1945**	**1949**
Year to	**1955**	**1963**	**1955**	**1963**
Bore (mm)	69	69 **3**	82·5	82·5
Stroke (mm)	93	93 **3**	93	93
Capacity (cc)	348	348	497	497
Compression ratio (to 1)	6·3 **4**	6·3 **4,5**	5·9 **6**	5·9 **6,7**
Valve position	ohv	ohv	ohv	ohv
inlet opens BTDC	32 **8**	32 **8**	32 **8**	32 **8,9**
inlet closes ABDC	63	63	63	63
exhaust opens BBDC	65	65	65	65
exhaust closes ATDC	30	30	30	30
Valve clear. (cold) in. (in)	nil	nil	nil	nil
Valve clear. (cold) ex. (in.)	nil	nil	nil	nil
Ignition timing (in.)	0·437 **10**	0·500	0·437 **10**	0·500
Points gap (in.)	0·012	0·012	0·012	0·012
Front tyre (in.)	3·25 × 19	3·25 × 19 **11**	3·25 × 19	3·25 × 19 **11**
Rear tyre (in.)	3.·25 × 19	3·25 × 19 **11**	3·25 × 19 **12**	3.50 × 19 **11**
Rim front	WM2	WM2	WM2	WM2
Rim rear	WM2	WM2	WM2	WM2
Brake front dia. (in.)	5·5 **13**	7	5·5 **13**	7
Brake front width (in.)	0·87 **14**	0·87 **15**	0·87 **14**	0·87 **15**
Brake rear dia. (in.)	5·5 **13**	7	5·5 **13**	7
Brake rear width (in.)	0·87 **14**	0·87	0·87 **14**	0·87
Front suspension	teles	teles	teles	teles
Rear type	rigid	s/a	rigid	s/a
Petrol tank (Imp. gal)	3·0 **16**	3·0 **16,17**	3·0 **18**	3·0 **18**
Oil tank (Imp. pint)	4·0	4·0 **19**	4·0	4·0 **19**
Box capacity (Imp. pint)	1·0	1·0	1·0	1·0
Ignition system	magneto	magneto **20**	magneto	magneto **20**
Generator type	dynamo	dynamo **21**	dynamo	dynamo **21**
Battery (Volt)	6	6	6	6
Wheelbase (in.)	54	55·2	54	55·2
Ground clear. (in.)	5·5	5·5	5·5	5·5

Model	16M/G3L	16MS/G3LS **1**	18/G80	18S/G80S **2**
Year from	**1945**	**1949**	**1945**	**1949**
Year to	**1955**	**1963**	**1955**	**1963**
Seat height (in.)	30	31	30	31
Width (in.)		28		28
Length (in.)	85	86·2	85	86·2
Dry weight (lb)	344	380	353	390
Power: bhp	16	16 **22**	23	23 **23**
@ rpm	5600	5600 **22**	5400	5400 **23**

1 1959—16/G3, 1962—also 16S/G3S. **2** 1959—18/G80. **3** 1962—74 × 81. **4** 1952—6·53.
5 1956—7·5, 1962—8·5. **6** 1952—6·26. **7** 1956—7·3. **8** 1954—36, 51, 50, 30. **9** 1956—18, 69, 50, 30.
10 1952—·500. **11** 1963—18 in. rims. **12** 1948—3·50 × 19. **13** 1948—7. **14** from 1948.
15 1963—1·12. **16** 1955—3·75. **17** 1962—4·2. **18** 1954—3·75. **19** 1956—5. **20** 1958—coil.
21 1958—alternator. **22** 1956—19/5750, 1962—23/6200. **23** 1956—26/5500.

Model	16MC/G3LC	16MCS/G3LCS	18C/G80C	18CS/G80CS
Year from	**1946**	**1951**	**1946**	**1951**
Year to	**1955**	**1955**	**1955**	**1955**
Bore (mm)	69	69	82·5	82·5
Stroke (mm)	93	93	93	93
Capacity (cc)	348	348	497	497
Compression ratio (to 1)	6·3	6·3 **1**	5·9	5·9 **2**
Valve position	ohv	ohv	ohv	ohv
inlet opens BTDC	32 **3**	32 **4**	32 **3**	32 **4**
inlet closes ABDC	63	63	63	63
exhaust opens BBDC	65	65	65	65
exhaust closes ATDC	30	30	30	30
Valve clear. (cold) in. (in.)	nil	nil	nil	nil
Valve clear. (cold) ex. (in.)	nil	nil	nil	nil
Ignition timing (in.)	0·437 **5**	0·500	0·437 **5**	0·500
Points gap (in.)	0·012	0·012	0·012	0·012
Front tyre (in.)	2·75 × 21 **6**	3·00 × 21	2·75 × 21 **6**	3·00 × 21
Rear tyre (in.)	4·00 × 19	4·00 × 19	4·00 × 19	4·00 × 19
Rim front	WM1	WM1	WM1	WM1
Rim rear	WM3	WM3	WM3	WM3
Brake front dia. (in.)	5·5 **7**	7	5·5 **7**	7
Brake front width (in.)	0.87 **8**	0·87	0·87 **8**	0·87
Brake rear dia. (in.)	5·5 **7**	7	5·5 **7**	7
Brake rear width (in.)	0·87 **8**	0·87	0·87 **8**	0·87
Front suspension	teles	teles	teles	teles
Rear type	rigid	s/a	rigid	s/a
Petrol tank (Imp. gal)	3·0 **9**	2·25	3·0 **9**	2·25
Oil tank (Imp. pint)	4·0	4·0	4·0	4·0
Box capacity (Imp. pint)	1·0	1·0	1·0	1·0
Ignition system	magneto	magneto	magneto	magneto
Wheelbase (in.)	53	55·2	53	55·2
Ground clear. (in.)	6·5	6·5	6·5	6·5
Seat height (in.)	32·5	32·5	32·5	32·5

Model	16MC/G3LC	16MCS/G3LCS	18C/G80C	18CS/G80CS
Year from	**1946**	**1951**	**1946**	**1951**
Year to	**1955**	**1955**	**1955**	**1955**
Length (in.)	82	85·2	82	85·2
Dry weight (lb)	300 **10**	320	307 **11**	323
Power: bhp	16	16 **12**	23	23 **13**
@ rpm	5600	5600 **12**	5400	5400 **13**

1 1954—9·4. **2** 1954—8·5. **3** 1954—36, 51, 50, 30. **4** 1954—59, 68, 74, 48. **5** 1952—0·500.
6 1949 to 54—3·00 × 21. **7** 1948—7. **8** from 1948. **9** 1950—2·25. **10** 1954—296.
11 1954—299. **12** 1954—26/6000. **13** 1954—32/5400.

Model	16MC/G3LC **1**	16MCS/G3LCS	18CS/G80CS	8/G5
Year from	**1956**	**1956**	**1956**	**1960**
Year to	**1963**	**1959**	**1965**	**1962**
Bore (mm)	69	72	86	72
Stroke (mm)	93	85·5	85·5	85·5
Capacity (cc)	348	348	497	348
Compression ratio (to 1)	6·5	9·9	8·7	7·5
Valve position	ohv	ohv	ohv	ohv
inlet opens BTDC	26	59	59	40
inlet closes ABDC	53	69	69	75
exhaust opens BBDC	64	74	74	70
exhaust closes ATDC	25	48	48	40
Valve clear. (cold) in. (in.)	nil	nil	nil	nil
Valve clear. (cold) ex. (in.)	nil	nil	nil	nil
Ignition timing degree	39	41	39	33
Points gap (in.)	0·012	0·012	0·012	0·015
Front tyre (in.)	2·75 × 21	3·00 × 21 **2**	3·00 × 21 **2**	3·25 × 18
Rear tyre (in.)	4·00 × 19	4·00 × 19	4·00 × 19	3·25 × 18
Rim front	WM1	WM1	WM1	WM2
Rim rear	WM3	WM3	WM3	WM2
Brake front dia. (in.)	7 **3**	7	7	6
Brake front width (in.)	0.87	0·87	0·87	1
Brake rear dia. (in.)	7 **3**	7	7	6
Brake rear width (in.)	0·87	0·87	0·87	1
Front suspension	teles	teles	teles	teles
Rear type	s/a	s/a	s/a	s/a
Petrol tank (Imp. gal)	2·0	2·0	2·0	3·25
Oil tank (Imp. pint)	4·0 **4**	4·0	4·0	2·5
Box capacity (Imp. pint)	1	1	1	3·0
Ignition system	magneto	magneto	magneto	coil
Generator type				alternator
Output (Watts)				54
Battery (Volt)				6
Wheelbase (in.)	54 **5**	55·2	55·2	54
Ground clear. (in.)	6·5 **6**	6·5	6·5	6
Seat height (in.)	32·5	32·5	32·5	29·5 **7**
Width (in.)	28	28	28	

Model	16MC/G3LC 1	16MCS/G3LCS	18CS/G80CS	8/G5
Year from	**1956**	**1956**	**1956**	**1960**
Year to	**1963**	**1959**	**1965**	**1962**
Length (in.)	83	85·2	85·2	
Dry weight (lb)	319	321	324	340
Power: bhp	18	27	33	
@ rpm	5750	6300	6200	

1 1959—16C/G3C. **2** 1958 option—3·50 × 19. **3** 1959—5·5. **4** 1959—2·75.
5 1959—52·2. **6** 1957—10. **7** 1962—30·5.

Model	16/G3	16C/G3C	18/G80	G85CS
Year from	**1963**	**1963**	**1963**	**1965**
Year to	**1966**	**1964**	**1966**	**1969**
Bore (mm)	72	72	86	86
Stroke (mm)	85·5	85·5	85·5	85·5
Capacity (cc)	348	348	497	497
Compression ratio (to 1)	9·0	7·0	7·3	12
Valve position	ohv	ohv	ohv	ohv
inlet opens BTDC	36	26	18	67
inlet closes ABDC	51	53	69	81
exhaust opens BBDC	50	64	50	69
exhaust closes ATDC	30	25	30	48
Valve clear. (cold) in. (in.)	nil	nil	nil	nil
Valve clear. (cold) ex. (in.)	nil	nil	nil	nil
Ignition timing degree	34	34	38	33
Points gap (in.)	0·015	0·012	0·015	0·012
Front tyre (in.)	3·25 × 18	2·75 × 21	3·25 × 18	3·00 × 21
Rear tyre (in.)	3·25 × 18	4·00 × 19	3·50 × 18	4·00 × 18
Rim front	WM2	WM1	WM2	WM1
Rim rear	WM2	WM3	WM2	WM3
Brake front dia. (in.)	8	5·5	8	7
Brake front width (in.)	1·25		1·25	1·12
Brake rear dia. (in.)	7	5·5	7	8·25
Brake rear width (in.)	1·25		1·25	1·25
Front suspension	teles	teles	teles	teles
Rear type	s/a	s/a	s/a	s/a
Petrol tank (Imp. gal)	4·0	2·0	4·0	2·0
Oil tank (Imp. pint)	4·0	2·75	4·0	5·0
Ignition system	coil	magneto	coil	magneto
Generator type	alternator		alternator	
Battery (Volt)	6		6	
Wheelbase (in.)	55	54	55	56·9
Ground clear. (in.)				8·5
Seat height (in.)				33
Dry weight (lb)	382	306	394	291
Power: bhp				41
@ rpm				6500

Model	14/G2	14CS/G2CS	14S/G2S	14CSR/G2CSR
Year from	**1958**	**1959**	**1961**	**1962**
Year to	**1963**	**1962**	**1962**	**1966**
Bore (mm)	69·85	69·85	69·85	69·85
Stroke (mm)	64·85	64·85	64·85	64·85
Capacity (cc)	248·5	248·5	248·5	248·5
Compression ratio (to 1)	7·8	10·0	7·8	8·0 **1**
Valve position	ohv	ohv	ohv	ohv
inlet opens BTDC	35·5 **2**	35	35	35
inlet closes ABDC	68·5	77	77	77
exhaust opens BBDC	65·5	77	77	77
exhaust closes ATDC	38·5	38	38	38
Valve clear. (cold) in. (in.)	nil	nil	nil	nil
Valve clear. (cold) ex. (in.)	nil	nil	nil	nil
Ignition timing degree	36	36	36	36
Points gap (in.)	0·015	0·012	0·015	0·015
Front tyre (in.)	3·25 × 17	3·00 × 19	3·25 × 17	3·25 × 17
Rear tyre (in.)	3·25 × 17	3·50 × 19	3·25 × 17	3·25 × 17
Rim front	WM2	WM1	WM2	
Rim rear	WM2	WM2	WM2	
Brake front dia. (in.)	6	7	6	6
Brake front width (in.)	1	0·87	1	1·375
Brake rear dia. (in.)	6	5·5	6	6
Brake rear width (in.)	1	0·75	1	1
Front suspension	teles	teles	teles	teles
Rear type	s/a	s/a	s/a	s/a
Petrol tank (Imp. gal)	2·75 **3**	2·75	3·25	3·25
Oil tank (Imp. pint)	2·5	2·5	2·5	2·5
Box capacity (Imp. pint)	3·0	3·0	3·0	3·0
Ignition system	coil	energy transfer **4**	coil	coil
Generator type	alternator	alternator	alternator	alternator
Output (Watts)	54			54
Battery (Volt)	6	6 **5**	6	6
Wheelbase (in.)	53	54	54	53
Ground clear. (in.)	5·5	7·2	5·5	6·5
Seat height (in.)	30 **6**	32	29	30
Width (in.)	28	28		
Length (in.)	82	81·5		
Dry weight (lb)	325	321	322	328
Power: bhp	18		19·5	
@ rpm			7400	

1 1965—9·5. **2** 1959—35, 77, 77, 38. **3** 1960—3·25. **4** 1961—coil. **5** from 1961. **6** 1961—30·5.

Model	20/G9	20CS/G9CS	20CSR/G9CSR
Year from	**1949**	**1958**	**1958**
Year to	**1961**	**1959**	**1959**
Bore (mm)	66	66	66
Stroke (mm)	72·8	72·8	72·8

Model	20/G9	20CS/G9CS	20CSR/G9CSR
Year from	**1949**	**1958**	**1958**
Year to	**1961**	**1959**	**1959**
Capacity (cc)	498	498	498
Compression ratio (to 1)	7·0 **1**	8·5	8·5
Valve position	ohv	ohv	ohv
inlet opens BTDC	35 **2**	37	37
inlet closes ABDC	65	77	77
exhaust opens BBDC	65	73	73
exhaust closes ATDC	35	43	43
Valve clear. (cold) in. (in.)	0·006	0·006	0·006
Valve clear. (cold) ex. (in.)	0·006	0·006	0·006
Ignition timing degree	39	39	39
Points gap (in.)	0·012	0·012	0·012
Front tyre (in.)	3·25 × 19	3·00 × 21	3·25 × 19
Rear tyre (in.)	3·50 × 19	4·00 × 19	3·50 × 19
Rim front	WM2	WM1	WM2
Rim rear	WM2	WM3	WM2
Brake front dia. (in.)	7	7	7
Brake front width (in.)	0·87	0·87	0·87
Brake rear dia. (in.)	7	7	7
Brake rear width (in.)	0·87	0·87	0·87
Front suspension	teles	teles	teles
Rear type	s/a	s/a	s/a
Petrol tank (Imp. gal)	4·0/3·0 **3**	2·0	4·25
Oil tank (Imp. pint)	4·0 **4**	5·0	5·0
Box capacity (Imp. pint)	1·0	1·0	1·0
Ignition system	magneto **5**	magneto	magneto
Generator type	dynamo **6**	dynamo	dynamo
Battery (Volt)	6	6	6
Wheelbase (in.)	55·2	55·2	55·2
Ground clear. (in.)	5·5		5·5
Seat height (in.)	30/31.5	31	31·5
Width (in.)	28		
Length (in.)	86·2		
Dry weight (lb)	394/400	377	379
Power: bhp	29 **7**		
@ rpm	6800		

1 1956—7·8, 1959—8·0. **2** 1957—24, 65, 63, 25; 1959—37, 77, 73, 43. **3** 1954—3·75, 1959—4·25. **4** 1956—5. **5** 1959, std model—coil, 1960—coil. **6** 1959, std model—alternator, 1960—alternator. **7** 1956—30·5.

Model	30/G11	30CS/G11CS	30CSR/G11CSR
Year from	**1956**	**1957**	**1958**
Year to	**1958**	**1958**	**1958**
Bore (mm)	72	72	72
Stroke (mm)	72·8	72·8	72·8
Capacity (cc)	593	593	593

Model	**30/G11**	**30CS/G11CS**	**30CSR/G11CSR**
Year from	**1956**	**1957**	**1958**
Year to	**1958**	**1958**	**1958**
Compression ratio (to 1)	7·5	8·5	8·5
Valve position	ohv	ohv	ohv
inlet opens BTDC	24	24	24
inlet closes ABDC	65	65	65
exhaust opens BBDC	63	63	63
exhaust closes ATDC	25	25	25
Valve clear. (cold) in. (in.)	0·006	0·006	0·006
Valve clear. (cold) ex. (in.)	0·006	0·006	0·006
Ignition timing degree	39		
Points gap (in.)	0·012	0·012	0·012
Front tyre (in.)	3·25 × 19	3·50 × 19	3·25 × 19
Rear tyre (in.)	3·50 × 19	4·00 × 19	3·50 × 19
Rim front	WM2	WM1	WM2
Rim rear	WM2	WM3	WM2
Brake front dia. (in.)	7	7	7
Brake front width (in.)	0·87	0·87	0·87
Brake rear dia. (in.)	7	7	7
Brake rear width (in.)	0·87	0·87	0·87
Front suspension	teles	teles	teles
Rear type	s/a	s/a	s/a
Petrol tank (Imp. gal)	3·75	2·0	3·75
Oil tank (Imp. pint)	5·0	5·0	5·0
Box capacity (Imp. pint)	1·0	1·0	1·0
Ignition system	magneto	magneto	magneto
Generator type	dynamo	dynamo	dynamo
Battery (Volt)	6	6	6
Wheelbase (in.)	55·2	55·2	55·2
Ground clear. (in.)	5·5	6·0	5·5
Seat height (in.)	31·5	31	31·5
Dry weight (lb)	394	386	
Power: bhp	33		
@rpm	6800		

Model	**31/G12**	**31CS/G12CS**	**31CSR/G12CSR**
Year from	**1958**	**1958**	**1958**
Year to	**1966**	**1960**	**1966**
Bore (mm)	72	72	72
Stroke (mm)	79·3	79·3	79·3
Capacity (cc)	646	646	646
Compression ratio (to 1)	7·5	8·5	8·5
Valve position	ohv	ohv	ohv
inlet opens BTDC	24 **1**	24 **1**	24 **1**
inlet closes ABDC	65	65	65
exhaust opens BBDC	63	63	63
exhaust closes ATDC	25	25	25

Model	31/G12	31CS/G12CS	31CSR/G12CSR
Year from	**1958**	**1958**	**1958**
Year to	**1966**	**1960**	**1966**
Valve clear. (cold) in. (in.)	0·006 **2**	0·006 **2**	0·006 **2**
Valve clear. (cold) ex. (in.)	0·006 **2**	0·006 **2**	0·006 **2**
Ignition timing degree	35	35	35
Points gap (in.)	0·012 **3**	0·012	0·012
Front tyre (in.)	3·25 × 19 **4**	3·00 × 21	3·25 × 19 **5**
Rear tyre (in.)	3·50 × 19 **4**	4·00 × 19	3·50 × 19 **5**
Rim front	WM2	WM1	WM2
Rim rear	WM2	WM3	WM2
Brake front dia. (in.)	7 **6**	7	7 **6**
Brake front width (in.)	0·87 **7, 8**	0·87	0·87 **8**
Brake rear dia. (in.)	7	7	7
Brake rear width (in.)	0·87 **8**	0·87	0·87 **8**
Front suspension	teles	teles	teles
Rear type	s/a	s/a	s/a
Petrol tank (Imp. gal)	4·25 **9**	2·0	4·25 **9**
Oil tank (Imp. pint)	5·0	5·0	5·0
Box capacity (Imp. pint)	1·0	1·0	1·0
Ignition system	magneto **10**	magneto	magneto
Generator type	dynamo **11**	dynamo	dynamo **12**
Battery (Volt)	6 **13**	6	6 **13**
Wheelbase (in.)	55·2	55·2	55·2
Ground clear. (in.)	5·5	6·5	5·5
Seat height (in.)	31	32·5	31
Dry weight (lb)	396 **14**	379	381 **15**

1 checked at 0·012 gap as 37, 77, 73, 43. **2** 1960—0·008. **3** coil—0·015. **4** 1963—18. **5** 1964—18. **6** 1964—8. **7** 1963—1·12. **8** 1964—1·25. **9** 1963—4. **10** 1959—std—coil, 1960—coil. **11** 1959—std—alternator, 1960—alternator. **12** 1962—alternator. **13** 1964—12. **14** 1964—403. **15** 1964—390.

Model	33/G15	33CS/G15CS	33CSR/G15CSR
Year from	**1964**	**1967**	**1964**
Year to	**1969**	**1969**	**1969**
Bore (mm)	73	73	73
Stroke (mm)	89	89	89
Capacity (cc)	745	745	745
Compression ratio (to 1)	7·6	7·6	7·6
Valve position	ohv	ohv	ohv
Points gap (in.)	0·012	0·012	0·012
Front tyre (in.)	3·50 × 18 **1**	3·50 × 18	3·25 × 18 **2**
Rear tyre (in.)	4·00 × 18	4·00 × 18	3·50 × 18 **2**
Brake front dia. (in.)	8	8	8
Brake front width (in.)	1·25	1·25	1·25
Brake rear dia. (in.)	7	7	7
Brake rear width (in.)	1·25	1·25	1·25
Front suspension	teles	teles	teles

Model	33/G15	33CS/G15CS	33CSR/G15CSR
Year from	**1964**	**1967**	**1964**
Year to	**1969**	**1969**	**1969**
Rear type	s/a	s/a	s/a
Petrol tank (Imp. gal)	4·0	2·2	4·0
Oil tank (Imp. pint)	5·0	5·0	5·0
Ignition system	magneto **3**	capacitor	magneto **3**
Generator type	alternator	alternator	alternator
Battery (Volt)	12	12	12
Wheelbase (in.)	56·5	55·4	56·5
Ground clear. (in.)	6	6·5	5·25
Seat height (in.)	31·5	33	33
Dry weight (lb)	410	400	398
Power: bhp	49		49
@ rpm	6400		6400

1 1967—3·25. **2** 1967—19. **3** 1968—capacitor ignition.

Model	7R	7R	7R	7R
Year from	**1948**	**1950**	**1953**	**1956**
Year to	**1949**	**1952**	**1955**	**1963**
Bore (mm)	74	74	74	75·5
Stroke (mm)	81	81	81	78
Capacity (cc)	348	348	348	349
Compression ratio (to 1)	8·45	8·85 **1**	10	10 **2**
Valve position	ohc	ohc	ohc	ohc
inlet opens BTDC	63	63	50	50
inlet closes ABDC	73	73	74	74
exhaust opens BBDC	62	62	70	70
exhaust closes ATDC	43	43	49	49
Valve clear. (cold) in. (in.)	0·005	0·005	0·008	0·008
Valve clear. (cold) ex. (in.)	0·014	0·014	0·012	0·012
Ignition timing degree	39	39	39	37 **3**
Points gap (in.)	0·012	0·012	0·012	0·012
Front tyre (in.)	3·00 × 21	3·00 × 21	2·75 × 19	2·75 × 19 **5**
Rear tyre (in.)	3·25 × 20 **4**	3·25 × 20	3·25 × 19	3·25 × 19 **5**
Rim front	steel **6**	LA	LA	WM1—LA
Rim rear	steel **6**	LA	LA	WM2—LA
Brake front dia. (in.)	8·25	8·25	8·25	8·25
Brake front width (in.)	1·75	1·75	1·75	1·75
Brake rear dia. (in.)	8·25	8·25	8·25	8·25
Brake rear width (in.)	1·25	1·25	1·25	1·25
Front suspension	teles	teles	teles	teles
Rear type	s/a	s/a	s/a	s/a
Petrol tank (Imp. gal)	4·75	4·75	5·25	5·25 **7**
Oil tank (Imp. pint)	8	8	8	8 **8**
Box capacity (Imp. pint)	1	1	1	1
Ignition system	magneto	magneto	magneto	magneto
Wheelbase (in.)	55·5	56	55·5	55

Model	7R	7R	7R	7R
Year from	**1948**	**1950**	**1953**	**1956**
Year to	**1949**	**1952**	**1955**	**1963**
Ground clear. (in.)		5	5	6 **9**
Seat height (in.)		32	32	31·5 **10**
Width (in.)				24
Length (in.)				85·5
Dry weight (lb)	298	300	293	298 **11**
Power: bhp	31	33		38 **12**
@ rpm	7000	7200		7600 **12**

1 1951—9·4. **2** 1959—11·5, 1961—12. **3** 1962—34. **4** 1949—3·50. **5** 1961—3·00 × 19, 3·50 × 19.
6 light alloy option. **7** 1960—4·75. **8** 1960—7. **9** 1962—6·75. **10** 1962–27.
11 1959—285. **12** 1957—39, 1959—40·5/7800, 1961—41·5/7800.

Model	G45	G50	G50CSR
Year from	**1953**	**1958**	**1962**
Year to	**1957**	**1963**	**1962**
Bore (mm)	66	90	90
Stroke (mm)	72·8	78	78
Capacity (cc)	498	496	496
Compression ratio (to 1)	9·4 **1**	10 **2**	11·2
Valve position	ohv	ohc	ohc
inlet opens BTDC	62		
inlet closes ABDC	64		
exhaust opens BBDC	63		
exhaust closes ATDC	47		
Valve clear. (cold) in. (in.)	0·004		
Valve clear. (cold) ex. (in.)	0·008		
Ignition timing degree	39	37 **3**	
Points gap (in.)	0·012	0·012	0·012
Front tyre (in.)	3·00 × 19	3·00 × 19	3·25 × 19
Rear tyre (in.)	3·50 × 19	3·50 × 19	3·50 × 19
Rim front	LA	LA	WM2
Rim rear	LA	LA	WM2
Brake front dia. (in.)	8·25	8·25	7
Brake front width (in.)	1·75	1·75	0·87
Brake rear dia. (in.)	8·25	8·25	7
Brake rear width (in.)	1·25	1·25	0·87
Front suspension	teles	teles	teles
Rear type	s/a	s/a	s/a
Petrol tank (Imp. gal)	6	5·5	2
Oil tank (Imp. pint)	8	7	
Box capacity (Imp. pint)	1	1	1
Ignition system	magneto	magneto	magneto
Generator type			dynamo
Battery (Volt)			6
Wheelbase (in.)	55·5	55	55·2
Ground clear. (in.)	6	6	

Model	G45	G50	G50CSR
Year from	**1953**	**1958**	**1962**
Year to	**1957**	**1963**	**1962**
Seat height (in.)	31·5	31·5	31
Width (in.)	24	24	
Length (in.)	85·5	85·5	
Dry weight (lb)	320		
Power: bhp	48 **4**	48 **5**	46·5
@ rpm	7200 **4**	6800 **5**	7000

1 1954—10. **2** 1960—10·7, 1962—11·2. **3** 1962—34. **4** 1957—52/7400.
5 1960—50/7200, 1961—51/7200.

Model	Double T	Alamos	Y4 **1**	37A—T
Year from	**1967**	**1967**	**1969**	**1969**
Year to	**1968**	**1968**	**1973**	**1969**
Bore (mm)	68	68	68	66
Stroke (mm)	68	68	68	72
Capacity (cc)	247	247	247	246
Compression ratio (to 1)			12·3 **2**	7·9
Front tyre (in.)		2·75 × 21	2·75 × 21	2·75 × 21
Rear tyre (in.)		4·00 × 18	4·00 × 18	4·00 × 18
Rim front	LA	WM1	WM1	WM1
Rim rear	LA	WM3	WM3	WM3
Brake front dia. (in.)			5	6
Brake rear dia. (in.)			5	6
Front suspension	teles	teles	teles	teles
Rear type	s/a	s/a	s/a	s/a
Petrol tank (Imp. gal)	2·75 + 1·25	1·75	2·0	1·75
Box capacity (Imp. pint)			1·0	
Ignition system			magneto	magneto
Wheelbase (in.)			55·5	51·5
Ground clear. (in.)			9	9·5
Seat height (in.)			31	30
Width (in.)			33·5	
Length (in.)			83	
Dry weight (lb)	198	205	218	212
Power: bhp	32	25	27 **3**	12·4
@ rpm	8400	6400	6400 **3**	5000

1 1971—Y41. **2** 1970—11·0. **3** 1970—25/7000, 1972—28/6500.

Model	Y40	Y5 **1**	Y50	410
Year from	**1970**	**1970**	**1970**	**1971**
Year to	**1970**	**1971**	**1970**	**1973**
Bore (mm)	68	83	83	83
Stroke (mm)	68	68	68	74
Capacity (cc)	247	368	368	400
Compression ratio (to 1)	11·0	10·5 **2**	10·5	10·75

Model	Y40	Y5 1	Y50	410
Year from	**1970**	**1970**	**1970**	**1971**
Year to	**1970**	**1971**	**1970**	**1973**
Ignition timing (mm)	2·5	2·5	2·5	3·2
Front tyre (in.)	2·75 × 21	2·75 × 21	2·75 × 21	2·75 × 21
Rear tyre (in.)	4·00 × 18	4·00 × 18	4·00 × 18	4·00 × 18
Brake front dia. (in.)	5	5	5	5
Brake rear dia. (in.)	5	5	5	5
Front suspension	teles	teles	teles	teles
Rear type	s/a	s/a	s/a	s/a
Petrol tank (Imp. gal)	2·0	2·0	2·0	2·25
Box capacity (Imp. pint)	1·0	1·0	1·0	1·0
Ignition system	magneto	magneto	magneto	magneto
Wheelbase (in.)	55·5	55·5	55·5	55·5
Ground clear. (in.)	9	9	9	9·5
Seat height (in.)	31	31	31	30
Length (in.)				83
Dry weight (lb)	218	221	221	229
Power: bhp	25	30	30	37
@ rpm	7000	6700	6700	6000

1 1971—Y51. **2** 1971—9·85.

Transmission

The heavyweight and twin cylinder AMC models used Burman or AMC gearboxes during the postwar era. These varied in type and internal ratio over the years and further variation in the overall gearing occurred due to changes in the sprockets. Up to 1963 the gearbox and rear wheel remained unaltered and the clutch only changed once after 1956. All gearing changes were obtained by altering the engine sprocket and these ranged from 15 to 21 teeth at first and later to 23 teeth. In the final years other gearbox and rear wheel sprockets were fitted.

To avoid repetition of the same notes for model after model the details of gearbox types and ratios are set out below followed by those of the sprockets, top gear ratio and gearbox fitted to each model by year. From this the intermediate ratios may be calculated.

Transmission on all models was by chain and all except the lightweights used $\frac{1}{2} \times \frac{5}{16}$ in. primary and $\frac{5}{8} \times \frac{3}{8}$ in. final drive. For the lightweights $\frac{3}{8}$ in. duplex primary was used for the 350 and CSR models, $\frac{3}{8}$ in. single for the standard and S models and $\frac{1}{2} \times \frac{5}{16}$ in. for the CS, hence the variation in number of teeth on the clutch sprocket. All lightweights used $\frac{1}{2} \times \frac{5}{16}$ in. final drive.

All road racing models used $\frac{1}{2} \times \frac{5}{16}$ in. primary and $\frac{5}{8} \times \frac{1}{4}$ in. final drive and were supplied with a range of engine and rear wheel sprockets to provide alternative gear ratios to suit the racing circuits. Alternative gearbox and rear wheel sprockets were available for the two stroke models and these had a $\frac{3}{8}$ in. duplex primary chain and $\frac{1}{2} \times \frac{5}{16}$ in. final drive for 1969 but $\frac{5}{8} \times \frac{1}{4}$ in. from 1970 on.

Gearboxes

type	years used	internal ratios top	3rd	2nd	1st
CP road	1945–51	1	1·278	1·761	2·667
CP trials	1945–51	1	1·287	2·087	3·161
BA	1951				
B52	1952–56	1	1·307	1·697	2·654
B52 close	1952–56	1	1·09	1·35	1·87
B52 trials	1952–55	1	1·422	2·02	3·11
AMC	1957–59	1	1·35	1·77	2·67
AMC (1960)	1960–66	1	1·22	1·70	2·56
AMC trials	1957–65	1	1·56	2·44	3·24
Lwt A	1958–64	1	1·30	1·85	2·92
Lwt B	1960–62	1	1·30	1·85	2·42
Lwt C	1965–66	1	1·23	1·79	2·76
7R	1948–49	1	1·136	1·35	1·936
7R50	1950–57	1	1·09	1·35	1·87
AMC race	1958–63	1	1·1	1·332	1·78
Std.	1969	1	1·255	1·53	2·03
Trials	1969	1	1·56	2·4	3·6
Close	1970–73	1	1·256	1·513	2·006
Wide	1970–73	1	1·256	1·661	2·528

Gearing

AJS	Matchless	year	sprockets E	C	G	W	top ratio	gearbox type
16M	G3L	1945–51	18	40	16	42	5·833	CP road
		1952–55	18	40	16	42	5·833	B52
16MS	G3LS	1949–51	18	40	16	42	5·833	CP road
		1952–56	18	40	16	42	5·833	B52
		1957–58	19	42	16	42	5·803	AMC

AJS	Matchless	year	sprockets E	C	G	W	top ratio	gearbox type
16	G3	1959	19	42	16	42	5·803	AMC
		1960–63	19	42	16	42	5·803	AMC (1960)
		1963–66	20	42	16	42	5·512	AMC (1960)
16MC	G3LC	1946–47	17	40	16	42	6·176	CP trials
		1948–50	16	40	16	42	6·562	CP trials
		1951	16	40	16	42	6·562	BA
		1952–55	16	40	16	42	6·562	B52 trials
		1956–58	17	42	16	42	6·485	AMC trials
16MCS	G3LCS	1951	16	40	16	42	6·562	BA
		1952–55	16	40	16	42	6·562	B52
		1956–58	17	42	16	42	6·485	AMC
16CS	G3CS	1959	17	42	16	42	6·485	AMC
16C	G3C	1959–64	17	42	16	42	6·485	AMC trials
18	G80	1945–51	21	40	16	42	5·00	CP road
		1952–55	21	40	16	42	5·00	B52
18S	G80S	1949–51	21	40	16	42	5·00	CP road
		1952–56	21	40	16	42	5·00	B52
		1957–58	22	42	16	42	5·011	AMC
18	G80	1959	22	42	16	42	5·011	AMC
		1960–63	22	42	16	42	5·011	AMC (1960)
		1963–66	23	42	16	42	4·793	AMC (1960)
18C	G80C	1946–47	19	40	16	42	5·526	CP trials
		1948–50	18	40	16	42	5·833	CP trials
		1951	18	40	16	42	5·833	BA
		1952–55	18	40	16	42	5·833	B52 trials
18CS	G80CS	1951	18	40	16	42	5·833	BA
		1952–55	18	40	16	42	5·833	B52
		1956–65	19	42	16	42	5·803	AMC trials
	G85CS	1965–69	19	42	16	54	7·46	AMC (1960)
14	G2	1958–63	21	50	19	55	6·892	Lwt A
14CS	G2CS	1959	17	37	19	70	8·019	Lwt A
		1960–62	17	37	17	70	8·962	Lwt B
14S	G2S	1961–62	21	50	19	55	6·892	Lwt A
14CSR	G2CSR	1962–64	22	46	18	55	6·389	Lwt A
		1965–66	22	46	18	56	6·505	Lwt C
8	G5	1960–62	22	46	18	55	6·389	Lwt A
7R		1948–49	21	42	21	54	5·143	7R
		1950–55	21	42	21	55	5·238	7R50
		1956–57	22	42	21	55	5·00	7R50
		1958	22	42	21	55	5·00	AMC race
		1959–60	23	42	21	56	4·869	AMC race
		1961–63	22	42	22	56	4·859	AMC race
	G45	1953–55	24	42	21	55	4·583	7R50
	G50	1958–63	23	42	21	56	4·869	AMC race
20	G9	1949–51	21	40	16	42	5·00	CP road

AJS	Matchless	year	sprockets E	C	G	W	top ratio	gearbox type
		1952–56	20	40	16	42	5·25	B52
		1957–59	21	42	16	42	5·25	AMC
		1960–61	21	42	16	42	5·25	AMC (1960)
20CS	G9CS	1958–59	19	42	16	42	5·803	AMC
20CSR	G9CSR	1958–59	21	42	16	42	5·25	AMC
30	G11	1956	20	40	16	42	5·25	B52
		1957–58	22	42	16	42	5·011	AMC
30CS	G11CS	1957–58	22	42	16	42	5·011	AMC
30CSR	G11CSR	1958	22	42	16	42	5·011	AMC
31	G12	1958–59	23	42	16	42	4·793	AMC
		1960–62	23	42	16	42	4·793	AMC (1960)
		1963–66	24	42	16	42	4·594	AMC (1960)
31CS	G12CS	1958–59	21	42	16	42	5·25	AMC
		1960	21	42	16	42	5·25	AMC (1960)
31CSR	G12CSR	1958–59	23	42	16	42	4·793	AMC
		1960–63	23	42	16	42	4·793	AMC (1960)
		1964–65	23	42	17	42	4·511	AMC (1960)
		1966	24	42	17	42	4·324	AMC (1960)
33	G15	1964–69	23	42	17	42	4·511	AMC (1960)
33CSR	G15CSR	1964–65	23	42	17	42	4·511	AMC (1960)
		1966–69	23	42	18	42	4·261	AMC (1960)
	G15CS	1967–69	21	42	17	42	4·941	AMC (1960)
37A-T		1969	20	43	15	58	8·313	Trials
Y4		1969	20	43	15	66	9·46	Std.
		1970	20	43	13	61	10·09	Close
Y40		1970	20	43	13	57	9·427	Wide
Y41		1971–73	20	43	13	59	9·758	Wide or close
Y5		1970	24	40	12	65	9·028	Wide
Y50		1970	24	40	12	61	8·472	Wide
Y51		1971	24	40	13	59	7·564	Wide or close
410		1971–73	24	40	13	59	7·564	Wide or close

Colours

Traditionally the AMC colour was black with the AJS having gold lining and the Matchless silver with a central red pin-stripe. When colour was used the AJS was normally blue with birch grey as a supplement, and the Matchless red with arctic white when in two-tone. In the notes, 'colour' means this unless otherwise stated.

The colours and finishes given below are for the home market models. For export these were often changed and on occasion special finishes were ordered.

Transfer details are not included for space reasons but these and supplies of transfers made to the works drawings and specifications can be obtained from the owner's club.

1945
Black for all major parts with tank lined and name as transfer. Chrome plated exhaust system, headlamp rim, push rod tubes and minor fittings. AJS or M on timing cover.

1946
Road: as 1945.
Comp.: as road, except alloy mudguards in black.

1947
Matchless flying M separate pressing, chrome plated. Rims chrome plated with lined black centres. Bars chrome plated, otherwise as 1946.

1948
As 1947 except chrome plated front brake backplate and battery strap.
Comp.: polished alloy mudguards.

1949
Rigid singles: as 1948 except chrome plated rear light body; chrome plated and crimson tanks for export models.
Sprung singles: as rigid except petrol tanks. AJS chrome plated with wide black line surrounding chrome inner side panel carrying AJS transfer, single silver line with blue pin-stripe outside black one, top tank panel in black. Matchless chrome plated with Aldwych red top and side panels silver lined, flying M pressing on each side. Both marques with chrome plated wheel rims with, for AJS black centres lined gold or for Matchless red centres lined silver, monogrammed kneegrips and timing covers.
Twins: as sprung singles except AJS tank with two silver lines outside and two inside wide black ones. AJS or M on timing cover.
Comp.: black, polished alloy mudguards, transfers and lining on tank in gold or silver.

1950
All models: as 1949.

1951
As 1949, AJS models with oval metal tank badges, sprung AJS singles with one inner gold line added to tank sides, Matchless sprung singles with the option of black rim centres, silver lined. Competition models with metal tank badges.

1952
Singles and **twins:** due to restrictions on plating, all-black finish with tanks lined gold or silver, the silver with a further thin red line on it. Polished lower fork legs and front brake backplates. Rims Argenized as matt aluminium without paint or lining. Light alloy, die-cast tank badges, AJS as three gold anodized letters on bar, Matchless round with letter M on red background and flying wings to each side.
Singles: cadmium plated push rod tubes.
Comp.: As 1951.

1953
As 1952, chrome plated rims and tanks for export.
Twins: seat piping in colour all spring frame singles and twins fitted with dual seats for 1953.

1954
Singles: as 1953, chrome plated push rod tubes. Round tank badges introduced. For AJS in blue and bronze for painted tanks and blue and silver for chrome-plated ones. Matchless badges in maroon or silver.
Twins: tanks chrome plated as in 1949 pattern but with plastic badges.

1955
All: as 1954.

1956
AJS badge 0·25 in. larger diameter.
Singles: as 1954.
Comp.: chrome plated rims.
Twins: 500 as 1954 with larger AJS badge, 600 tanks chrome plated and painted black (AJS), or red (Matchless).

1957
Singles: as 1956, option of chrome plated tank side panels with coloured plastic edge beading for road models.
Twins: 500 tanks black, 600 tanks in blue for AJS and red for Matchless, all tanks with chrome plated side panels as standard.

1958
All: chrome plated rims without painted centres except AJS model 30 which had blue centres silver lined.

Singles: as 1957 with further tank panel option colours in gold with blue beading for AJS and in off-white with red beading for Matchless, as well as chrome plated.

Twins: As 1957.

CS models: in black, tanks lined in gold or silver and with name transfers, light alloy mudguards. For export—petrol tank, oil tank and toolbox in colour.

CSR: black frame, coloured petrol tank, oil tank and toolbox; chrome plated tank side panels, fork covers and rear unit shrouds. Light alloy mudguards.

Lightweight single: Black frame, forks, chaincase, mudguards, mudguard stay, side covers, rear units and cylinder barrel. Coloured petrol tank and engine side flashes. Tank lining in gold or silver. Chrome plated headlamp rim, wheel rims, exhaust pipe. Plastic tank badges. AJS in Mediterranean blue.

Mid-year option for heavyweight **singles** and **twins** only: black frame and forks. AJS with Mediterranean blue petrol tank, oil tank, mudguards and toolbox; tank panels in silver with blue beading. Matchless with silver mudguards and petrol tank, red oil tank, toolbox and tank panels with black beading.

1959

Range of colour options offered for larger **singles** and **twins** fitting 3·75 or 4·25 gallon petrol tank. Frame and forks black for all models; mudguards, oil tank and toolbox black or coloured option; chrome plated wheel rims. All standard models supplied with lined black tank. De-luxe fitted with black tank with chrome plated side panels which were optional for all road models. Colour options applied to tank alone or tank, oil tank, mudguards and toolbox. **Single** colours were AJS blue or Matchless white. Two-tone applied to tank only as AJS blue upper and grey lower, or Matchless white upper and red lower with chrome plated separating strip on each side. **Single** colour tanks had chrome plated side panels. Lists indicate that all options were available to all road models but **CSR** twins came as standard with AJS blue or Matchless red (not white) tanks and coloured oil tank and toolbox plus alloy mudguards. **CS** models were in black with colour option for tank, lined in all cases, and with alloy mudguards.

Trials: black with gold or silver lining and transfers, alloy mudguards.

Lightweight: as 1958, alloy mudguards for **CS.**

1960

Singles, twins, 250 CS: as 1959.

Lightweight 250: options of black tank, coloured tank with chrome plated side panels or two-tone as range.

350: as standard **250**.

1961

All: larger tank badges and larger transfers on lightweights only, rest as 1959 except AJS blue changed to birch grey and Matchless white to cardinal red and for export to Hades red. Two-tone options changed to birch grey upper tank and blue lower for AJS, cardinal red upper and arctic white lower for Matchless. Effect of change was grey mudguards, oil tank and side panels for AJS with petrol tank the same in single colour option, and those items in red for Matchless.

Lightweight: standard—black, option in blue or red or in two-tone, as others; **S**—chrome plated mudguards, chainguard and rims; coloured petrol tank and side covers; black frame and forks, polished engine sides.

1962

Singles and **twins:** new tank badges, AJS with letters set in an oval in side panel with horizontal ribs, Matchless as large flying M on side panel with pronounced ribs top and bottom, badges chrome plated die-cast zinc alloy. Lightweight knee grips fitted.

Singles: black standard, all coloured option with white mudguards. **Sports 350** has chrome plated mudguards and chainguard.

Twins: standard models in black with colour option as singles with white mudguards; red shade called tartan red.

CSR: frame and forks black, light alloy mudguards, coloured petrol tank, oil tank and toolbox; option in all coloured with alloy mudguards.

Lightweights: standard—black frame, forks, mudguards, side panels, engine flashes, rear units and chainguard; coloured tank with gold lined, white flash running forward from kneegrip. **S**-chrome plated mudguards and chainguard, coloured tank and side covers, polished engine sides, option of all coloured with white mudguards. **CS**—as 1959, red remained cardinal red. **CSR**-black frame and forks; coloured tank with chrome plated sides, chrome plated mudguards and chainguard; silver cylinder; polished engine sides, head fin edges and rocker cover.

1963

Singles and **standard twin:** black with coloured option for tank, oil tank and toolbox only. Double zig-zag lines in gold or silver on tank shoulders with thick lower and thin upper lines—all models.

CSR twin: as 1962, no option, zig-zag tank lining.

250 Standard and **250 CSR:** as 1962.

1964

Singles and **twins:** as 1963, AJS blue changed to polychromatic blue. **CSR twin** with coloured top, chrome plated

sides, coloured oil tank and toolbox, chrome plated mudguards.
250CSR: as 1962.
1965
AJS badge diamond-shape, Matchless just 'M' with flying wings without background of 1962–64 both in plastic.
Singles: black only as 1964.
Comp.: as before.
650 twin: standard in black only, **CSR** as 1964 except coloured tank without chrome sides.
750 standard: as 1964 **CSR twin.**
750CSR: black frame and forks; light alloy mudguards; chrome plated tank sides below smooth lining, headlamp shell, rear chainguard and instrument panel; coloured tank top, oil tank and toolbox.
250CSR: as 1964, black side covers.
1966
Singles: black with lined tank.
G85CS: red tank, silver frame.
Twins: 650 standard—black as 1965; **650CSR** and **750** standard—black frame and forks, tank coloured and chrome with zig-zag divide as 1965, **750CSR** coloured oil tank and toolbox, chrome plated mudguards; **750CSR**—as 1965.
250CSR: polished alloy mudguards.
1967
G85CS: as 1966.
750 standard: black frame and forks, chrome plated mudguards, tank blue for AJS or black for Matchless.
750CSR: as 1965.
1968/69
G85CS and **Matchless twins:** as 1967.
G15CS: black, candy apple red tank, chrome plated mudguards.

Engine and frame numbers

Up to 1963 the dating of AMC engines was made very easy by the code system used. This comprised the last two digits of the year followed by the model type and then a serial number. Thus 48/16/1234 was a 1948 AJS model 16M and 61/G12/3456 was a 1961 Matchless model G12.

After 1963 a number alone was used and the details and dates are as follows:

	Model		Engine number	
Date	**AJS**	**Matchless**	**AJS**	**Matchless**
9/63	14CSR	G2CSR	13275	13274
9/64			14107	13956
9/65			14833	14757
7/66			15506	15468
8/64	16C	G3C	4827	4802
9/64	18CS	G80CS	4619	4958
8/65		G80CS		5179
7/66		G85CS		296
9/64	16	G3	42791	42761
7/66			43066	43171
9/64	18	G80	134658	134939
7/66			135289	135336
9/64	31	G12	10212	10254
7/66			10509	10784
9/64	31CSR	G12CSR	10211	10175
7/66			10659	10715

The frames are less easy to determine for a number of reasons. Each frame type was numbered from zero upwards but could be fitted to more than one model. On occasion prefix or suffix letters were used, usually A or FA when full width hubs were introduced and the suffix of C or CS for the all welded off-road competition models prior to 1956. AMC were not totally consistent to their own rules in this as the rigid and springer singles had common front frames and hence common frame numbers for a few years. To assist owners in dating frames some dates, models and numbers are listed as a guide. This information should be used in conjunction with parts lists and model recognition data to help determine marque, model and year. Often the owners club can assist in this matter and all AMC enthusiasts are recommended to join this helpful organisation.

Heavyweight road singles and twins—frames

Date	Number	Date	Number
1946	500	9/54	A21057
1947	12760	9/55	37700
1948	23358	9/56	49350
1949	35000	9/57	59492
1950	47000	9/59	72300
9/50	59744	9/60	76550
9/51	74100	9/62	A83900
9/52	89501	9/63	85669

Date	16	G3	18	G80	31	G12	31CSR	G12CSR
9/64	87183	87120	86850	87144	86815	86828	86786	86712
7/66	88277	88307	87891	88257	87387	88405	88108	88339

Notes

1 September 1959 number is for 20/G9 std model; de luxe, CS and CSR number is 72228.

2 Start number for 30 is 38294 and for G11 is 38253.

3 August 1958 end number for 30 is 65925, for G11 is 65864, for 30CS and 30CSR is 65662 and for G11CS and G11CSR is 65967.

Competition frames

	Trials	Trials	Scrambles	Scrambles	Trials	Trials	Scrambles	Scrambles
Date	**16MC**	**G3LC**	**16MC/S**	**G3LC/S**	**18C**	**G80C**	**18CS**	**G80CS**
1946	464C	463C			457C	467C		
1947	574C	680C			575C	576C		
1948	958C	981C			979C	978C		
1949	1746C	1542			1500C	1547C		
1950	F2220	2200			2107C	2105C		
9/50	F2642	2911C	F2642	2806CS	2604	9604	2604	9604
9/51	2642C	3117	2642C	3104	2712C	2694C	2833CS	2754CS
9/52	3193C	3704	3106	3704	3704	3218C	3704	3221
9/53	3775C	4725	3861CS	4942	F4609	3969C	F4609	3967
9/54	4880C	5651	4956CS	5212	5012	4615	4747CS	4616
9/55	5660C	6243	5267CS	F6391	5658C	5711	5093C	5251

	Trials **16MC, 16C**	Scrambles **16MCS, 16CS**	Scrambles **18CS**	Scrambles **G80CS**	Scrambles **G85CS**
Date	**G3LC, G3C**	**G3LCS, G3CS**			
11/55		6396	6401	6395	
9/56	7350	7350	7350	7350	
9/57	7952	7952	7952	7952	
9/58	8490	8633	8572	8550	
9/59	8860	8671	8880	8880	
9/60	9500		9500	9500	
9/62			C10550	C10550	
7/63	C10499				
8/64	10871 (16C) 10841 (G3C)				
9/64			10728	10936	
8/65				11082	
7/66					328
6/67					5348

Lightweights

Note

First number given in each pair is for the frame and the second is for the engine.

Date	14/G2	14CS/G2CS	14CSR/G2CSR	8/G5
6/58	1001/501			
9/59	5270/4756	5270/4756		6020/500
9/60	10183/7979	10183/7979		10183/2237
5/62			12500/8750	
9/63			16800/13275	
9/64			17536/14107	
9/65			18283/14833	
7/66			19033/—(14CSR)	
7/66			18932/—(G2CSR)	

Road racing

7R

Date	Engine	Frame
1948	501	1201
1949	580	1280
1950	678	1378
1951	801	1401
5/53	901	1501
1954	1001	1601
1955	1071	1671
1956	1500	F1500
9/57	1600	F1600
1959	1650	1650
9/63	1900	1900

G45

Date	Numbers
9/53	102
9/54	205
9/55	300
8/57	354

G50

9/58	1700
9/63	1900

Carburettor settings

AJS	Matchless	Year	Type	Size	Main	Pilot	Slide	Needle pos.	Needle jet
14	G2	1958–61	376	$1\frac{1}{16}$	180	25	$3\frac{1}{2}$	3	·106
14CS		1959–61	376	$1\frac{1}{16}$	180	25	3	4	·106
14CSR	G2, G2S, G2CSR	1962–66	389	$1\frac{1}{8}$	200	20	3	3	·106
	G3 (ex-WD)	1940	276	1	150		6/4	3	std
	G3L (ex-WD)	1941–45	275	$\frac{7}{8}$	160		5/5	4	std
16M, 16MC, 16MS	G3L, G3LC, G3LS	1946–53	76	1	150		6/4	3	std
16MCS	G3LCS	1950–53	76	1	150		6/4	3	std
16M, 16MS, 16MCS	G3L, G3LS, G3LC, G3LCS	1954	76	$1\frac{1}{16}$	150		6/4	3	std
16MCS	G3LCS	1954–56	TT	$1\frac{1}{16}$	300		5	4	·109
16M, 16MS, 16MCS	G3L, G3LS, G3LC	1955–61	376	$1\frac{1}{16}$	210	30	$3\frac{1}{2}$	3	·106
		1955–56	376	$1\frac{1}{16}$	200	30	$3\frac{1}{2}$	3	·106
	G3LC	1955–57	376	$1\frac{1}{16}$	240	30	3	3	·106
16MCS	G3LC	1957–59	389	$1\frac{1}{8}$	280	30	3	3	·106
16MC	G3LC	1956–61	376	$1\frac{1}{16}$	210	30	3	3	·107
8	G5	1960–61	389	$1\frac{1}{8}$	220	25	$3\frac{1}{2}$	3	·106
8, 16	G5, G3, G3S	1962–63	389	$1\frac{1}{8}$	230	25	$3\frac{1}{2}$	3	·106
16C	G3C	1962–63	376	$1\frac{1}{16}$	210	30	3	3	·107
16	G3	1964–66	389	$1\frac{1}{8}$	260	25	3	3	·106
18, 18C, 18CS, 18S	G80, G80C, G80S	1946–53	89	$1\frac{3}{32}$	180		29/4	3	std

18	G80,G80C,G80S,G80CS	1954	89	$1\frac{5}{32}$	180		29/4	2	std
18, 18S, 18C	G80, G80S	1955–59	389	$1\frac{5}{32}$	260	30	$3\frac{1}{2}$	3	·106
18, 18C, 18S, 18CS	G80, G80S	1955–56	389	$1\frac{5}{32}$	250	30	$3\frac{1}{2}$	3	·106
18CS	G80CS	1955	TT	$1\frac{3}{16}$	340		7	4	·109
18CS	G80C, G80CS	1958–61	389	$1\frac{3}{16}$	440	30	3	3	·106
	G80R	1957–61	GP	$1\frac{3}{8}$	320		7	3	·109
	G80R	1959	GP	$1\frac{1}{2}$	450		4	3	·109
18, 18S, 18C		1960–61	389	$1\frac{5}{32}$	300	25	$3\frac{1}{2}$	3	·106
	G80CS	1960–61	GP	$1\frac{3}{8}$	290		6	5	·109
18	G80	1962–63	389	$1\frac{5}{32}$	300	25	$3\frac{1}{2}$	3	·106
18	G80	1964–66	389	$1\frac{1}{8}$	290	25	$3\frac{1}{2}$	3	·106
18CS	G80CS	1962–65	GP	$1\frac{3}{8}$	290	25	6	5	·109
18CS	G80CS	1966	389	$1\frac{3}{16}$	440	30	3	3	·106
	G85CS	1966–68	GP	$1\frac{3}{8}$	310	25	6	5	·109
	G85CS	1967–68	932	32 mm	270	30	3	2	·107
20	G9	1949–54	76	1	180		6/4	3	std
20	G9	1953	pair 76	1	180		6/4	3	std
20	G9	1955–61	376	1	220	30	4	3	·106
20	G9	1955–56	376	1	230	30	4	3	·106
30	G11	1955–57	376	1	260	30	4	3	·106
30, 30CS	G11, G11CS	1957–58	376	$1\frac{1}{16}$	280	30	$3\frac{1}{2}$	3	·106
30 (2 carbs)	G11 (2 carbs)	1957–59	376	$1\frac{1}{16}$	220	25	$3\frac{1}{2}$	3	·106
31	G12	1957–59	389	$1\frac{1}{8}$	400	30	3	3	·106
31	G12	1960–66	389	$1\frac{1}{8}$	390	20	4	4	·106
31CS, 31CSR	G12CS, G12CSR	1960–66	389	$1\frac{1}{8}$	450	20	4	4	·106
31CSR (speed kit)	G12CSR (speed kit)	1962–65	pr 389	$1\frac{1}{8}$	280	25	3	4	·106
	G15	1962–63	389	$1\frac{1}{8}$	410	20	4	4	·106
33P	G15P	1964–66	pr 389	$1\frac{1}{8}$	420	20	3	3	·106
33CS	G15CS	1964–66	pr 389	$1\frac{1}{8}$	380	20	3	3	·106
33	G15	1965	pr 389	$1\frac{1}{8}$	350	20	3	3	·106
33CSR	G15CSR	1965–66	pr 389	$1\frac{1}{8}$	360	20	3	3	·106
33, 33CSR		1967–68	pr 930	30 mm	220	25	2	2	·106
	G15, G15CSR	1967–68	pr 930	30 mm	230	25	2	2	·106
7R		1949–53	TT	$1\frac{1}{8}$	400		4	4	·109
7R		1955–59	GP	$1\frac{1}{8}$	220		7	1	·109
7R		1955–59	GP	$1\frac{5}{32}$	270		5	2	·109
7R		1959–61	GP	$1\frac{3}{8}$	360		5	3	·109
7R		1962–63	GP	$1\frac{3}{8}$	330	25	5	3	·109
	G45	1954	TT	$1\frac{3}{16}$	340		7	4	·109
	G45	1955–57	GP	$1\frac{3}{32}$	240		5	4	·109
	G50	1960–61	GP	$1\frac{1}{2}$	450		4	3	·109
	G50	1962	GP	$1\frac{1}{2}$	430	25	4	3	·109
	G50	1962	GP	$1\frac{3}{8}$	280	25	5	3	·109
Y4		1969–71	932	32 mm	270	20	$3\frac{1}{2}$	2	·107
Y5		1970–73	1034	34 mm	300	25	$2\frac{1}{2}$	3	·107
410		1973	1034	34 mm	290	25	$3\frac{1}{2}$	3	·107

Prices

The prices of the machines are set out in the following tables. In each case the AJS machine type is given above the Matchless one except in the few cases where no equivalent was built, these being the racing models and in the final days. UK purchase tax is included except where the price is given as basic and a good few of the changes that occurred were solely due to budget alterations in the rate of that tax. In all cases, except the early 500 cc twins, the price was the same regardless of marque and in that instance the specification differed in the matter of seating and petrol tank size.

AJS Matchless	16M G3L	16MC G3LC	16MS G3LS	16MCS G3LCS	7R	 G45
1945	£91 basic					
3.46		£96 basic				
30. 5.46	£124. 9s. 2d.					
24.10.46	£134.12s. 5d.	£140.19s. 5d.				
16.10.47	£142. 4s.10d.	£148.11s.10d.				
1. 4.48					£323.17s. 0d.	
11.11.48			£128 basic			
13.10.49	£147. 6s. 6d.	£160. 0s. 6d.	£167.12s.10d.		£323.17s. 0d.	
28. 9.50				£180. 6s.10d.		
19. 3.51	£161. 5s. 9d.	£173.19s.10d.	£182.17s. 7d.	£195.11s. 8d.		
13. 9.51	£172.10s. 0d.	£185. 5s. 7d.	£194. 4s. 6d.	£207. 0s. 0d.		
18. 9.52	£172.10s. 0d.	£185. 5s. 7d.	£197. 8s. 4d.	£207. 0s. 0d.		
20.11.52					£376.18s.10d.	£376.18s.10d.
23. 4.53	£163. 2s. 6d.	£175. 4s. 2d.	£186.13s. 9d.	£195.15s. 0d.	£356. 9s. 2d.	£356. 9s. 2d.
10. 9.53	£166.16s. 0d.	£179. 8s. 0d.	£191. 8s. 0d.	£204. 0s. 0d.	£366. 0s. 0d.	£366. 0s. 0d.
9. 9.54	£170. 8s. 0d.	£183. 0s. 0d.	£196. 4s. 0d.	£211.16s. 0d.	£390. 0s. 0d.	£390. 0s. 0d.
28. 4.55	£176. 8s. 0d.	£189. 0s. 0d.	£204.12s. 0d.	£220. 4s. 0d.		

		16MC G3LC (s/a)		16MCS G3LCS (s/s)		
15. 9.55		£212. 8s. 0d.	£204.12s. 0d.	£218. 8s. 0d.	£390. 0s. 0d.	£390. 0s. 0d.
17.11.55					£403. 0s. 0d.	£403. 0s. 0d.
26. 4.56		£219. 9s. 7d.	£211. 8s. 5d.	£225.13s. 7d.		
2. 5.57		£235.12s. 0d.	£226.18s. 5d.	£243. 0s. 9d.		
12. 9.57		£243. 5s. 3d.	£233.18s. 2d.	£250.14s.11d.	£417.18s. 3d.	£417.18s. 3d.

	16 G3	16CS G3CS	16C G3C	18 G80	18CS G80CS	7R	 G50
2.10.58	£231. 8s. 3d.	£247. 0s. 0d.	£243. 5s. 3d.	£244.10s. 2d.	£268. 4s. 3d.	£417.18s. 3d.	£430. 7s. 9d.
23. 4.59	£223.15s. 3d.	£238.16. 5d.	£235. 4s. 5d.	£236. 8s. 6d.	£259. 6s.11d.	£404. 1s.11d.	£416. 3s. 2d.
1.10.59	£224.19s. 4d.		£235. 4s. 5d.	£237.12s. 8d.	£265. 7s. 6d.	£422. 3s. 9d.	£434. 5s. 0d.
5. 5.60	£236. 8s. 6d.		£247. 5s. 8d.	£249.13s.10d.	£278.12s.10d.		
25. 8.60						£443. 5s.11d.	£455.19s. 3d.
27. 4.61	£236. 8s. 6d.		£236. 0s. 0d.	£249. 0s. 0d.	£278.12s.10d.		
10. 8.61	£240. 9s. 4d.		£240. 0s. 9d.	£253. 5s. 2d.	£283. 8s. 2d.	£450.17s. 6d.	£463.15s. 2d.

	16 (s/s) **G3**	**16S** **G3S**					
14. 9.61	£240. 6s. 9d.	£247.13s. 2d.	£240. 6s. 9d.	£254. 7s. 5d.	£284. 5s. 2d.		
16.11.61						£512. 8s. 0d.	£527. 0s. 9d.
27. 9.62	£248. 4s. 5d.		£236. 8s. 0d.	£262.14s. 2d.	£293.11s. 7d.	£420. 0s. 0d.	£432. 0s. 0d.
3.10.63	£263. 7s. 6d.		£261.16s. 5d.	£268.16s. 7d.	£289. 1s.10d.		
19.11.64	£279.15s.11d.			£282.19s. 0d.	£289. 1s.10d.		
9. 9.65	£290. 1s. 3d.	**G85CS**		£297.16s. 5d.			
6.10.66	£294.15s. 8d.	£390.19s. 1d.		£302.13s. 4d.			
	18 **G80**	**18C** **G80C**	**18S** **G80S**	**18CS** **G80CS**	**20**	**G9**	
1945	£99 basic						
3.46		£104 basic					
30. 5.46	£135. 7s.10d.						
24.10.46	£147. 6s. 5d.	£153.13s. 5d.					
16.10.47	£154.18s.10d.	£161. 5s.10d.					
11.11.48			£138 basic				
25.11.48					£165 basic	£167 basic	
13.10.49	£160. 0s. 6d.	£172.14s. 5d.	£180. 6s.10d.		£214.12s. 8d.	£217. 3s. 6d.	
28. 9.50				£193. 0s.10d.			
19. 3.51	£176.10s. 7d.	£189. 4s. 8d.	£198. 2s. 5d.	£210.16s. 4d.	£232. 8s. 2d.	£234.19s.10d.	
13. 9.51	£190. 7s.10d.	£203. 3s. 4d.	£212. 2s. 3d.	£224.17s.10d.	£246.12s. 3d.	£249. 3s. 4d.	
18. 9.52	£190. 7s.10d.	£203. 3s. 4d.	£215. 6s. 1d.	£224.17s.10d.	£249.16s. 1d.	£248.10s. 6d.	
23. 4.53	£180. 0s.11d.	£192. 2s. 6d.	£203.12s. 1d.	£212.13s. 5d.	£236. 4s. 7d.	£235. 0s. 5d.	
10. 9.53	£184. 4s. 0d.	£196.16s. 0d.	£208.16s. 0d.	£221. 8s. 0d.	£240. 0s. 0d.	£240. 0s. 0d.	
9. 9.54	£187.16s. 0d.	£200. 8s. 0d.	£213.12s. 0d.	£229. 4s. 0d.	£240. 0s. 0d.	£240. 0s. 0d.	
28. 4.55	£193.16s. 0d.	£206. 8s. 0d.	£221. 8s. 0d.	£237. 0s. 0d.	£249.12s. 0d.	£249.12s. 0d.	
				18CS **G80CS** **(s/s)**	**20** **G9**	**30** **G11**	**30CS** **G11CS**
15. 9.55			£216.12s. 0d.	£235. 4s. 0d.	£246. 0s. 0d.	£252. 0s. 0d.	
17.11.55					£254. 4s. 0d.	£260. 8s. 0d.	
26. 4.56			£223.16s. 5d.	£243. 0s. 9d.	£254. 4s. 0d.	£260. 8s. 0d.	
2. 5.57	**30CSR**		£240.11s. 2d.	£262.17s. 7d.	£272.16s. 0d.	£280. 4s. 9d.	
12. 9.57	**G11CSR**		£247.12s. 7d.	£271.19s. 1d.	£281. 6s. 3d.	£288.15s.11d.	£299. 8s. 0d.
23. 1.58	£299. 8s. 0d.						
	20 **G9**	**20 dl** **G9 dl**	**20CS & CSR** **G9CS & CSR**	**31** **G11**	**31 dl** **G11 dl**	**31CS** **G11CS**	**31CSR** **G11CSR**
2.10.58	£270. 1s. 8d.	£280.13s. 9d.	£291.18s. 4d.	£275. 1s. 6d.	£285.13s. 7d.	£296.18s. 0d.	£296.18s. 0d.
23. 4.59	£261. 3s. 1d.	£271. 8s. 2d.	£282. 5s. 4d.	£265.19s. 7d.	£276. 4s. 8d.	£287. 1s. 8d.	£287. 1s. 8d.
1.10.59	£262. 7s. 2d.			£267. 3s. 8d.	£277. 8s. 9d.	£287. 1s. 9d.	£288. 5s.11d.
5. 5.60	£275.12s. 7d.			£280. 9s. 1d.	£291. 6s. 2d.	£301.11s. 3d.	£302.15s. 5d.
27. 4.61	£252. 0s. 0d.			£256. 0s. 0d.	£267. 0s. 0d.		£280. 0s. 0d.

	20 G9	20 dl G9 dl	20CS & CSR G9CS & CSRR	31 G11	31 dl G11 dl	31CS G11CS	31CSR G11CSR
10. 8.61	£256. 6*s.* 2*d.*			£260. 7*s.* 6*d.*	£271.11*s.* 4*d.*		£284.15*s.* 9*d.*
14. 9.61				£262. 6*s.* 0*d.*			£289.15*s.* 0*d.*
27. 9.62	**33**			£270.18*s.* 0*d.*			£299. 5*s.* 0*d.*
3.10.63	**G15**	**G15CSR**		£321. 0*s.*10*d.*			£331. 3*s.* 5*d.*
19.11.64	£355. 4*s.* 2*d.*	£366. 3*s.* 7*d.*		£335. 1*s.* 1*d.*			£342.14*s.* 2*d.*
9. 9.65	£367.12*s.* 6*d.*	£370.14*s.* 6*d.*		£342. 8*s.* 4*d.*			£354. 8*s.*10*d.*
6.10.66	£373.12*s.* 2*d.*	£376.15*s.* 2*d.*		£347.19*s.* 9*d.*			£360. 4*s.* 2*d.*
16. 3.67	£381. 1*s.* 7*d.*	£384. 4*s.* 7*d.*					

	14 G2	14CS G2CS	14S G2S	8 G5
19. 6.58	£196. 9*s.* 8*d.*			
2.10.58	£196. 9*s.* 8*d.*	£209.11*s.* 7*d.*		
23. 4.59	£189.19*s.* 9*d.*	£202.13*s.* 0*d.*		
1.10.59	£191. 3*s.*10*d.*	£202.13*s.* 0*d.*		£208.13*s.* 8*d.*
5. 5.60	£200.16*s.*10*d.*	£212.18*s.* 1*d.*		£218.18*s.* 8*d.*
25. 8.60	£203.17*s.* 2*d.*	£217.14*s.* 6*d.*		£221.19*s.* 0*d.*
10.11.60	£203.17*s.* 2*d.*	£217.14*s.* 6*d.*	£209.17*s.* 9*d.*	£221.19*s.* 0*d.*
27. 4.61	£199. 0*s.* 0*d.*	£215. 0*s.* 0*d.*	£205. 0*s.* 0*d.*	£214. 0*s.* 0*d.*
10. 8.61	£202. 8*s.* 1*d.*	£218.13*s.* 6*d.*	£208.10*s.* 1*d.*	£217.13*s.* 2*d.*
14. 9.61	£204.19*s.* 2*d.*	£227.10*s.* 7*d.*	£212. 5*s.* 7*d.*	£220. 4*s.*2*d.*
27. 9.62	£211.13*s.* 7*d.*			

	14CSR G2CSR
10. 5.62	£228.10*s.* 0*d.*
2.10.63	£234.10*s.*11*d.*
19.11.64	£243.17*s.*11*d.*
25. 2.65	£224.18*s.* 5*d.*
9. 9.65	£248. 0*s.* 0*d.*
6.10.66	£252. 0*s.* 9*d.*

Racing models

Works road racers

1947

Porcupine first used, horizontal cylinders, downdraught carbs, spike fins, swinging fork frame, candlesticks, twin leading shoe brakes front and rear.

1948

7R used by works.

Porcupine: curved inlet tracts, horizontal carbs, top feed float chamber, new Lucas racing magneto, finned oil cooler anodized and dyed black, oil tank anodized and dyed black, frame gusseted for top of rear units and megaphone mountings, simpler rear brake pedal, shorter seat, brazed on control pivots, new rear hub, torque stay for brake, smaller rear sprocket.

1949

7R: magnetic sump plug.

Porcupine: new carburettor mounting, shorter inlet tracts, mixing chambers at angle, carb support incorporated front tank rubbers, shock absorber in clutch.

1950

7R: engine modified internally with pressed in timing side mainshaft, smaller flywheels, timing side roller main, stiffer crankpin, 79° valve angle, larger inlet valve; sump plate added, exhaust pipe curved inside right down tube, smaller pipe and megaphone, revised clutch, 7R50 gearbox, primary chain lubricated via engine sprocket holes.

Porcupine: raised compression ratio, splayed carburettors, prototype GP, twin float chambers mounted to frame downtubes, cooling flutes on rear hub side, bars moved.

Both: front brake drum bolted into hub shell, slimmer oil tank, petrol tank with knee recesses, tail fairing.

1951

7R: 74° cylinder head, narrower crankcase, no engine shock absorber, engine moved forward in frame, tyre sections of 2·75 and 3·25 in., jet control for lubrication of both chains.

Porcupine: non-spike cylinder heads at first separate and later in one piece, oil pump in crankcase, one gallon oil sump under engine, revised carburettors with central float with extensions to support mixing chambers, tyre sections 3·00 and 3·50 in.

Both: shorter wheelbase, shorter forks with alloy top crown,

clip-ons, shorter seat with plug storage, 19 in. wheels, jampots with alloy spring boxes, longer rear mudguard.
Prototype G45: twin engine in works **7R** frame, single carburettor, well finned cylinder head, 19 in. wheels, rev-counter driven from magneto gear.

1952
7R: 3 valve engine with chain camshaft drive, small megaphones, new frame, new gearbox mounting and gearbox bearings.
E95: inclined engine, chain driven rotating magnet magneto, transverse gear lever, new frame, jampots, new rear hub, unsprung rear mudguard, petrol tank strap.

1953
7R3A: new frame with vertical seat tubes.
E95: new frame, carburettors tilted to 49 degrees, modified jampots, return spring on gear lever, spike fins on one model.

1954
7R: revised chain oiler, slimmer oil tank.
7R3B built.
Both: lowered frame, shorter forks, deep pannier tanks, special fuel system with pump.

1955
Raced modified standard **7R** and **G45** models.

Model recognition

1948
7R: First model, wrap round oil tank, side bolt petrol tank, very large megaphone.

1949
7R: magnetic sump plug.

1950
7R: modifications as works model.

1951
7R: 1950 works cam and piston, 9·4:1 compression ratio, oil feed to cams modified, jet control for chain lubricant, more extensive primary chain guard, jampots.

1952
7R: continued.

1953
7R: 74° valve angle, roller rockers, revised bottom half, three bolt exhaust pipe collar, shorter pipe and megaphone, new frame, shorter forks, 19 in. wheels, twin leading shoe front brake, single leading rear, forged gearbox bridge, remote gearchange, tank strap, shorter seat, jampot, primary chainguard extended round chain, tyre sections 2·75 and 3·25 in.
G45: twin cylinder engine in **7R** cycle parts, rev-counter driven from exhaust camshaft, finned exhaust rocker caps, machined steel crankshaft, tyre sections 3·00 and 3·50 in.

1954
7R: drive side main modified.
G45: Y alloy cylinder head, modified rockers, valves and springs, cam follower needles made smaller and number increased, forged steel crankshaft, main bearings locked into crankcase.
Both: primary chainguard drain added, holes for cooling air in front of chainguard, gear linkage modified.

1955
Both: twin feed primary chain oiler.

1956
7R: engine dimensions altered, Dykes piston ring.
Both: rotating magnet magneto, new tank shape, narrower oil tank, reverse cone megaphones, clip-ons, works controls, positive stop twistgrip, magnetic rev-counter, revised rear units, large brake air scoops, direct gear pedal, slotted hub side covers.

1957
Girling units, last of **G45** models.

1958
7R: 14.5° downdraught for inlet, longer inlet tract with insulating block in place of plate between head and carburettor, diaphragm float mount, exhaust cam change, piston change, timed engine breather, AMC gearbox, 3 spring clutch, rear engine plates in place of casting, rear units near vertical, lower seat and hump, one piece fibreglass for front number plate plus rev-counter and screen mounting, chain oiler supply to final chain.
G50: prototype at TT, model introduced late in year.

1959
7R: bigger carburettor, raised compression ratio, new big

end cage, gearbox changes, raised gearing.
7R and **G50:** rear frame narrowed, exhaust pipe tucked in more, fork changes, fairing lug on headstock, fibreglass seat with hump and tail.

1960
Both: lower frame tubes raised, timing and gearbox end covers altered to allow exhaust pipe to tuck in more, footrests and rear fork narrowed, tank top lowered an inch, knee recesses and seat hump moved forward an inch, oil tank cut away, cable rear brake, steering damper wing nut, quicker twistgrip, new inlet cam, port changes, magneto vernier made finer, modified clutch centre.
G50: larger inlet valve.

1961
7R: 22 tooth sprockets for engine and gearbox, 12:1 compression ratio, tyres as **G50**.
Both: multi-rate springs for forks, fork gainters, matched Girlings, larger front brake air scoop, smaller oil tank cap, revised timing case, exhaust pipe tucked in and megaphone further back.

1962
7R: flexibly mounted carburettor.
7R and **G50:** flap valve in drive side mainshaft, chain line moved in, forged big end cage, shim under barrel to set squish clearance, 34° ignition timing, alloy gear pedal, rubber tank strap, new gearbox mounting, matchbox float chamber, two brake linings per shoe.
G50CSR: **G50** engine in CSR cycle parts with quickly detachable electrics, belt driven dynamo, sheet steel cover over primary chain and dynamo drive, oil tank on left, battery on right, full width hubs, steel rims.

Colours
1948–55
7R: black frame, forks, and mudguards, petrol tank black with AJS and lining in gold, oil tank black with gold lining, AJS on timing cover, gold finish to crankcase, cambox and timing covers.

1953–55
G45: as **7R** but with silver lines on tanks and flying M transfer.

1956–57
No lining on oil tank, otherwise as before.

1958
7R unchanged, **G50** with M on timing cover and tank finished in a maroon red with silver lining and flying M tank transfer. Later models also seen finished in black.

1959–62
No changes.

1962
G50CSR: blue frame, forks and tanks, polished mudguards, silver petrol tank lining and flying M transfer.

Model recognition

1945
Single: all iron engine, coil valve springs, teles, rigid, saddle, magneto in front for AJS and to rear for Matchless, 350 cc exhaust pipe above footrest, 500 below.

1946
Comp.: upswept exhaust, competition tyres, heavy gauge spokes, alloy mudguards, duplicated cables.

1947
Single: two-start oil pump, shorter rod, lower gudgeon pin hole in piston, plain flanged main, three-rate fork springs plus buffer, 350 pipe as 500, modified number plates, flared chainguard, lifting handle in rear stay.

1948
Single: oil system changes, 7 in. brakes, four-bolt handlebar clamp, revised forks, 3·50 section rear tyre for 500, adjustable saddle springs, domed headlamp glass. During year wire-wound piston for 500 and 500 crankcase and crankshaft used for 350 to make them common.

1949
Single: hairpin valve springs, deeper barrel fins, valve lifter in rocker box, dynamo speed raised, wire-wound piston in 350, air filter option, new frame with sidecar lugs, larger oil tank, new handlebars, new headlamp shell, rectangular rear lamp, cvc on rear of battery carrier. Swinging fork models introduced with candlestick units with clevis ends and cvc mounted to frame behind the battery.
Twin: introduced with s/a frame and single cycle parts; Matchless with dualseat and megaphone silencers, AJS with saddle, tanks differed.

1950
All road: ribbed mudguards, offset silencer (not Matchless twin), five-spring clutch (not on 350).
Single: long carburettor body, centre stand for s/a models, tookbox between chainstays on rigid models, front brake torque arm adopted.
Comp.: all alloy engine, Lucas wader magneto, five-spring clutch, shorter wheelbase, smaller fuel tank, tubular toolbox under saddle, front brake torque arm.

1951
All road: jampots, new fork internals, recessed fork drain plugs, forged steel lower fork crown, controls and wiring tidied up, horn button in right bar, new chaincase seal.
Single: alloy head, alloy push rods, new Matchless magneto drive cover, all ball race dynamo, flexible horn mounting.
Comp.: s/a frame listed, type BA Burman gearbox.
Twin: frame altered for air filter provision, longer legs on centre stand, magneto cut-out button on points cover, vynide seat cover for Matchless.

1952
All models: B52 Burman gearbox, clutch access cap in chain-case, alloy front brake backplate, malleable iron top crown.
All road: underslung pilot lamp, flexibly mounted cvc, positive earth, colour coded wiring.

All singles: magneto at front for Matchless, chrome top ring, new timing main, modified hairpin seat.
Road singles: horn behind cylinder for Matchless, no compression plate on 500
Twin: engine breather in crankshaft drive end.

1953
All models: front brake cam lever points forward, endless chaincase seal.
All road: fork shrouds free to turn, steering lock bar, rear mudguard tail detaches, Diacon rear lamp, stop lamp option, dualseat for all s/a models.
All singles: small magneto shield.
Twin: two-bolt rocker covers, modified cam followers.

1954
All models: full width, light alloy front hub with straight spokes, clutch dome cover on chaincase.
All road: twin pilot lights, flared mudguards, new propstand spring, flexible fuel lines.
All singles: cable lubricators, change to rocker lubrication, new cams, bigger carbs.
Road singles: cvc under seat, bigger petrol tank for 500 (same as twins), auto-advance for 500 and bulge in timing cover.
Sprung singles and **Comp.:** larger timing mainshaft, lighter flywheels, oil tank modified.
Comp.: internal gearbox changes, improved gearbox to chaincase seal, altered oil filler cap, alloy tank; on rigid only—all welded front frame; on springer—new rear units and dualseat.
Twins: oil tank modified, common petrol tank to both marques as used on 500 single.

1955
All models: Monobloc, narrower front hub with fins in barrel profile, new silencer shape (not for Matchless twin), full width rear hub, larger diameter forks, modified jampots.
All road: frame with hole for air filter tube, pressed steel lugs for pillion rests, deeper headlamp shell carrying speedometer, deeper chainguard, rear reflector, simplified oil tank and battery carrier mounting, new front mudguard without front stay, qd rear hub and screw chain adjustors on s/a models.
All singles: timing side main with larger flange, larger inner drive side main, revised oil tank connections, 350 with larger petrol tank and auto ignition advance with bulge in timing cover, rigid models with barrel saddle springs.
Comp.: 2·75 × 21 in. front tyre on rigid models, new dualseat for s/a and TT carb for scrambler.
Twin: grooved rockers, shallower cap over oil filter. Late in year rigid and CS models stopped.

1956
Road singles and **twins:** new frame with vertical seat tube, long thin oil tank in right subframe angle, toolbox on left to match, cross panel to join, cover over grearbox with primary chain adjustor under, front brake cam lever at top of backplate, rear brake adjustor at front end of brake rod, no front stand, rear brake alloy backplate, horn under seat, longer seat, fork legs modified, cables grouped and routed to fork crown, horn button and dipswitch combined.
Single: compression ratio increased, magnetic sump oil filter.
Trials: new model with s/a frame, low compression ratio, shorter wheelbase.
Scrambles: short stroke, all alloy engine, integral push rod tunnels in barrel, Monobloc, road type frame, forged steel flywheels.

Twin: introduction of 600, raised compression ratio for 500, panel over coil.

1957

All: AMC gearbox, Norton-type clutch with shock absorber, no engine shock absorber, smaller dome in chaincase, Girling units with clevis lower ends.

Road models: ribbed oil tank and toolbox lid, oil tank panel on twins, push-on oil pipes.

Single: new inlet cam.

Twin: modified cams.

1958

Road models: twin pilot lights dropped, alloy chaincase, modified rear units giving lower ride height.

Road singles: ac electrics, rectifier under seat, ignition coil under tank, small timing cover with points.

Scrambers: new seat, wider mudguards, oil tank more set in, qd lights as for trials model.

CS twins: siamesed pipes, scrambles frame, full width hubs, 2 gallon tank, fat tyres, qd lights, speedo on fork crown, old type headlamp shell, high bars, comp mudguards.

CSR twins: engine as CS, scrambles frame, siamesed exhaust, standard tank and bars, comp dualseat, qd lights.

Lightweight: introduced during year.

Late in year 600 twin range stopped.

1959

Road singles: deeper section mudguards.

Trials: new frame, long inclined Girling units, rear fork without bridge with one arm held by cotter, small offset brakes.

Twin: introduction of 500 and 650 in standard, de-luxe, CS and CSR forms. 650 engine with longer barrel and one extra fin Standard and dl; frame with vertical rear units and deep front mudguard; standard only—alternator and distributor; CS and CSR; performance engine, siamesed pipes, alloy mudguards, scrambles frame with inclined units; tanks—CS had 2 gallon rest 4·25 gallon with central welded seam.

Lightweight: CS model introduced with performance engine, heavier gauge down tube, modified sub-frame, longer Girling units, stronger forks, alloy mudguards, 19 in. wheels, comp tyres, open exhaust, offset hubs, energy transfer ignition. Late in year 350CS, 500dl twin, 500CS twin, 500CSR twin stopped.

1960

Road models: duplex cradle frame, smaller headlamp shell, two-level dualseat, closer gearbox ratios.

Road singles: revised cylinder head and new piston for 500.

Scrambles: oil tank on left, GP carb, air filter in old oil tank position, for road use battery fitted under air filter and alternator supplied.

Twin: new cylinder head with added fin with three small diagonal fins each side on underside near exhaust, thicker head steady lug, reduced valve angle, two-rate valve springs, three-point tank mounting, smaller battery. Use of modular iron crankshaft begun.

Lightweight: standard—roll-on centre stand, roller main, two-level seat, 3·25 gallon tank; CS—first gear raised, gearing altered; 350 introduced—as 250, quadrant flywheel, 11 barrel fins (250 has 8), 18 in. wheels, Teledraulics.

Late in year 650CS stopped.

1961

Road models: shorter mudguards, larger badges.

Road singles: oil pump drive strengthened, inlet valve guide circlip located.

Twin: oil system modified.

Lightweight: standard—changes to gearbox and breather, full chaincase fitted as standard; CS—stronger crankpin, coil ignition, Varley dry battery, chainguard; S introduced—semi drop bars.

Late in year 350 long stroke, std 500 twin and 650 de-luxe stopped.

1962

Road models: breather tower on oil tank (as CSR twins), ignition key in place of knob switch, roll-on centre stand, stronger kickstart spring, new horn.

Road singles: new 350 with push rod tunnels integral with barrel, larger petrol tank; sports version with downswept bars.

Twin: new tank mountings, 1959 type battery, fork springs for standard model made stronger and as CSR. Road frame in place of CS frame for CSR, modified exhaust system for CSR.

Lightweight: all—longer kickstart lever; S—new narrower bars; 350—breather change, roller inner main; CSR—internal changes, raised gearing, British Hub full width alloy drums, front air scoop, forks as CS, bars S.

Late in year 250S, 250CS and 350 stopped.

1963

Road singles and **standard twin:** new front hub with five fins and wider brake shoes, new subframe and rear fork, standard Girling units without clevis end, restyled and more

rounded oil tank and toolbox, 18 in. wheels, narrower seat, D-section mudguards, direct action stop light switch, tank with kneegrips in recesses, silencer without tailpipe.
Single: chaincase option.
Comp.: new front hub, works-type air cleaner.
Twin: standard—gearing changed, wider oil pump gears; CSR—silencer, petrol tank and oil pump as standard model.
Lightweight: no change, standard 250 stopped in mid-year.

1964
Road models: Norton Roadholder forks and hubs, frame altered to suit.
Single: scramble type engines with integral push rod tunnels in barrel, 85·5 mm stroke, raised compression ratio, steel flywheels, single row big end, roller and bush timing main, Norton gear oil pump, scavenge feed to rockers.
Comp.: scrambler with Norton oil pump, trials with fixed seat with fibreglass base, revised sub-frame, shorter Girlings.
Twin: 12 volt electrics, standard with two sets of contact points; CSR with 18 in. wheels, new subframe, oil tank and toolbox as 1963 standard model; also gearing altered.
Lightweight: no change.
Late in year 350 trials model stopped.

1965
Single: no changes.
Twin: introduction of standard 750 with Norton Atlas engine in 650 frame; also 750CSR with low bars, rearsets, folding footrests, sweptback exhaust, forks with gaiters, no lower covers on rear units.
Lightweight: raised compression ratio, coil valve springs, closer gears, silencer with no tailpipe.
Late in year scrambler single stopped.

1966
Single: no changes.
Twin: CSR gearing altered.
Comp.: introduction of G85CS with duplex welded frame, AMC front hub with fins machined off, 7R rear hub, all-alloy engine, central oil tank, three-point footrest mounting.
Lightweight: alloy mudguards, semi-sweptback exhaust pipe.
During year 250CSR, all road singles and 650s stopped.

1967
G85CS: improved output oil pump.
Twin: oil system improved in Atlas engine.
CSR: 19 in. wheels.
CS: introduction under Matchless label only, small tank, trail tyres, capacitor ignition.
During year end of AJS production.

1968
Matchless models only.
G15 became G15MkII with capacitor ignition which was also fitted to CS and CSR models.

1969
Production ceased.

Model charts

AJS	Matchless	b × s	From	To
16M	G3L	69 × 93	1945	9 1955
16MC	G3LC	69 × 93	1946	9 1958
16MS	G3LS	69 × 93	1949	9 1958
16MCS	G3LCS	69 × 93	9 1950	11 1955
16MCS	G3LCS	72 × 85·5	11 1955	9 1958
16C	G3C	69 × 93	9 1958	7 1963
16	G3	69 × 93	9 1958	9 1961
16CS	G3CS	72 × 85·5	9 1958	9 1959
16	G3	74 × 81	9 1961	9 1963
16S	G3S	74 × 81	9 1961	9 1962
16	G3	72 × 85·5	9 1963	7 1966
16C	G3C	72 × 85·5	9 1963	8 1964
8	G5	72 × 85·5	9 1959	7 1962
14	G2	70 × 65	6 1958	7 1963
14CS	G2CS	70 × 65	1 1959	9 1962
14S	G2S	70 × 65	11 1960	9 1962
14CSR	G2CSR	70 × 65	5 1962	7 1966

AJS	Matchless	b × s	From	To
18	G80	82·5 × 93	1945	9 1955
18C	G80C	82·5 × 93	1946	9 1955
18S	G80S	82·5 × 93	1949	9 1958
18CS	G80CS	82·5 × 93	9 1950	9 1955
18CS	G80CS	86 × 85·5	11 1955	8 1965
18	G80	82·5 × 93	9 1958	9 1963
18	G80	86 × 85·5	9 1963	7 1966
	G85CS	86 × 85·5	9 1965	1969
7R		74 × 81	1948	1955
7R		75·5 × 78	1955	1963
	G45	66 × 72·8	1953	1957
	G50	90 × 78	1958	1963
	G50CSR	90 × 78	1962	1962

AJS	Matchless	b × s	1948	49	50	51	52	53	54	55	56	57	58	59	60	61	62	63	64	65	66	67	68	69
20	G9	66 × 72·8	—	—	—	—	—	—	—	—	—	—	9											
20 dl	G9 dl	66 × 72·8											9	9										
20 std	G9 std	66 × 72·8											—	—	—	9								
20CS	G9CS	66 × 72·8											9	9										
20CSR	G9CSR	66 × 72·8											9	9										
30	G11	72 × 72·8								9	—	—	8											
30CS	G11CS	72 × 72·8										9	8											
30CSR	G11CSR	72 × 72·8											1 8											
31	G12	72 × 79·3											9	—	—	—	—	—	—	—	7			
31 dl	G12 dl	72 × 79·3											9	—	—	9								
31CS	G12CS	72 × 79·3											9	—	9									
31CSR	G12CSR	72 × 79·3											9	—	—	—	—	—	—	—	7			
33		73 × 89																	9	—	—	8		
33CSR		73 × 89																	11	—	—	8		
	G15	73 × 89																	9	—	—	9		
	G15Mk2	73 × 89																				9	—	—
	G15CS	73 × 89																				4	—	—
	G15CSR	73 × 89																	11	—	—	—	—	—

7R turned roadster, quite a common fate for the early models which would accept a silencer and a soft plug